8 to Great

HOW ARR THE CHILDREN?

THANK YOU FOR ALL
THAT YOU DO

INJOY

Ed
"LINCOLN"

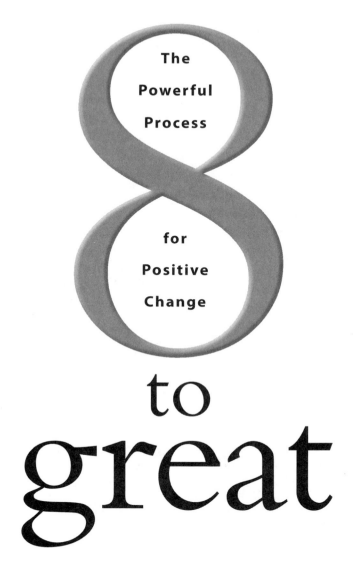

The
Powerful
Process

for
Positive
Change

to
great

MK MUELLER

Foreword by Mike Dooley

Insight Inc.
Omaha, Nebraska

insight
inc.

Published by:
Insight Inc.
www.mkmueller.com
mk@mkmueller.com
1-800-419-0444

8 to Great: The Powerful Process for Positive Change
by MK Mueller

Copyright © 2010 by MK Mueller

Publisher's Cataloging-In-Publication Data
(Prepared by The Donohue Group, Inc.)

Mueller, Mary Kay.
   8 to great : the powerful process for positive change /
MK Mueller ; foreword by Mike Dooley.

   p. ; cm.
   Includes index.
   ISBN-13: 978-0-9654372-8-8
   ISBN-10: 0-9654372-8-0
1. Happiness. 2. Self-actualization (Psychology) I. Dooley, Mike.
II. Title. III. Title: Eight to great
BF637.S4 M841 2009
158.1   2009927641

Content edit by Gail M. Kearns, www.topressandbeyond.com
Copyedit by Gary Anderson
Book production coordinated by To Press and Beyond, www.topressandbeyond.com
Book and cover design by Peri Poloni-Gabriel, Knockout Design, www.knockoutbooks.com

Printed in the United States of America

Table of Contents

FGH – The World's Simplest Positive Attitude Formula —193

Foreword

I met **MK Mueller on** a cruise I hosted in the Caribbean in 2007. It was an "adventure" sponsored by my website, where likeminded people could explore the philosophical "jungles of time and space" in between my every-other-day lectures. She was easy to recognize as somebody special. Kindness and enthusiasm shown from her eyes. Yet, admittedly, and I am not proud of this, I didn't grasp the depth of her understandings nor the passion of her conviction to change the world.

Reading **8 to Great** has changed everything. It's not just a powerful book from cover to cover, revealing the greatest secrets to thriving within time and space that have ever been shared, but its lessons are made easy. They're taught in plain English by the kind of teacher we need. Someone real. Someone who's learned by trial and error. Someone skilled at telling stories with a message and humor. She's turned ancient wisdom into modern day tools, and above all, she's remained authentic, conceiving of and framing each of the 8 High-Ways in one of the most original presentations I have ever read.

I'm often asked what's going to rock the world, psychologically, next. What, after *The Secret*, that is. And the answer is that people are going to be discovering the truth about their *absolute* power and their *absolute* responsibility for living their lives consciously and deliberately. People will be learning that *The Secret* was about far more than positive thinking or a way at looking at life; it's literally how reality unfolds. The concepts of victimhood, failure, luck, and blame are about to be swept into extinction like the philosophical dinosaurs they are.

We're now at the dawn of a new era: spiritual giants waking from a deep slumber, during which we reacted to the world around us instead of molding it. People will soon be realizing for the first time in recorded history that we are *all* capable of living as richly and happily as we can imagine, and that *nothing* can rob us of our power to conceive of, believe in, and achieve whatever our heart desires (using MK's *C-B-A Formula*). Whether this next wave of enlightenment will be sparked by a single book or a collection, I'm not sure, but I do know that **8 to Great** will be part of it.

Mike Dooley
As featured in *The Secret*, and author of *Infinite Possibilities: The Art of Living Your Dreams*

Acknowledgments

Words are incredibly inadequate for the gratitude I feel to all who loved and supported me through this work, but until I write the song that's in my heart, they will have to do.

First, my forever thanks to the Source of all Truth. I feel like I downloaded the 8 High-Ways because they came to me so quickly. Being an envoy for a process this powerful has reminded me that the branch with the most fruit bows the lowest.

Then, for the numerous books that this one turned out to be (once you count the secondary education handbooks it birthed along the way) I must thank the village that helped me raise my "children:"

Zach, your daily "How was your day, Mom?" and caring about my answers were sunshine on the cloudiest days. The song I sang to you when you were little still shines true.

Jo Bear, your "bearing" with me in loving patience meant more than you will ever know. I'm so proud and grateful to be your Mom!

Kaylene, how many times did you open my eyes and my heart with your loving listening and insights? We are joined at the hip-hip-hooray because this book is both of ours, dear friend.

Tessa, when I count my blissings, you're on the page twenty times. Thank you for the miracle that you are. May I support your dreams half as much as you have supported mine.

Jules, green truly is the new color of unconditional love. Thank you for the beautiful "shutter release" that you have been for my soul.

JoAnn, the supersis and focus coach I was reunited with while writing this book, thank you. I love you so much!

Coco, even when we miss our morning intendings, your delightful dreamings fill my days with love and laughter.

Abraham, Esther, and Jerry, my heart is full of appreciation for your lighting the way and clearing the path.

John, your generous gifts to the kids freed me to find my inner CEO. Namaste.

Momma Ruth, thank you for your unconditional love even when I had more questions than answers. We have found our perfect harmony!

And sincere thanks to Phil Dawson for the grounding, Cindy Osterloh for the learning lab, Gail M. Kearns for the kindest of kick butt, Mike Dooley for the spirit-lifting *Daily Notes from the Universe*, Teresa Cunningham and Amy Krance for holding the vision, and Gary Anderson for the eloquent editing.

Finally, to the man who left his wings behind so that I could fly: Dad, I never learned bridge, but have dedicated my life to becoming one. Thank you for the love I feel from you every day and for following your dream so that I could do the same.

Gratefully,
MK

I cannot tell you any truth
that deep within you don't know already.
All I can do is remind you of what you have forgotten.

Eckhart Tolle

༄

The Foundation

If you can't describe what you're doing as a process,
you don't know what you're doing.

W. Edwards Deming

⁣◦∞◦⁣

There are four kinds of people in the world: those who are unhappy and don't know why, those who are unhappy and believe they know why, those who are happy and don't know why, and those who are happy and know why. Your picking up this book indicates that you are ready to move solidly into the fourth category, not only for your own bliss and blessings, but so that your happiness and insight might benefit others. The power is in the process.

I recall the day years ago when I walked through a study hall at an alternative high school. A young man looked up without raising his head. There was sadness in his eyes. It seemed somewhere inside he knew that life could be easier and better, if only someone would show him the way.

Six weeks later, that same young man had learned the **8 to Great** process. The light in his eyes as he passed me in the hall was unmistakable. He, like thousands of others, had discovered that when we learn the *process* for success, the *progress* follows.

Over the years, I have not only used this process every day of my life, I have also trained hundreds of thousands of business people, health care professionals, and educators in **8 to Great**. Meanwhile, as this edition goes to press, over 500 certified trainers have taught countless middle school, high school, and college students the **8 to Great** process with amazing results. I have seen its power so clearly that I can make you three promises:

Promise #1:
It will take you no more than three hours to **learn** this process.

Promise #2:
It will take you no more than three minutes each day
to **apply** this process.

Promise #3:
This process will help everyone who surrenders to it.

How can I make these promises? Because successful people know that success is a science more than an art. It's the result of practices that have been taught for thousands of years by the greatest among us. How else could every bookstore be filled with "How-To" guides that top the best-seller charts?

The reason so many people fail to make lasting changes is that they don't commit to one path long enough to see results. When we jump from process to process, it's like someone on a diet alternating days between Atkins (low carb) and Weight Watchers (low fat). In doing so, they would not only *not* lose weight, they would *gain it!* There's no one way to succeed at anything. Many roads will get you there, but you must *choose one and trust it.*

Some of us want to get to Hollywood; others just want to get out of hell. The 8 High-Ways have helped one individual lose 140 pounds, another get a gold ticket to Hollywood with *American Idol*, a 50-year old man find his first true love, a 40-year-old woman find the courage to open her first business, a teenager who lived on a farm get a scholarship to MIT, a young adult move from addiction to a happy and sober life, and so much more. No matter what your dream, *these High-Ways can get you where you want to go.*

When you're ready, write down the following and keep the sheet of paper where you can see it: *"Today is the first day of the best of my life."* Sign it and date it. Then congratulate yourself and buckle your seatbelt, because you're in for the High-Ways ride of your life!

Defining Attitude

You are living the life you've imagined. You always have been. Your imagination is where your future comes to life, so you're living the result of what you've expected to happen so far. Are you ready to expect and imagine bigger and better? As soon as you make that simple shift, using your imagination to design a life you love, your life will change dramatically.

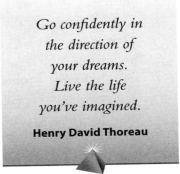

Go confidently in the direction of your dreams. Live the life you've imagined.

Henry David Thoreau

And there's more good news. While your imagination determines your future, your *attitude* determines your present. Everyone talks about "the importance of attitude," but no one has ever offered a definition simple and powerful enough to be universally accepted. Look at how various texts have defined the concept. The only thing that's clear is how *unclear* we are:

"Attitudes have to do with your orientation towards something…"
(*Boundaries*, Dr. Henry Cloud and Dr. John Townsend)

"My definition for attitude is simple: Life!"
(*Attitude Is Everything*, Keith Harrell)

"Attitude: a manner of showing one's feelings or thoughts; a state of mind; one's disposition, opinion, etc; a manner of acting…"
(Webster's Dictionary)

It's time for a definition of attitude we can all agree on. If you could only choose one of the following three answers, would you say attitude is a set of feelings and emotions, thoughts and beliefs, or behaviors and actions?

When I ask executives, parents, nurses, educators, or counselors this question, about one-third of *every* group chooses *each* option. If a fourth option is offered—"all of the above"—90 percent will choose that answer, even though it's *wrong*. There's only *one* correct response. Your attitude is based on your thoughts and beliefs. Attitude is *mental,* not emotional or behavioral. Emotions and behaviors are the *result* of our thoughts and beliefs. Once we get this, we can better understand how *we* are in charge of our attitudes.

Years ago, I created a diagram to demonstrate how attitude works. Since positive attitude is the key to personal power, I refer to it as...

The Power Pyramid

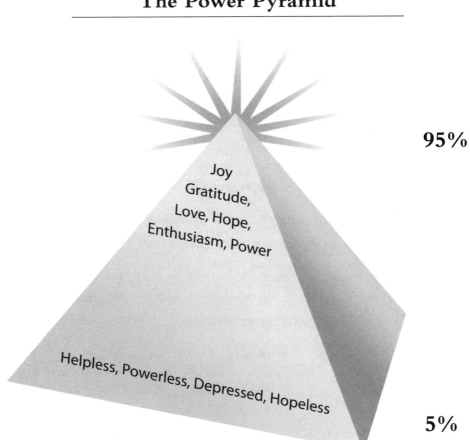

95%

Joy
Gratitude,
Love, Hope,
Enthusiasm, Power

Helpless, Powerless, Depressed, Hopeless

5%

*We are at "95" on the **Power Pyramid** when 95 percent of our thoughts feel good.* Another way of saying that is when 95 percent of our thoughts feel good, we're using 95 percent of our power.

*We are at "5" on the **Power Pyramid** when only 5 percent of our thoughts feel good.* That's because when only 5 percent of our thoughts feel good, we're only using 5 percent of our power.

Most of our lives we are hovering somewhere between "5" and "95." As you become more aware of how your thoughts feel with the 8 High-Ways, you'll not only be able to move up the **Power Pyramid**, you'll be able to do it quickly, by selecting the focus of your next thought.

Misery Loves Company, But...

Complete the following phrases:

What goes around...

Birds of a feather...

When it rains, it...

Misery loves...

The adages above are familiar to most of us. What goes around comes around. Birds of a feather flock together. When it rains, it pours. Misery loves company. But so does *joy*! The thoughts and beliefs you have about the world are like boomerangs: they come back to you, often immediately. This universal truth is often referred to as the Law of Attraction.

On the **Power Pyramid**, at any moment in your day, you're between the bottom (5 percent) and the top (95 percent). When you're down at a "5" and only 5 percent of your thoughts feel good, you feel like a victim—hopeless and powerless. As a result you either attract others who feel the same or you bring out the worst in those around you.

Conversely, when you're at the top at "95" and 95 percent of your thoughts feel good, you attract others who feel powerful, grateful, joyful, and hopeful, and bring out the best in those around you. At the top of the pyramid, you're full of energy, enthusiasm, and appreciation. You're confident about your destiny because you understand that what you focus on determines how your life will play out.

Your Attitude Score

You can use the **Power Pyramid** at any time to gauge how positive your attitude is. Are you feeling powerful right now, focusing on fun, gratitude, excitement, or anticipation ("95-ing")? Or are you giving away your power by complaining, blaming, and focusing on problems ("5-ing")? We all have something we could be complaining about or worrying about right now. We also all have something we could be grateful for right now. The decision we make between those good feeling (powerful) and not good feeling (powerless) thoughts is the deciding factor for which direction our life is going.

> *Success is not the way to happiness.*
> *Happiness is the way to success.*
>
> **Albert Schweitzer**

As you grasp the concept of the **Power Pyramid**, more and more aspects of life will start to make sense. For example, you'll see that "5" and "95" personalities do not choose to be around each other. When we're "5-ing" and having a bad day and come across a "95-er" who is having a great day, we tend to write them off, label them as fake, or assume they're just "lucky."

Not only that, but when we look at the "what goes around" principle, it's clear that because there is a smaller circumference at the top, what goes around (the good stuff) comes around *faster* up there. At this speed, we often call those manifestations "luck" or "miracles." But this wonderful power we've been given by our creator is not sporadic. It's at work every moment of every day, and is always available to bring you your next dream.

Choosing Your Thoughts

So how can you choose to focus your thoughts more deliberately? Right now, remember your last great vacation. See how much fun you were having. There you go. You just changed your focus. It's that simple. You may not be motivated to be selective with your thoughts yet, but the next time something goes "wrong," remember that focusing on something you're grateful for is a painless way to feel better *immediately*. That in itself will be your motivator.

Will it work? The truth that *your thoughts create your reality* has been written about in myriad ways by some of the greatest teachers of all time.

> *There are two ways to live your life— one is as though nothing is a miracle, the other is as though everything is a miracle.*
>
> **Albert Einstein**

In ancient scriptures:

"Everything you ask for, believe you have it already, and it shall be yours."

Mark 11:24

In government:

"The empires of the future are empires of the mind."

Winston Churchill

In motivational literature:

"You must understand that seeing is believing but also know that believing is seeing."

Denis Waitley

In sports:

"I won (Mr. Universe four times) because I saw myself so clearly, being up there on the stage and winning."

Arnold Schwarzenegger

The message is consistent: *Your life is like it is because of what you choose to focus on and believe.*

Thoughts That Feel Good

You're thinking about something right now. That thought either feels good (moving you higher on the **Power Pyramid)** or it doesn't (taking you lower on the **Power Pyramid**). Your homework is to travel the road of the thoughts that feel better. When you get de-toured onto thoughts that don't feel so good, catch yourself, make a legal "you-turn," and return to joy.

For example, you've just finished a presentation at work and are feeling good about it as you drive home, but then realize you forgot a key point. There's nothing you can do about it now, but you can focus on gratitude for the car you're driving, or your great spouse, or your health. Or perhaps you awaken feeling good but then hear your teens arguing about who's been in the bathroom too long. You could take a deep breath, accept that teenagers argue, and be grateful they're so "normal" (more on this in High-Way 3)!

I'm often asked how long it takes to change your life using the High-Ways. My reply is always, "As long as it takes you to think your next thought." Try it right now. In the next moment, choose a "95" thought that feels good, such as...

- ✔ *admiring the beauty of a tree outside your window*
- ✔ *appreciating the love and support of a good friend*
- ✔ *delighting in your child, grandchild, or pet*
- ✔ *relishing a recent accomplishment*
- ✔ *dreaming of a "Won't it be wonderful when..."*

Next, take a moment to be grateful for *your ability to read the words on this page.* Finally, wiggle your toes. Realize that when you were born, someone was very grateful that you had ten of them! Notice how these thoughts are affecting how you feel? That's the work we'll be doing in this process, but it will often feel more like *play.*

The *FGH* Formula

So what are the best ways to get to the top of the **Power Pyramid** and stay there? Simply choosing your mental focus and going to positive attitude thoughts. Since every thought is about the past, present, or future, I define *Positive Attitude* in a simple three-letter formula, **FGH:**

Forgiveness of the past,
Gratitude for the present,
and **H**ope for the future.

Once I discovered the power of **FGH,** I shared it with anyone who would listen. I began seeing its effects in my children as well as in the lives of thousands of my coaching clients and seminar participants. The results were never short of astounding.

Nearly every holy book, guru, saint, and mystic has spoken of these three virtues in some manner as the path to peace, freedom, enlightenment, and heaven. Growing up, I used these three because I was told to. Today I use the **FGH** formula because *it works*.

This book will take you through the 8 High-Ways process to a positively powerful life. Before explaining how the 8 came to be, let me summarize them.

The 8 High-Ways in a Nutshell

High-Way 1: *Get the Picture*

Visualizing the outcome until it feels good is the first step to any dream or goal. Once you're clear on your destination, keep thinking about it until you can get excited *by what it will be like*. Then, from that good-feeling place, the next step will reveal itself as surely as the next yellow brick showed up on Dorothy's road to Oz. Visualize yourself getting the diploma, driving the new car, or laughing with loved ones. It'll take you straight to "95" on the **Power Pyramid**.

High-Way 2: *Risk*

Once your dream starts to take shape, your next step will be to take a risk to follow it. Cowards have the same amount of fear as heroes, but while cowards use their fear as an excuse to stay stuck, heroes feel the fear and do it anyway. Whether it's the risk of telling the truth or pursuing a dream, the bigger the risk, the bigger the reward. Risking is letting go of security as the world defines it for a larger safety net—being true to yourself. *Risk* is never running from (our fears)—it's always running to (our dreams), so ask yourself, *"If I had no fear, what would I do?"*

High-Way 3: *Full Responsibility*

Great men are those who see that thoughts rule the world.

Ralph Waldo Emerson

As we travel down the *Risk* High-Way, obstacles and detours will inevitably appear. We can curse our "bad luck," but not without being pulled off course. *Full Responsibility* is the fundamental shift that allows us to take charge of our lives by owning that *we* were the ones who chose to go down the road of thoughts that didn't feel good. Until we see that we're in charge of our lives, we can feel trapped in a prison of resentment, bitterness, and confusion. When we acknowledge the power of our focus, we realize that we were never prisoners in the first place.

High-Way 4: *Feel All Your Feelings*

As challenges arise, allowing yourself to *Feel All Your Feelings* returns you to the freedom of childhood, when emotions came and went without guilt or denial. When we realize that there are no "bad" feelings, we stop getting stuck in one feeling to prevent feeling another. We realize that we can feel mad and sad and still have a positive attitude. Once we're freed up emotionally, we "feel" better physically as well. Finally, as we overcome the fear and judgment of our own emotions, we can more easily accept the feelings of others.

High-Way 5: *Honest Communication*

Once we get in touch with our emotions through High-Way 4, we're ready to practice communicating them honestly with others in a self-responsible way. The practice of non-defensive listening and assertively asking for what we want will empower us and deepen our connection to those around us. When we risk taking responsibility for our feelings rather than blaming others for them, we combine the first four High-Ways into an "inner-state" of loving joy.

High-Ways 6,7,8: *The FGH Formula*

The sixth, seventh, and eighth High-Ways make up *the world's most powerful positive attitude formula*. Since attitude is mental, not emotional, and since all thoughts are either about the past, present, or future, we only need to practice three kinds of thoughts: ***FGH***.

High-Way 6: *Forgiveness of the Past*

...is knowing we were all doing the best we could at the time with the information we had.

High-Way 7: *Gratitude for the Present*

...is focusing on appreciation and celebration of the good in every person and situation.

High-Way 8: *Hope for the Future*

...is the light within us, no matter how small, that helps us persevere through the darkness. It's knowing that our destiny awaits us.

How *8 to Great* Came to Be: The First Five High-Ways

As simple a concept as ***FGH*** has been for my clients and audiences to understand, when I first began to teach it, there were often people who seemed unable to change their negative thought patterns. Despite their longing for greater happiness, they acted almost hostile toward the concepts of forgiveness, gratitude, and hope. I was determined to find out why.

By talking with them week after week, I learned that some were stuck in rage and depression—angry about their anger and sad about their sadness. They didn't realize that it's possible to be mad and sad and still have a positive attitude because they'd been taught to label those feelings as "negative." I saw that their inability to accept and acknowledge *all their feelings* was keeping them stuck. At that point, I added High-Way 4: *Feel All Your Feelings* to my process.

Next I saw that once an individual got in touch with their feelings, good communication skills were necessary to give those emotions a voice. Because many had never learned those skills in childhood, I added High-Way 5: *Honest Communication*.

Next I noticed another pattern as I came across those who had lost touch with their dreams. They had forgotten their purpose and were simply going through the motions. *Get the Picture* became High-Way 1. For those who could verbalize their dreams but were hiding in their comfort zones and afraid to follow them, I added High-Way 2: *Risk*. Finally, for those stuck in blaming and complaining and who didn't understand that power only comes in tandem with *Full Responsibility*, I added that as High-Way 3.

In coaching clients to greater freedom and fulfillment, I now teach the first five High-Ways to clear the way for 6, 7, and 8—**F, G,** and **H**. The exciting reality has been that the 8 High-Ways process works for *every* person willing to work it!

The Science of Luck

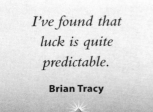

I've found that luck is quite predictable.

Brian Tracy

Most of us claim we don't believe in luck, yet refer to it almost daily when discussing coincidental occurrences. When things go very well or terribly wrong for someone we know, we talk about that person being "fortunate" or "down on their luck." But good and bad fortune are neither random nor mysterious. On the contrary, the way your life plays out is the direct result of your thoughts and beliefs. When we get this, we get it all.

Luck or the Law?

I got to see The Science of Luck in action a few years back after speaking at the International Jaycees conference in Barcelona. I started to feel sad about leaving. As the airport shuttle pulled up, I decided to change my mood by imagining a truly interesting and fun ride to the airport.

Once I got on the shuttle, I was "fortunate" to enjoy a half-hour chat with the winner of the World's Top Young Person award. I knew as I listened that Tim Lawrence lived all eight of the High-Ways. He is upbeat and optimistic and has a contagious "can-do" and "will-do" confidence that has helped him accomplish everything from running for office to swimming the English Channel.

Was this wonderful encounter a coincidence? Of course not. I intended joy and received it. I hope that through these High-Ways you'll see that there is actually a "science of luck."

It All Adds *Up*

You've had a thousand little regrets—a thousand and one big and little disappointments. So, have you had enough? Are you ready to release those old patterns and live the life of your dreams? If the answer is yes, do the math. Figure out what percentage of your life isn't working right now—10 percent, 50 percent, 90 percent? Even if it's 99 percent, just be honest with yourself. What percentage would you like to trade in for an upgrade? Okay, got the number? That's the percentage of your thinking that has to be reprogrammed. That percentage tells you how often you have forgotten your power to shift your focus. When you choose thoughts that feel good, your thoughts will all add *up*.

When You Feel Good

Before we move on, here's an activity you can use to feel better right now. **Complete this phrase 5 times: "When I feel good..."** (For example, "I have more energy.")

Answers like "I smile more," "I laugh more," or "I'm more patient" often show up on this list. You may have written: I feel better, am kinder, more creative, or more productive. Whatever your answers were, they can be summed up this way:

When you feel good, good things happen.

Ever noticed how often people say, "I'll be happy when..." but *when* never arrives? Happiness is your choice in this moment, and it's an inside job.

Getting Started

If you're ready to feel better *right now*, complete the *Gratitude* exercise on the next page. You'll be amazed how quickly your mood and attitude will improve.

> *There is no way*
> *to happiness.*
> *Happiness is the way.*
>
> **Dr. Wayne Dyer**

Your Gratitude Homework

The secret of getting ahead is getting started.
The secret of getting started is breaking your overwhelming tasks
into small manageable tasks, and then starting on the first one.

Mark Twain

Although Gratitude is its own High-Way (7), it's such a simple way to get to "95" quickly, I'm going to start you on that part of the process now. It will make all of the other High-Ways easier, I promise.

Each day, take one minute to *write down three things you're grateful for from the past twenty-four hours, no repeats,* in a journal or notebook. In order to see the best results, do this each morning or evening *for the next 30 days.*

The most important components of this homework are writing it down and remembering not to repeat. If you write down "sunshine" tomorrow morning, for example, you're done with sunshine for life! Why? Because repeating the same phrases over and over (health, job, family, etc.) can get stale and lose their ability to evoke good feelings. Stay fresh by looking for new things every day to be grateful for. You'll be amazed at how easy this will become over time.

My *Gratitudes* on an average day might look like:

1. *the gurglings of my guinea pig*
2. *new blooms on my Peace Lilly*
3. *the taste of bananas on my French toast*

Or:

1. *the beautiful full moon last night*

2. *my sweetheart's midday phone call*

3. *that someone figured out how to make the next Kleenex pop up!*

That's it! Whether it's your nice big deck, your iPod, your mail carrier, the change in your pocket, or your contact lenses, you'll start to see life through grateful eyes. There may be some days that are more challenging, but trust the process and write three *Gratitudes* a day, even if one of them is *"I'm grateful I remembered to write down my Gratitudes today!"* If you ever forget for a few days, weeks, or months, just **FGH** yourself: *Forgive* yourself for forgetting, be *Grateful* that you remembered when you did, and have *Hope* that you'll remember better next time.

If you're feeling down, off balance or like your heart is broken, keeping a gratitude journal will change your life.
I guarantee it!
Oprah Winfrey

❧

High-Way 1:
Get the Picture
Think It 'til
You Feel It

∞

Defining *Get the Picture*

We're never given a dream without the power
to make it come true.
Richard Bach

⚒

Emma's Dream Job

I met Emma at one of my workshops. She sought me out at lunch-time to talk about how unhappy she was at her accounting firm. She didn't feel as if she shared the values of her employers and longed for things to be different.

When I asked what her dream job looked like, she chuckled, as though the concept of finding it was ludicrous, but eventually she not only told me, but also started to write it down. It was the first step on her road to success.

What would your life be like if you woke up tomorrow with a magic wand?

Imagine that all you had to do was wave your magic wand in a *figure eight,* say your wish aloud, and it would come true in the next day, week, or month. How would that power change your life? I hear some of you thinking, "I'd win the lottery." Great. Then what? Where would you go? What would you do? Who would you be?

High-Way 1 is a reminder that you *do* have the power to co-create wealth, health, romance, and the job of your dreams—powers you've forgotten and therefore haven't been using to their full capacity. Your power has nothing to do with your bank account, your job title, your waistline, or your age. Your power lies within.

Spend any time around toddlers and you'll recall that we were all born with the boldness to ask for what we want, but as we grow, the litanies of "life is hard" and "get your head out of the clouds" take their toll. As a result, too many of us abandon our dreams. We start to see ourselves as helpless prey to life's circumstances, unworthy of life's greatest gifts.

The exciting news is that we can release those self-imposed limits by using the first **8 to Great** High-Way: *Get the Picture.*

The Magic Want

Instead of a wand, you have a magic *want*. Every time you *Get the Picture* and think about something you desire, your thoughts send out energy—like a magnet—to attract that very thing to you. The more you think about it, the more real it becomes until the thought of it feels as real as the chair you're sitting on. The easiest way to move from conceiving (thinking a new thought) to believing (feeling excited) is by using our imagination.

The C-B-A Formula:
If you **C**onceive it and **B**elieve it, you will **A**chieve it.

> *The biggest thing I've been thankful for is my imagination. When people said, "It's impossible; it can't be done," that's where my imagination came into play.*
>
> **Michael Phelps**

As children, daydreaming and pretending came naturally and dominated our free time. Then, as we grew, many of us started to forget the fun and magic of "acting as if." Yet the most successful adults *never stop* daydreaming. They understand that their thoughts become their beliefs which then become their future.

Goals vs. Dreams

Part of understanding the power of dreams is to see how they differ from goals. Most books on goal-setting remind us that a *goal* is a target or destination achieved by following specific steps to a particular outcome. In the *Gratitude* homework at the end of the Foundation chapter, for example, I coached you on *how many Gratitudes* to do and *when* to do them. Your goal might be to do them five days this week. Goals are extremely beneficial to a healthy life.

Leap and the net will appear.

Julia Cameron

Dreams—the ones you have when you're awake—are very different. Books on dreams are even in a separate section on the bookstore shelves. That's because *a dream is bigger*—so large in fact that people are often reluctant to share theirs out loud. If they do, it's only to a select few, because tears can flow when we touch this sacred place within. Meanwhile, when you first get clear on what your big dreams are, the steps necessary to achieve them are hidden from view, which can feel frightening or overwhelming. Following a dream is a leap of faith that can discourage weaker hearts from ever getting started.

A simple way to distinguish between a goal and a dream is as follows:

A *Goal* is S.M.A.R.T. =
Specific, Measurable, Attainable, Realistic, and Time-Based

When we set a goal, we know *Who, What, When, Where, Why, How,* and *How Long.* For example: *I will walk for thirty minutes five days a week in my neighborhood to get back in shape.*

A *Dream* is B.I.G. =
Bold, Innovative, and Grand

When we allow ourselves to dream, we disregard *Who, When, Where, How and How Long.* Instead, we focus only on *What (we want) and Why (we want it).* The other W and H questions are *head* questions that can take us from fantasizing to fretting, while *What* and *Why* are *heart* questions. They're the "turn-ons" that we can feel in the depths of our being.

"Johnny, Stop Paying Attention and Start Daydreaming!"

Remember the well-meaning teachers in our past who would scold daydreamers during class, telling them to "pay attention" and to "snap out of it?" Some such "challenging" students known for "excessive daydreaming" were Albert Einstein, Thomas Edison, George Lucas, Lewis Carroll, and Eleanor Roosevelt. Not a bad gang to be associated with!

So how do you start believing the impossible is possible? I once asked an airline pilot how much his plane weighed. He lit up as he told me, "That's my favorite question! About 266,000 pounds, fully loaded!" That day I realized that if I could believe that a one-hundred-ton metal machine could fly, I could believe anything. So can you. As the White Queen pointed out to Alice in Wonderland, it just takes practice.

> *Alice laughed. "There's no use trying," she said. "One can't believe impossible things." "I daresay you haven't had much practice," said the Queen. "When I was your age, I always did it for half an hour a day. Why, sometimes I've believed as many as six impossible things before breakfast."*
>
> **Lewis Carroll's**
> **Through the Looking Glass**

Why is this such good news? Because the imagining is almost as much fun as the experiencing. Since the mind can't tell the difference between thought and reality, you can feel better instantly by going to that place in your imagination and crafting your ideal scene. Think of it as a free Virtual Reality ride. Often we only dream dreams that are similar to our daily experience, but the more we read and listen to the stories of great dreamers, the more we realize that even the sky isn't the limit when our heart is in it.

What can you expect from expecting miracles? Recently, a high school student told me that using *Get the Picture* to imagine working with his dad to restore an old car helped him stop fighting at school, thereby allowing him to graduate. *Imagine* that!

Strong Desires and Big Dreams

As children, many of us were warned by well-meaning adults that strong desires were "bad." Yet the word for "de-sire" is French for "of the Father." (Even the desire for *no* desire is a desire.) Desires naturally burn within us from the moment of birth and are the fuel for our dreams.

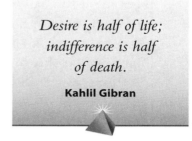

Passionate desires and big dreams are the common thread linking the most successful and "luckiest" people in the world. This can be seen in the true stories that have become film classics such as *Coach Carter, Music of the Heart, Rudy, Sea Biscuit, Miracle, Invincible,* and *Pursuit of Happyness.* Each of the heroes in these stories were branded as "out of their minds" by those around them. They were *out of their minds* and *into their hearts*. As with all dreamers, their dreams had moved from a thought place into a feeling place.

Desire is half of life; indifference is half of death.

Kahlil Gibran

Mary Lou Retton

In 1984, the first perfect ten score in the history of the United States Olympic team was achieved by a sixteen-year-old by the name of Mary Lou Retton. When the reporters swarmed around her after her flawless performance on the vault, someone asked, "How does it feel to have received the first perfect ten for the U.S. team?"

Her answer was, "Like it's always felt!"

"But no one has ever done it before!" the reporter challenged.

"I've done it thousands of times in my mind," was her reply.

A belief is a thought you keep thinking until you *feel* it.

Mary Lou understood that nothing is impossible once you believe it to be true. For years she thought about the excitement of achieving a perfect ten until she felt it. At that point, the only impossibility was that she would *not* achieve it.

Barcelona Baby

Years ago, when speaking to a group in Minneapolis, I was "95-ing." Sharing the docket with Patch Adams for a large healthcare organization, I was getting paid to do what I loved! My talk and products that day were well received by the 500+ who attended and I got to see some dear friends. One was Brian McDermott, my agent, who had come to hear me speak. Add to that the warm first-week-of-spring weather, and you can imagine how good I felt. When we're "buzzing" at this high level, we're like Jack and his Magic Beans. Anything we plant will manifest quickly.

> *Your hopes, dreams, and aspirations are legitimate. They are trying to take you airborne, above the clouds, above the storms, if you only let them.*
>
> **William James**

After I finished my talk, Brian and I went for a walk. "So, what's new with you?" I asked.

"The wife and kids and I are leaving for Spain next week," he replied, glowing.

He then went into colorful detail of what markets, music, and museums they were looking forward to, as well as the bullfights they'd probably skip. It was a glorious daydreamy discussion, during which we both got more and more excited about his trip to Barcelona. (Let me note that I had never had the tiniest desire to travel to Spain before that day when the seeds were planted.)

The following day, as I was unpacking my bags back at home, the phone rang. It was Brian.

"How would you like to go to Barcelona in November?"

"With you?" I asked, stunned.

"No, with the International Jaycees. They want you to be the keynote speaker. Pack your bags, baby. You're going to Barcelona!"

So it was that my first international talk was translated into seven languages and I got to share the stage with one of my favorite authors, Edward de Bono. It is a memory that can still take me to "95."

The *Get the Picture* Process:
Believing Is Receiving

The **8 to Great** process defines success as "setting a goal or dream and achieving it." What always amazes me is that the greatest stumbling block for most people is the *first half*—expressing the goal or dream. The majority of us don't take the time to get clear about our desires because we've never learned how powerful this process can be. Yet it's as simple as listing what you want.

What You Want to Receive/Experience

Take a moment now to create in a journal or on your computer a list of things you'd like to receive or experience. It could be three things or thirty things. You may ask for anything, as long as you're willing to believe it's possible. For the fun of it, make your intentions different sizes—some smaller and some larger.

Smaller Intentions

Surprise money
Receiving a compliment from a stranger
An "aha" insight
Hearing your favorite song
Eating your favorite food
Having a great laugh
Hearing from an old friend
Finding something you've misplaced
Receiving flowers
Attracting a new client

Larger Intentions

Getting a promotion or job offer
Finding a solution to a long-standing problem
Meeting your true love
Finding out you're going to have a baby

Selling your house, your car, or your book rights
Winning a competition or getting a scholarship
Meeting someone famous
Having a health challenge disappear
Receiving a surprise gift of $25,000
Receiving an invitation to travel to a beautiful resort as someone's guest

Every one of the above has happened to me or someone I was coaching through this process. I recall teaching this process to a client who had just finished reading *Slow Waltz at Cedar Bend* by Robert Waller. On her list she wrote that she wanted to meet a "wild and free" gent like the protagonist of that book, despite the fact that she lived in a fairly small Midwestern town.

> *Your dream must be bigger than what you think you can do.*
>
> **Mary Manin Morrissey**

She informed me a week later that she had met a man who had *ten* characteristics of the book's hero, (shoulder-length hair, a motorcycle man, a great athlete who had blown out his knee during his senior year in high school, etc.) and that they'd just gone out on their third date.

When you're ready to allow miraculous manifestations into your experience, pick one of your intentions and do the following visualization.

Get the Picture 3-Minute Visualization

Sit up in your chair, put both feet on the floor, and take a nice deep breath. When you're comfortable, close your eyes.

In your mind, go to the day when your dream is coming true. See it in full color. Notice what you're wearing, who's there with you, what people are saying, and especially how you're feeling. Stay there for a minute.

Next, in your dream, notice someone walking excitedly toward you. Once they reach you, hear them tell you that they have a dream similar to yours. Hear them ask you how you did it. Take a minute to tell them that you released the "How," simply imagined the good feelings of the end result, and *Got the Picture* of it coming true. Enjoy that conversation for a minute.

Then, keeping your eyes closed, imagine yourself returning home after that dream-come-true day. In your mind's eye, walk into your home and see your mail lying on the counter. Notice that the top letter is addressed to you. See yourself sitting down and opening it. As you read it, discover that it's full of even *more* good news. It may be a love letter, a check, an announcement that you've won an award, a scholarship, or a thank-you letter from someone whose life you've touched. Be there with your feelings for a minute.

When you're finished, open your eyes.

How did that feel? After completing this 3-minute visualization in an **8 to Great** class, one high school student answered, "Freakin' awesome!" When we focus on our dreams, it fills us with awe and lifts us to "95!"

> *What we **think** determines what we **feel**, which determines what we **do**, which determines who we **are**.*
>
> **Anonymous**

Flexing Your Dream Muscle

People sometimes tell me that they've "forgotten how to dream," but that simply means they're out of practice. When you read a book before seeing the movie, the characters in the film inevitably look different from those you *imagined*. Imagination is what a child exercises while packing for summer camp, what an actor uses to create a role, or what a chef draws on to create a new dish. It's a muscle we all have that can be flexed and strengthened whenever we're ready.

Get the Picture is learning to harness that wonderful power—to *see* the checks as though they're already coming in, *feel* your clothes fitting loosely, *smell* your new love's cologne, or *hear* the laughter as your co-workers interact with all your new customers. In that instant, you are powerfully drawing your dreams into physical manifestation.

Thinking a Thought Until You Feel It

As we think a new thought, we're transformed. I can start thinking of myself as having a great memory for names. You can practice thinking of yourself as healthier and more energetic than you've ever been. Who do you *think* you are? That's who you're becoming. On any given day, you can practice believing that:

✔ *money is hard to come by*

✔ *there's no time to do what you really want*

✔ *you have trouble making new friends*

OR you can practice believing that:

✔ *more than enough money flows to you easily and often*

✔ *you get everything that needs to be done accomplished with time to spare*

✔ *you make and keep good friends easily and naturally*

> *You have within you a GPS system that never asks where you've been or why you've been there so long. It simply listens to the now, and is set up to take you where you want to go by following thoughts that feel good.*
>
> **Abraham-Hicks**

How can you tell what you believe now? Look at your life. Are you getting what you desire? I have a dear friend named Phil who always gets the parking spot right in front of the restaurant we're meeting at, no matter how full the parking lot. He jokingly calls it "Phil's Space." He expects to get the perfect parking space, and life becomes a mirror of his thoughts.

Waiting vs. Expecting

Perhaps the most challenging piece of dreaming is releasing the **How** and **When** and allowing a dream to show up in its own time and in its own way. *Expecting* is an apt description of the "95" frame of mind. Like the mother anticipating the birth of her child, you take your focus off of "wondering if" and move it into "preparing for."

When we stay focused on ***What*** we want and ***Why*** we want it, it will come to us at just the right time. This understanding is crucial because when we can release our attachment to the ***When*** of our dreams, we'll have the freedom to enjoy each and every moment in the present.

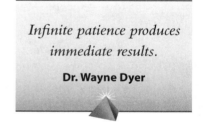

Infinite patience produces immediate results.

Dr. Wayne Dyer

Getting frustrated can actually delay your desire from reaching you to the point of stalling. So whenever you're drumming your fingers and looking at your watch as you await a particular dream-come-true, get back to "95" by noticing three things you're grateful for. Then let your imagination paint a picture of how perfect your dream will be when it arrives!

Remember to be gentle with yourself. Intensity isn't a characteristic of a "95" attitude. Think of the stereotypical "car salesman" as someone you want to avoid becoming. One easy way to remember this is to "intense-shun." Tension doesn't work when you're doing your intentions. We need focus, not force, to bring our dreams to life.

Why Pushing Against Doesn't Work

Our brains are like computers—they can't take a joke. Whatever mental picture comes in the clearest on our cerebral screen is the one coming our way. I recall speaking to a woman after one of my talks in North Dakota. Her two friends were a few feet away and loudly exclaiming how they did *not* want to slip on the ice on the way to the car because they were all dressed up.

"They're going down," I said softly to the woman next to me. She looked confused, so I continued. "Even though their focus is all about *not* slipping, the picture in their minds is of slipping."

"You should warn them!" she told me.

"I just spent two hours warning them. I don't think they'd believe me."

As we spoke, the two women headed out the door and fell down within seconds. Fortunately, we were able to help them up and walk them safely to their cars.

This concept—that pushing against something actually attracts it to us—can take awhile to wrap our minds around. We start to realize that:

✔ *Every time we criticize someone for a mistake, we are encouraging them to make more mistakes.*

✔ *Every time we think about how fat we are, we are more likely to gain weight.*

✔ *Every time we complain about bills, we attract more bills.*

So how do you *not* fall into these thought patterns? Impossible. Trying *not* to do them will simply bring *more of them*. Instead of worrying about a problem, we can imagine the feeling of having the solution. Fortunately, positive thoughts are a thousand times more powerful than negative thoughts, and so it only takes a few minutes of dreaming a day to see amazing results.

Plugging into Your Power

You can't access your power while you're focused on what you don't want. You'll be like a lamp whose plug can't find the outlet. But once you "plug in" by focusing on thoughts that feel good, there's no dream or goal you can't bring to light.

After hearing about these concepts in his *8 to Great* class, one high school junior took the message to heart. During class, he did the gratitude exercises, then spent three minutes visualizing winning first place in his swim meet against a tough team later that afternoon.

Five hours later, he not only won first place, but took *two full seconds* off his best-ever time. After seeing his time, he jumped out of the water and ran up to his coach yelling, "She was right! That lady was right! When I believe it, I can achieve it!"

He became the motivational coach for his team that season, and the last time I saw him, was fully enjoying his full scholarship to art school.

> *Stay away from people who belittle your aspirations. Small people do that. But the truly great people in the world will make you believe that you, too, can one day become great.*
>
> **Mark Twain**

Why We Don't Ask and Believe

We handcuff the heavens when we don't ask.

Caroline Myss

⊂∞⌐

Take a moment to answer the following:

When it comes to asking for what you want:

    A. *The most selfish people do it all the time.*

    B. *We should only ask when people are in good moods.*

    C. *It's a risk that often ends up badly.*

    D. *The happiest and healthiest people do it all the time.*

The amazing thing is that *only 10 percent* of people get the answer correct the first time. The answer is D. One morning I got a glimpse as to *why...*

Santa Claus or Fairy Godmother?

"Can I talk with you for a minute?" asked a handsome twenty-something man after my **8 to Great** class at a homeless shelter. (I later discovered that although he was homeless, he'd been a professional model.) He walked me to my car and along the way told me how much he'd appreciated my presentation. Then he shared what was on his mind.

"If I start asking for things every day like you suggest, isn't that like believing in Santa Claus? If it were that simple, why wouldn't we all have what we want?"

I thanked him for his powerful question, then asked him to sit with me for a few minutes to do a visualization. He agreed, sat down, and closed his eyes as I began:

"Imagine that your fairy godmother appears to you tonight while you're sleeping. She sprinkles magic fairy dust over you and says, 'As of tomorrow morning, you'll be blessed with more money than you could ever spend. Everywhere you go, you'll increase your wealth.

But there's one spending rule: You may keep it or spend it on yourself, but you may only give it to others *if they ask.'*

"Now imagine it's a month later. You're grateful for having money and all the things money can bring, and excited about visiting family members in another state. As you drive up to their small home, you can't wait to begin sharing your wealth. They greet you with hugs and start asking questions about your amazing new car. You explain about your fairy godmother and that all they have to do is ask and you can give them as much abundance as they want.

"'No way,' says your brother. 'That money's not mine. I can't take any of it.'

"'We haven't done anything to deserve it. It wouldn't be right,' explains your sister-in-law.

"'I don't believe that crazy story,' challenges your nephew.

> To know that one is worthy of happiness is the essence of self-esteem.
>
> **Nathaniel Branden**

"'I'm happy the way I am, son, but thank you,' adds your mom.

"A few days later, you drive away, confused and sad that you couldn't give your nephew a scholarship, your brother a hunting trip up north, your mom a comfortable recliner, or your sister-in-law a new minivan. You understand now why most people don't get. Most people don't ask."

Tears were rolling down his cheeks by the time I finished. He hugged me, thanked me, and walked back to his living quarters. The next day, he started to dream of getting back into shape. That week, someone donated like-new tennis shoes in his size to the shelter. Six weeks later, he had a good job and had lost twenty-five pounds. Six months later, he called to thank me for helping him turn his life around.

The Reasons We Don't Ask

Happiness is always knocking at the front door, yet many of us run out the back. As I discussed at length in my first book, *Taking*

Care of Me: The Habits of Happiness, here are the four main reasons why:

1. We're afraid of getting our dream.
2. We're afraid of being disappointed by losing our dream.
3. We believe we don't deserve our dream.
4. We'd feel guilty about enjoying happiness when others are still unhappy.

Think about the following:

> *If the entire world woke up tomorrow happy and contented*
> *and you were the only one left with any misery or frustration,*
> *what would be your excuse for holding onto your pain?*

A phone call I received one day made me shake my head and smile. An intelligent, happy, and healthy friend who'd been listening to me talk and receiving my monthly Key-Mails for years was helping me proofread an article. In the middle of reading about High-Way 1, he decided to give this stuff a try. He picked up the phone to tell me:

"I got it. Today I got it! I'd been trying to get through to this one business for an hour on the phone, so I finally got fed up and stopped trying. Then I read your *Get the Picture* article and decided to test it.

"I said to myself, 'Someone will pick up on the third ring and we'll have a wonderful and loving conversation.' I only half believed it, but that's exactly what happened—third ring and all! Today was the first day I really and truly understood this isn't just a formula, it's the *truth*!"

Clearly, the reasons we don't ask or believe make no logical or rational sense. They're thought patterns we learned from our parents, who learned them from their parents and passed them along. They were

> *The reason some of your thoughts haven't yet become things is because other thoughts of yours have.*
>
> **Mike Dooley**

all doing the best they could at the time, but with new information, we can now do *better*.

If He Would Have Asked...

How important is asking for what we want to our happiness and well-being?

The following is an excerpt from a letter I received from a fifteen-year-old boy who had been sentenced to twenty years in prison:

"I find it hard to ask for help from friends and family," he began. "I've always been this way—as far back as I can remember. When I ask for help, it feels like I make the person I ask a better person than me and I'm less of a person for having to ask. I feel like there's something wrong with me and that if I need help I'm not a whole person. I also feel that when someone is helping me I must be lazy. This is the way I've felt all my life, but now as a person aware of himself, it is something I wish to change. I know you are helping me do that."

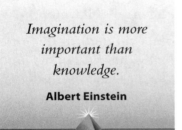

Imagination is more important than knowledge.

Albert Einstein

When I asked him a few weeks later what one message he'd send to young adults if he could share his insights with them, he said, "Reach out for help. There's always someone there. People really do care. God cares. Just ask for help."

Whether it's asking another person or the Source of all that is, many of us are out of practice. When I was growing up, I often heard adults say to the kids in the neighborhood, "You asked for it." We're *always* asking for it. *Every thought is a request.* Knowing this, we can become more focused and better and better at hitting our mark.

Get the Picture Success Stories

Wealth consciousness comes before the physical
manifestation of abundance, not after.

John Randolph Price

⌒∞⌒

I was once asked by a young man if he should follow his dream or follow the dollars. I replied that as I've watched people succeed and fail and succeed again, it had taught me that when you follow your dream, eventually it will take you to the dollars. If you follow dollars, however, they can detour you from your dream.

Asking for Money

Over the years, one of my favorite intentions has been asking for surprise money. I quickly realized that I had nothing to lose in asking and that when I received it, it felt like winning the lottery without buying a ticket!

At first, I found dimes and quarters everywhere I went. Then one summer day, I asked for hundreds of surprise dollars for a project I was working on. When I came back from the mailbox, my son noticed that I was frowning.

"What's the matter, Mom?" he asked.

"Oh, nothing, honey. I just asked for some surprise money, but there weren't any checks in the mail. I expected it, so I'm a bit confused."

"Money can come in more ways than just the mail," my brilliant twelve-year-old pointed out.

"That's true," I said. "Thanks for the reminder. I'll just keep expecting it and let you know how it shows up."

I do voice work at four recording studios in my area, most often phone messages for Fortune 500 companies. It's fun work that pays well. Only one of the four studios pays me the same day I do the work. An hour after the conversation with my son, I got a phone call from *that* studio, asking if I could come in on short notice because they had a boatload of work they needed to get out right away. I was paid hundreds of surprise dollars that afternoon.

A few months later, I was explaining the concept to a friend, but she'd have none of it.

"That's so silly," she said. "That wasn't an answer to your request. It was a coincidence."

I asked her to pick an amount of money she wanted me to ask for to convince her.

"OK, $10,000," she said without hesitation.

I got excited and agreed that I'd receive at least that much in the next week. Two days later, I got a surprise phone call from my printer.

"What do you want to do with these boxes of books?" he asked.

"What boxes are you talking about?" I replied.

"Last year, when you moved into your new home, you asked us to hold half the shipment. They're all paid for, but we have forty boxes sitting here that we need to deliver somewhere."

The total value of that book "find" far exceeded the $10,000 amount I'd requested. My skeptical friend started asking for and receiving surprise money the next day.

One Harvard study showed that ten years after graduation, the MBA graduates who were writing down their dreams were making an average of ten times as much money as those who were not.

Helping Our Children *Get the Picture*

When he was twelve, my son's nationally renowned children's choir was invited to China to sing at the Great Wall. I immediately contacted the director.

"Don't tell me I can't go," I challenged him. (He sometimes was concerned that having parents along was too great a distraction.) Eventually he gave me permission to lead a parents' tour, with a warning that I'd have to find nineteen other parents to join me. Eight e-mails and one month later, thirty-nine of the singers' family members had signed on.

Throughout that time, my company's finances were tied up in a video we were producing. Between that and writing, I wasn't sure where the money for the trip would come from, but I wasn't worried. I continued to get our group ready for what promised to be a glorious time, never giving the money a second thought. Two months into the planning process, I received a call from the tour director's office that my trip would be paid for due to my efforts in coordinating the group.

A few days later, Zach asked me for $250 to spend in China on gifts for family and friends. I knew I could have said yes, but I also knew it was a perfect opportunity for him to learn to manifest abundance for himself.

"Believe that you'll have that much spending money by June, honey," I told him.

"But how will I get it? Shoveling walks? Doing chores for you?" he asked.

"The opportunities will present themselves," I said. "*Intend* that you'll get it easily and quickly, and be grateful that it's already on its way!" He decided to give it a try.

On a snowy day two weeks later, he was in a friend's car on the way to choir practice when they were in a fender bender. Neither of them was hurt, but a month later, we got a call from the other driver's insurance company.

"Ms. Mueller," a voice asked, "who did you want this check made out to?" I assured him that Zachary had no injuries whatsoever, but the man was insistent. "You don't understand, ma'am. The money has already been issued. I have to write a check to someone. Who would you like it to go to, Zachary or yourself?"

The check addressed to Zach arrived two days later—for $250.00.

Intending a Delightful Surprise

My favorite type of intention is "a delightful surprise." I always ask for these to be "knock your socks off" surprises—and they always are!

> *The important thing is this: To be able at any moment to sacrifice what we are for what we could become.*
>
> **Charles Dubois**

One day I hosted a Gratitude Group in my home and nine people showed up. We spent an hour sharing what we were grateful for and saying our intentions out loud. Then we practiced feeling the good feelings we would experience once our intentions showed up. At the end of the evening amid the hugs and goodbyes, one woman asked if she could stay after for some help.

"I'd love to get some CDs to listen to on the days I don't have this group," she began. "Can you recommend some?" We went to my computer and I pulled up a list.

"I have everything by this author except Volume Two," I said. "They're all good, and I'm going to order Volume Two soon because I hear it's great."

She thanked me, gave me a hug, and left. I walked across the room to where my son had left the mail and sat down to read through the pile. When I got to the last item, a small package, I didn't recognize the return address.

"Who do I know in Vermont?" I wondered. I opened the package to find a note from someone I hadn't seen in a year. The note read, "MK, I know you love this author and I've listened to this set many times, so wanted to share it with you."

It was Volume Two.

The Oscar Dream

I love watching the Oscars—but not for the dresses. I watch the show to hear the inspiring acceptance speeches, like Hilary Swank's when she received her first Oscar for Best Actress.

> *"This is for those dreams that started all those years ago…*
> *in a mobile home court…"*

I love nothing more than imagining little Hilary, reading a book or looking out the window and imagining winning an Oscar in a gorgeous dress, smiling in front of millions of viewers. If you don't know her story, Google it. It's a classic example of a mother and daughter *Getting the Picture* while everyone around them was saying, "Impossible!" It is the hallmark of all the greats of ours and every age.

Love Was Looking for Her

I have seen countless examples of how, when we are looking for our dream to be realized, it is looking for us.

Kathleen attended one of my trainings six happy years into her marriage. Over dinner one evening she shared a wonderful story. A few months before her graduation from college, her boyfriend had broken up with her, leaving her devastated. Soon after receiving her diploma, she decided to take charge of her attitude and her love life. It started with a *Gratitude* list for all the good times they had shared with each other.

> *I'd be lying if I said I hadn't made a version of this speech before.*
> *I was probably eight years old and staring into the bathroom mirror. And this (holding up her statuette) would've been a shampoo bottle.*
> *Well, it's not a shampoo bottle now!*
>
> **Kate Winslet, 2009 Oscar winner of Best Actress**

"There were so many things to be grateful for, I focused on those and then started dreaming about finding my True Love," she told me.

She was amazed that just a few days after making her list, love songs were no longer painful to listen to. Instead, she heard the songs as though "he" (her imagined new love) had requested them for her. It wasn't long before "he" had a name.

It happened when she went to the movie *A Walk to Remember* and was completely taken by the actor Shane West. She began to daydream about him because it was so much fun and soon started talking about him to her friends as though they were a couple.

"I'd tell people that Shane was taking me out on Saturday" she told me, "but he wanted to surprise me and wouldn't tell me where we were going. It was our silly game."

A few weeks later, a classmate of hers called to say she was looking for someone to ride across country with her as she moved to

> *You've been telling the truth. You've just been telling it in advance.*
>
> **Zig Ziglar**

Arizona. Kathleen thought the adventure sounded like great fun and agreed to go.

"I'll never forget the day we drove through Iowa. We were both in "95" moods. It was a picture perfect summer day—blue skies, just the right amount of white fluffy clouds, green rolling hills as far as the eye could see—and then I saw it: a lovely white church steeple peeking out from between the hills.

"I squealed, 'Look at that. It's perfect! I could live here. I could meet someone wonderful, fall in love, and be deliriously happy!'"

High on hills and hope, Kathleen and her friend stopped at the next town to find a motel for the night. As they were checking in, Kathleen caught the eye of the gentleman behind the counter. Once they started talking, he wouldn't let her out of his sight.

You guessed it. The gentleman's name behind the counter was Shane. They fell in love over the next few months, and a year later, Kathleen married *Shane*, the man she had met while driving *West*.

Emma Gets Her Job

Remember Emma, the woman I asked to write down her dream job requirements? Before I tell you how things turned out, I need to note that Emma's son was such a phenomenal hockey player that his parents sent him to a year-round hockey instruction program in Colorado at fifteen years of age. He hadn't lived at home for two years. Now see if you can guess what happened. The list of specific intentions for her new job included:

- ✔ *A team-oriented environment*
- ✔ *A growing company that encourages me to venture into new arenas*
- ✔ *An environment that enables me to reach out and meet others*
- ✔ *A job where I don't just sit at a computer all day*
- ✔ *A job where I can mesh my accounting with my operational and management skills*

After not getting the third job she had interviewed for that month, Emma came home one evening to a circled paragraph in the local paper. "Look, honey," her husband began, "a professional hockey team is relocating here. They're gonna be hiring, why not check it out?"

She did and passed through one interview after another. At the end of her final interview for the highest-paying position for her skills, the team's manager leaned forward at his desk and got serious. "Emma, we're very impressed with you. I'd like to hire you, but I have to ask one more question. Do you know anything about hockey?"

As of this writing, Emma manages the budget for a multi-million-dollar professional hockey team, gets to work in a "team-oriented" environment, and regularly ventures into "new arenas" as she lives the life she'd imagined!

All big men are dreamers. They see things in the soft haze of a spring day, Or in the red fire of a long winter's evening. Some of us let these great dreams die, But others nourish and protect them, Nurse them through bad days till they bring them to sunshine and light, Which always come to those who sincerely believe.

Woodrow Wilson

Putting *Get the Picture* into Practice

When you're ready to follow the **8 to Great** process, it will start with your first thoughts each day.

Your Daily *Gratitude Rich-ual*

Take a minute to write your 3-5 *Gratitudes* each morning or evening. Recount on paper or via e-mail, 3-5 things you're grateful for from the past twenty-four hours with no repeats. If you write them down at night, begin your day by reading them over the next morning.

Then, at least once a week, take time to do the 3-Minute Visualization technique outlined earlier. As you start having fun with this, you may also want to add a little variety into your gratitude and visualization diet with a *Gratitude Sand-Wish*.

The *Gratitude Sand-Wish*

Here's how it works:

When you awaken each day to write down three things you're grateful for, select one from the past, one from the present, and one for the future. This third *Gratitude* is actually an intention. Your gratitude emanates from the feeling of having already received it. Again, that's:

One Gratitude from the Past: "I'm so grateful that I received/experienced…"

One Gratitude from the Present: "I am so grateful right now for…"

One Gratitude for the Future: "I am so grateful now that…"

(Pick one dream that's coming your way and be grateful for it as if it has already arrived.)

For this third *Gratitude*, remember to stay proactive rather than intending that things "stop happening." That's focusing on the things you don't want, which will only manifest more of them.

One of my favorite stories about using the *Gratitude Sand-Wish* happened many years ago but is still clear in my mind. I realized that I was feeling unsupported (low on the **Power Pyramid**), so as I was getting on a plane to keynote at a national education conference, I decided to spend a minute making a delicious *Gratitude Sand-Wish*.

The first slice of bread was my *Gratitude* for the *past*. I wrote:

I'm grateful for the way the earth supports me every day.

Then I wrote down the meat of my Sand-Wish—a *Gratitude* for the *present*:

I'm grateful for the airline crew offering me drinks and a pillow this afternoon.

Finally, I topped it off by writing my intention in gratitude form as if it had already happened:

I'm grateful now that I have met wonderfully supportive people at the hotel.

Those three *Gratitudes* shifted my mood and I had a great flight. Then I watched in amazement as my visualization unfolded. After we landed, I was met by a driver who took me to my hotel. I never touched my bags, got checked in within two minutes, and as the conference keynote, was given a key to a private floor.

Once on that floor, I had an exquisite view of the evening's gentle snowfall on the river, chocolates waiting on my pillow, a beautiful welcome gift on the dresser, a whirlpool tub, a fireplace, and a valet in the room next to mine *asking if I wanted bottled water or to have my suit pressed* for the following day. (I asked for both!)

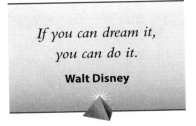

If you can dream it, you can do it.

Walt Disney

When creating a Sand-Wish, the "no repeat" rule applies to past and present, but you may repeat in the dreaming (future) section. Let's review why the Sand-Wish works so well:

1. I got to a "95" place (with Gratitudes), where what goes around comes around quickly.

2. I asked clearly for what I wanted.

3. I moved into grateful expectation as I imagined receiving my request.

The result was that I was able to receive what I had asked for—all in a matter of hours.

If you have that one big dream that you want to visualize every morning or once a week, using the *Get the Picture* 3-Minute Visualization is the way to go. The Sand-Wish helps you ask for and manifest various sizes of intentions, keeping your *Hope* muscle "nourished" as you build your belief in your biggest dreams.

With either the basic gratitude activity or the *Gratitude Sand-Wish*, the total time elapsed is less than three minutes per day. Are your dreams and happiness worth it?

Why Writing Helps

Every thought is an intention, but the ones you write down will manifest more quickly because *thinking*, then *writing*, then *seeing* it on paper is a triple dose of affirming its truth. It will also build your confidence in this process as you check back and see the dreams and intentions you've written down start to appear. Many of today's intentions will turn into tomorrow's *Gratitudes*. I've never known anyone to do this process and *not* have some of their intentions start showing up within a week or two.

> *The only limit to our realization of tomorrow will be our doubts of today.*
>
> **Franklin D. Roosevelt**

One of my dear friends loves this process but "isn't a journal keeper." Even so, she decided to try the Sand-Wish out of curiosity. For her future Gratitude, she wrote that she was "grateful now that I'm enjoying more travel."

When she got four invitations to great vacation spots in the *next two weeks*, she *Got the Picture!*

Super-Sizing Your Dreams

It doesn't matter what size your intentions are. Intending little things at first can build up your *Believing muscle* and prepare you to believe you can manifest bigger things. Remember to focus on *how you want to feel* with phrases such as: "I'm so grateful now that I have such great close friends" or "I'm so grateful now that I'm hearing so many congratulations." Being disappointed means you're impatient. Remember to let go of the when's and who's and just have fun with the what's and why's. Soon your friends will be asking for your secret—and you'll be the perfect one to tell them.

I recall the day I did a visualization of this book being completed. In my mind, I saw myself signing books in New York in the spring. My friends were all around me, laughing and talking. They knew we were going (in a white limo) to a classy restaurant that evening to celebrate and that they'd be in the audience the next day as I gave my first national television interview. We were all in a great mood—it felt wonderfully real!

"Hogwash!" shout the skeptics. "Tom Foolery!" cry the critics. Maybe it's a truth only fools and children can see. Ever wonder why they call it *"make-believe?"* Because by *believing* it, we access our God-given power to *make* it so.

The Teacher's Story

As part of my high school curriculum of *8 to Great,* I recommend a special graduation ceremony, during which students are able to share their success stories and receive certificates of completion. I'll never forget one young English teacher in our first inner city school.

At the *8 to Great* graduation ceremony that May afternoon, we went around the circle and learned that one junior had added thirty-four points to his competitive bowling score while a classmate of his had contacted her father for the first time in years. Each student had an amazing story to share.

I believed in belief for its own sake. To believe in the face of utter hopelessness, every article of evidence to the contrary, that's what's most important. Dispiritedness and disappointment are the real perils of life, not some sudden illness or cataclysmic millennium doomsday. My advice to each of you is never stop believing.

Lance Armstrong

As the circle ended, I turned to their teacher and said, "You've been participating through all the sessions. Have you seen any changes in your life that you'd like to tell us about?"

She teared up as she began, "I wasn't planning on sharing today, but I guess this is as good a day as any. In college, I was in the pre-med program. My first science test my junior year was especially difficult and I flunked it. Panic-stricken, I went to the instructor to request special help, telling him I needed a good grade to get into medical school.

"He laughed at me and said, 'There's no way that someone who flunks my exams can make it in med school.'

"Heartbroken, I dropped his class and changed my major the following day."

She paused to compose herself before continuing.

"I love teaching, but after hearing this program, I realize that I need to follow my dream, so last week I turned in my resignation. I'll stay until the end of this year, but I've already applied to medical school." Her students applauded her.

That woman was—and still is—one of my heroes. She taught in the most powerful way, through her example, how to *Get the Picture* as well as how to practice High-Way 2: *Risk.* We're not only much stronger than we imagine, we're much stronger *when* we imagine.

Q & A on *Get the Picture*

Q: *I went to lunch with a friend last week and we had so much fun talking about our dreams and memories that I went home feeling great. When I got to the office the next day, I had a message about a huge contract. Is it true that people can be "good luck" charms?*

A: Anything that makes you feel good—a smell, a taste, a touch, a beautiful sight, or a fun lunch with a friend—instantly moves you up the **Power Pyramid**. If you and your friend spent almost an hour "95-ing," that positive vibration was building on itself, heightening the effect. Staying at a high vibration for an hour will have a greater impact than a minute a day for sixty days. It's like a laser beam. The longer you hold a laser in one place, the more intense the effect.

Q: *When I was in my mid-30s, I was the golden boy at a huge advertising firm, often handling million-dollar accounts. Before every major project started, I'd spend two days mentally "walking through" what I'd wear, what I'd say, every meeting, every shoot, and every editing session in my mind. Sometimes I'd replay a "scene" in my mind three or four times until it felt right. I thought I was doing it because I was afraid of making a mistake. Now you're telling me that all along I was Getting the Picture?*

A: Yes. Welcome to the *fourth category of people*—those who are happy and *know* why!

Q: *When I discovered the* Get the Picture *concept years ago, it worked beautifully for me, but then I lost my "magic touch." How can I get back to manifesting what I desire with ease?*

A: You may be experiencing a very natural effect of taking the process for granted. What happens is that rather than imagining having what we want, we sometimes just think about thinking about it. We don't ever get to the feeling excited place.

"Yes," we think, "there's that yellow convertible. I could think about owning that." Then we stop there. *Get the Picture* doesn't work that way. You have to really put yourself in the picture and let it change how you feel. Don't just dip your toes in the water. Swim in the pictures of your imagination. Go test drive the car. Go visit the college. Take time each week to feed your imagination through listening to CDs, journaling, or daydreaming until you feel *grateful for already having it!*

Q: *What does being at "95" have to do with asking for what I want? Can't I ask for what I want when I'm in a really crummy mood, too?*

A: You can ask from there; you just can't receive from there. Let's say you're in an unhealthy relationship and want a better one, so you break up with boyfriend X and imagine boyfriend W (for Wonderful). In the moment you're imagining Mr. W, you're at "95."

Now it's the next day. You don't do your *Gratitudes*. Instead, you look in the mirror and tell yourself you hate your puffy eyes. You almost trip over the cat, so you start yelling at him. You listen to the news on the radio on the way to work and decide the world's falling apart. Once you get to work, you mutter to yourself about all the impossible deadlines.

Look where you are. From your position at the bottom of the **Power Pyramid**, that new salesman who is your "95" prince charming is going to stop by your office today, but neither of you will notice the other. You're not a match. He's "95-ing" and you're "5-ing." Instead, your ex-boyfriend is going to call and ask you to forgive him, and you'll consider it because you have lost hope that anybody "really good" is out there. *Now, let's replay the day.*

Take 2: Another possible scenario…

You wake up to a phone call from your *Gratitude Partner*. You both take a few minutes to do a *Gratitude Sand-Wish* with each other. Your future intention is "I'm so grateful now that I've had a delightful surprise that's so big it bowled me over." You really believe this will happen and are on the lookout for it!

You look in the mirror and are grateful for your nice smile and the stylist who helps bring out the best in your hair. From this relaxed state, when you see your cat sitting in your path, you pick him up and know that he just wants a little extra attention today. After a few minutes of cat time, you make your favorite breakfast, grateful that the milk hasn't soured, even though it's past its due date.

On your drive to work you play a CD of your favorite song. You imagine you and your sweetheart dancing to it in the living room. You see your date as you hear it live in concert.

You get to work, look at the number of e-mails you have to return, and are grateful that you have a job where you're busy, unlike the last one, where you were bored.

Now what happens when the new sales guy walks into your office? He only has eyes for "95's," and his eyes are on *you!*

Q: *I had a question come up in my ninth-grade class today and I told them I'd e-mail you. The student asked, "Will there ever come a time when I say, 'I can do it' but it just doesn't work out for me and ends up that I really couldn't do it?"*

A: No. If your thoughts create your reality, they create your reality. The only thing that might stop your "success" is that you got attached to the "when" and gave up one minute before the end of the game. You might consider having the students watch the movie *Rudy*, about a college student who gave up very close to the finish line and had to be talked back into a "95" place.

Q: *How do you continue believing when you've been waiting for your dream for a long time?*

A: I read success stories to remind me that everything is coming in its own perfect time. Find yourself a *Chicken Soup for the Soul* book full of hopeful stories and remember that its creator, Jack Canfield, was rejected by 123 publishers when he first proposed the idea for his book. At this book's printing, that series has sold over 80 million copies in over fifty languages. More on *Hope for the Future* in High-Way 8.

Q: *What do I do with the naysayers in my life?*

A: I suggest you only share your dreams with dreamers. The ancient Scriptures remind us not to cast our "pearls before swine." It's not that some people are swine. It's that they don't know the value of dreams and will treat them just like everything else in the trough.

Arguing with naysayers is draining. Simply say something like, "Thanks for sharing," without malice or cynicism. Then go *prove them wrong*.

Q: *When are dreams just fantasy? I have a dream of driving a black Mercedes—it's something I've always wanted. I don't know that it would serve much of a bigger purpose. Isn't that selfish?*

A: First, the "purpose" of getting your Mercedes is that you'll remember who you are and that you've been given the power to manifest anything in your life. You'll become so joy-filled with this understanding that you'll spread it to people, young and old, who are caught up in darkness and despair. Now that's a lot of "mileage" to get out of one Mercedes!

When you're ready you'll upgrade your definition of dreams from "fantasy" to "fantastic." You'll see that your dreams are sacred and realize that being called a "dreamer" is a very high compliment.

Finally, remember that the Mercedes won't bring you genuine happiness. It's your genuine happiness that will bring your Mercedes. Remembering your power to *Get the Picture* and choose your focus is the key that unlocks it all.

As long as you're going to think anyway,
think big.

Donald Trump

❧

High-Way 2:
Risk
Run to, Not from

Defining *Risk*

Only those who dare to fail greatly
can ever achieve greatly.

Robert F. Kennedy

⧼∞⧽

Webster's dictionary describes *risk* as: "a chance of suffering or harm or loss...danger." Most parents would agree. Yet the skill of creative risk-taking and thinking out of the box is a pre-requisite for success in business and in life. Obviously, our culture sends us very mixed messages about risk, but the greats among us have always agreed—*Risk* is the road to rewards.

There is no security on this earth. Only opportunity.
Douglas MacArthur, Chief of Staff, U.S. Army

If you want to increase your success rate, double your failure rate.
Thomas Watson, Sr., founder of IBM

Do one thing every day that scares you.
Eleanor Roosevelt, former first lady

Teaching this High-Way over the years, I've found that even those who acknowledge that moving out of our comfort zones is a good idea sometimes hesitate to take the chance. Why? Because risks are *risky*, and when they don't turn out, they can deal a seemingly crushing blow to our self-esteem. Therein lies the catch: on our lowest days, when we least want to risk, risk is the only way back up the **Power Pyramid**.

When we take a risk and it doesn't turn out, we can use this supposed "failure" as an excuse for guilt, regret, or self-doubt. From this lower place on the **Power Pyramid**, the courage to risk can feel out of reach, yet risk is necessary to redirect our focus. Whether it is daring to dream, feel, hope, or forgive, traveling on each of the High-Ways of *8 to Great* is its own risk.

The Happiest People

As children, risking was as normal for us as breathing. Ever see a child standing at the bottom of a large slide, yelling up to his playmate, "Now be careful up there?" No way. We all start out as risk-takers, but over the years we slowly shut down in order to play it safe.

> *to be nobody but yourself, in a world which is doing its best to make you everybody else—means to fight the hardest battle which any human being can fight; and never stop fighting.*
>
> **E. E. Cummings**

Two psychotherapists went around the world in the 1960s to study thirty-three different cultures with one intent: to find out *what the happiest people had in common.* The most common characteristic wasn't love, money, or fame. Neither was it good looks, lots of friends, perfect health, or perfect grades. It was *Risk*.

When people hear that for the first time, their response is interesting. One young GED student moved right to the heart of it by asking: "What kind of risks am I supposed to take?"

I looked into her wise young eyes and asked, "What's the greatest risk you could take from now 'til the day you die?"

"To be myself," she replied.

"And that, young woman, will remain your greatest risk for as long as you live."

A Different Drummer

One sure sign of maturity is when we begin to follow our inner voice more than the outer voices around us. The challenge is that internal wisdom will often lead in the opposite direction of external wisdom. "Follow your heart" may directly contradict your co-worker warning you not to "rock the boat." Your family of origin may want

The reward for conforming is that everyone likes you except yourself.

Rita Mae Brown

you to take a job close to home while your intuition is telling you to do what you love and follow your dreams.

Whether you refer to this inner counselor as your gut, your instinct, or your sacred knowing, you've undoubtedly heard it tell you to do something that would result in disapproval from those around you. The journey of a risk-taker inevitably includes times of trial, pain, and solitude. Yet risk we must.

Risk vs. Escape

In *8 to Great*, we define risk as facing our fears as opposed to trying to escape from them.

Risk is running to, not from.

Notice in the following list that some risks are *running to* and others are *running from:*

✔ sharing your improvement idea with your boss
✔ asking for a raise
✔ lying to a friend
✔ quitting a job with no notice
✔ getting drunk
✔ parasailing

Sharing your improvement idea, asking for a raise, and parasailing are *risks* because they are running *to* a goal or dream. On the other hand, all my audiences reply in unison that lying, quitting a job with no notice, and getting drunk are *escapes*—examples of running *from* our fears.

Fear Has No Favorites

Who do you think has the most fear, cowards or heroes? Most people assume it's one or the other, but the surprising fact is that we all have exactly the same amount. The high dive at the swimming pool is scary to *every* ten-year-old. Heroes feel the fear and do it anyway.

On any given day we can use fear as an excuse to stay stuck or we can tap into our innate courage and dive into our next risk. If you haven't been taking risks, your resistance to what's new and different has probably grown strong. As one CEO told me after my seminar, "I've created a security blanket that's suffocating me." He was ready to throw off his fear of change and start living again.

> *A ship is safe in harbor, but that's not what ships are for.*
>
> **William Shedd**

Fear has no favorites. It plagues us all from time to time. I'll always remember the evening a good friend of mine called to ask if he could come over to talk. The next morning he planned to ask his bank for a ten million dollar loan, even though he already owed them double that amount. I listened as he talked and held him as he shook with fear. Today he's worth many times his original debt.

There are some who could not imagine being in such a situation. Those who are the most miserable and stuck often criticize risk-takers and are quick to point out when we fall and skin our knees. The fact is that in order to find happiness and success, instead of being scared to death we must risk being "scared to life."

Who Makes More Mistakes?

When I teach High-Way 2 to adolescents, I ask this multiple choice question:

Successful people make how many mistakes as compared to unsuccessful people?

    a) half as many

    b) the same number

    c) twice as many

    d) five times as many

    e) twenty times as many

Very few guess the correct answer: e) twenty times as many.

Risks don't have to be huge. Everyone has the potential to take small risks every day. Maybe *American Idol* auditions aren't for you, but there's always the risk of singing a solo at church. Maybe you won't be called on to donate a kidney, but there's always an opportunity to donate blood, join a dance class, run for the school board, learn to roller blade, or strike up a conversation with your new neighbor.

The *Risk* of *Risking*

As I've shared earlier, I love the Academy Awards. It never fails to amaze me how top entertainers continue to grow and risk. I recall watching one year to learn that Clint Eastwood was not only a magnificent actor and director, but also a producer, a former mayor of Carmel, California, and an Academy Award nominated composer of film scores.

But, I hear you saying, *it's easy for him to risk, he's Clint Eastwood.*

I would rephrase that as: *It's easy for him to be Clint Eastwood because he risks.*

> *It is not because things are difficult that we do not dare. It is because we do not dare that things are difficult.*
>
> **Seneca**

What Have You Got to Lose?

What do you fear losing most? Time? Money? The respect of others? Your self-respect? These are all common anxieties we'll examine in the coming sections. Another reason many of us avoid venturing into new territory is because we fear that we'll lose *hope*.

In the past, perhaps we tried something new, hit a snag, and jumped to the conclusion that we weren't "supposed to" be on that particular path. We mistakenly interpreted a detour as a cosmic STOP sign.

Perhaps you wanted to go back to school but didn't get a loan. Perhaps you called to ask someone out but they turned you down. Perhaps your first month of sales yielded no results. None of those are out of the ordinary or a sign of defeat. Rather than failures, they were *feedback*. Those who want success on a silver platter have forgotten what the road to success looks like.

> *The jump is so frightening between where I am and where I want to be...*
>
> *but because of all I may become, I will close my eyes and leap!*
>
> **Maryanne Radmacher-Hershey**

The Road to Success

On a sheet of paper or in the air in front of you, draw what you think the road to success looks like. Start at *A* on your left-hand side (signifying where you *are* in your social life, work life, health goals, etc.) and end at *Z* on your right-hand side (signifying where you want to *arrive*). About half the people in my seminars draw a zigzag line from point to point, while the other half draws a straight line. The confusion reminds me of a student who once asked, "Do you want me to draw what I believe or what's true?" **8 to Great** teaches that:

The road to success is *never* a straight line.

Great courage in the face of great adversity is the norm for those who soar above the crowd. That understanding will come in handy when it's your turn to look fear in the eye and, like Dorothy, say to the Wicked Witch, "I'm not afraid of you!"

The *Risk* Process:
Run to, Not from

Life is an ongoing process of choosing between
safety (out of fear) and risk (for growth).
Make the growth choice a dozen times a day.

Abraham Maslow

Once you're ready to face your fears and move through them, you can begin using this formula for making the best, most loving decisions *every time*. The next time you have a decision to make, just ask yourself:

"If I had no fear, what would I do?"

Once I was sharing this with a group in recovery and a young woman blurted out, "Then I'd get drunk!" When I asked her if that was truly the case, she said no.

I worked with homeless people every week for over ten years. Sometimes they had only been off the streets a couple of days when I first met them. I've never heard any of them say they began abusing substances because they were *running to*. Rather, they acknowledged that it was the *fear of facing their pain* and *running from* that led them to use.

> *Some people live for ninety years. Others just live one year ninety times.*
>
> **Dr. Wayne Dyer**

A-ffair Question

The first time I asked a large audience the decision-making question, "If you had no fear, what would you do?" I received a surprising response.

A gentleman sitting in the back of the room yelled out, "Did you say if I had an affair, what would I do?"

After the laughter subsided, we were all able to agree that if you had no fear, you'd never have an affair, because you'd be open and honest with those concerned, including yourself, about what was going on. Addictions always involve secrets and are always running *from*.

The 95-Year-Old Vote Is In

When 95-year-olds are asked what they'd do differently if they got to do life over again, they most often reply they'd have taken more risks. It isn't the risks they *took* that they regretted, but the risks they *didn't* take. That would mean that raising your hand to ask the "stupid question" might be the *smartest* thing you can do!

The *Risk* of Believing in Our Dreams

The word "courage" comes from the French word *coeur*, meaning *heart*. The most courageous people are those who follow their hearts to places their minds would never approve of. Believing in our dreams takes great courage because our dreams often don't make logical or financial sense.

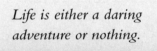

Life is either a daring adventure or nothing.

Helen Keller

I once knew a man who was rising to great heights as a corporate dealmaker. One day at lunch I asked him the "if fear wasn't a factor" question.

He challenged me, saying, "You don't understand. I just closed a five-million-dollar deal. I don't have any fears."

I continued, "Then tell me, if fear wasn't a factor, who would you *be?*"

He paused for a moment before he shared something he'd never told anyone.

"I'd be a math teacher to fifth graders at an inner city school." Then he added, "But if you ever tell anyone it was me who said that, you're dead."

No Risk, No Reward

When an employee can't risk saying no, they're headed for burnout, for no one can do it all. The ability to say no is the only way our *yes* means anything. When we agree to something, we are agreeing *not* to do other things. The glory of the human experience is that we can *have* it all—but not all at once.

Boundaries are honoring that something is important enough to you not to do something else. Whether we're in a recovery program, on a diet, or making sales calls, there are always distractions attempting to lure us away from our path. Assertiveness is needed to stand our ground and stay the course. At a time in my life when I was new at *no*, I found the following tenets from S. R. Lloyd extremely helpful:

Tenets of Assertiveness

1. By trying to govern our lives so we never hurt anyone, we end up hurting ourselves and others.

2. Not letting others know how we feel and what we think is a form of selfishness.

3. Sacrificing our rights usually results in training other people to mistreat us.

4. If we don't tell others how their behavior negatively affects us, we are denying them an opportunity to change their behavior.

5. We have the right to refuse requests, to feel and express anger, fear and hurt, to make mistakes in order to learn, to have opinions that are different from those of our family and friends, to be treated as capable adults, and to have our needs be as important as anyone else's.

Rewarding Your Risks

I'm a firm believer in recognizing and rewarding risks, regardless of whether or not they are successful. As a business owner, there aren't any gold watches or banquets in someone's honor among our little staff. Instead we might announce, "When *this* happens, we'll have lunch at the top of the Hilton."

Rewarding children for risks can also be rewarding. When my son turned six, I was concerned because he wasn't going underwater at the pool. To try and "fix" that problem, I signed him up for swim

> *To believe yourself brave is to be brave; it is the only essential thing.*
>
> **Mark Twain**

lessons, certain that the lifeguard would help remedy the situation. Unfortunately (for my agenda), Zach was smart enough to simply move to the back of the line when the instructor wasn't looking every time there was an underwater activity.

One day as I watched this fascinating foil take place, the teacher announced that as a special treat at the end of the class, anyone who wished to could jump off the diving board. Knowing that such a thing was out of the realm of possibility for my son, I started to walk toward the locker rooms—but my thirteen-year-old daughter stayed put at the fence.

"Psst! Zach! Come here!" she whispered.

Her younger brother obeyed and walked over to her. I was curious, too.

"If you jump off the low diving board, Mom'll take you to Dairy Queen!"

"Will you, Mom?" Zach asked.

"Um...of course I will, sweetheart."

To my amazement, after many small swimmers backed down from the diving board, Zach walked out to the edge, looked at the instructor holding out her arms to catch him, jumped into the water in the opposite direction, and swam over to the ladder.

Zach got his ice cream cone that day—and I got an amazing life lesson. My daughter knew that while waiting for life to reward us for risks, we can often reward ourselves.

Getting a Return on Your Risk

Here are some examples of how you can reward yourself for little risks. Note that it isn't the *outcome* that earns the rewards, it's the *output* of risk-taking!

Making ten cold sales calls—taking yourself and a friend to a movie

Asking someone out—a professional massage

Showing up for your first racquetball lesson—lunch at the best restaurant

Asking for a raise—taking a whole Saturday off without doing anything

Trying out for a play—going to dinner with a friend before the cast is announced

> *Courage is the price*
> *that life extracts for granting peace.*
> **Amelia Earhart**

✖

Why We Don't *Risk*

*There came a time when the risk to remain tight in the bud
was more painful than the risk it took to blossom.*

Anais Nin

∽

If so many self-help and motivational gurus agree that risk is the key to happiness, health, and wealth, why don't more of us turn off Reality TV and embrace our own adventures? Perhaps the answer is nestled somewhere between stock market and insurance industry jargon, which teaches that "low-risk" is the way to go.

I recall a high school junior who barely blinked during the first hour of my program because he was so engrossed. He shared with me after class that he had never considered the possibility that risk could be a good thing.

When he left for school the following morning, his mother sent him off with her usual, "Okay honey, be safe!"

"No, Mom!" he countered. "I'm learning from this lady at school that successful people take *risks*, so from now on, tell me to take some risks."

"Okay, honey," she replied hesitantly, taking her own gamble. "Go take some risks!"

Over the next six weeks, that young man went from all Cs and Ds to As and Bs, excelled as a football player, improved his relationship with his girlfriend, and according to his mother, "was barely recognizable as the same person because he was so helpful."

> *People can do extraordinary things if they have the confidence and take the risks. Yet most people don't. They sit in front of the TV and treat life as if it goes on forever.*
>
> **Philip Adams**

The Myth of Job Security

According to research done in 2008 by educator Karl Fisch and Creative Commons, the *top ten* in-demand jobs in 2010 did not exist in 2004. In addition, the average student, Fisch states, will have 10-14 jobs by the age of thirty-eight. In that light, what is job security, and does it make sense to pressure young people to decide what they want to do with their lives? Such pressure can discourage students from pursuing "risky" careers (such as entrepreneurial endeavors or the arts) and steer them toward more monetarily "secure" jobs. The false promise of security often entices us away from our dreams.

A Question of Who and When

One day after realizing a certain book agent wasn't going to work out for us, I was feeling disappointed and discouraged. My then 16-year-old son came in and gave me a hug. The next day as we were sitting and talking, he asked me a powerful question: "Mom, why don't you use the stuff you know to stop having ups and downs?"

I thanked him for his question and then asked him to show with his fingers how big a risk most people take. He showed me an inch. Then I asked how big the risks were that I usually took. He showed me about twelve inches. I agreed with his guestimate.

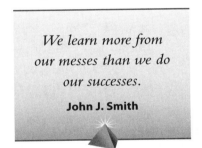

We learn more from our messes than we do our successes.

John J. Smith

"They're called risks because they're risky," I reminded him. "There's no way to protect yourself from big losses or big disappointments when you're going for the gold."

Somehow he had heard what I'd been saying all those years as something like "once you do these steps, your road to success will be a straight line," so I had to set the record "straight."

"Honey, what I teach is to believe that good stuff is coming and to let go of the *how* and the *when*. You and I thought this agent was going to be the *how* and we got all excited. Now we just have to step back, take a deep breath, and watch for *when* the real *who* shows up."

Making Friends with Change

Want to make friends with change? Rather than dreading its knock at the door, try inviting it over for dinner. I once spoke to a

> *Those who say it cannot be done should not interrupt the person doing it.*
>
> **Chinese Proverb**

group of men who had worked for the railroad an average of twenty-seven years. The topic for my talk was: "Shift Happens: Tools for Transition."

I asked them to write down what changes they would incorporate into their workplace if they were in charge. Out of seventy-nine men, seventy-eight wrote: "profit-sharing." We then spent thirty minutes brainstorming risks they could take to unite as one voice on that issue to get the attention of those in charge, amid mutterings such as, "She just doesn't understand how this place works."

The talk was so well received that I was invited back the following year. Again I asked everyone to list the changes they'd like to see at work. Not one of them listed profit-sharing. When I asked why, they told me, "Oh, we have that now!"

Their willingness to take a risk and dream about the solutions led to their desire being fulfilled.

The Money Excuse

It's common to hear people say that they can't take risks because they don't have the money. The book *Do What You Love, The Money Will Follow* by Marsha Sinetar adds some interesting points to this discussion. Here are some famous businesses whose founders refused to "buy" into the money excuse:

- ✔ Domino's pizza was started with a $900 loan.
- ✔ Pink's Hot Dogs in Hollywood was started with a hot dog cart in 1939 and in 2007 made 2.5 million in revenue.
- ✔ Calvin Klein was started when a friend loaned him $10,000.
- ✔ Ben and Jerry's began when they took a $5 correspondence course on making ice cream and got a $4,000 loan.
- ✔ Apple got its start when Jobs and Wozniak sold their van and two calculators. That $1,300 provided their initial funding.

Great risks don't need great amounts of money; they need great courage, great belief, and great perseverance.

Jim Carrey's Early Risks

Some of us run from risk because we don't want to "hit the rocks." The great news is that *there are no rocks*. Rock bottom is really a trampoline. The harder you hit it, the higher you can spring back, if you'll only release your self-judgment. The same "rocky" experience that deters one person from risking will be the catalyst for another to take a chance.

> *Avoiding danger is no safer in the long run than outright exposure.*
>
> **Helen Keller**

Dozens of life stories such as actor Jim Carrey's reveal that many people took their greatest risks when their life picture looked the gloomiest. When Jim was ten and his family needed money to pay the bills, he sent his resume to the star of the top comedy show on TV—Carol Burnett. Although he never heard from her, it did not deter him from dreaming big dreams and taking big risks later in life.

Nineteen years later, when he had only a few dollars to his name, he drove to the most beautiful area of Beverly Hills in the middle of the night and got out of his car. He sat on the curb and stared at his dream home until he could believe that he lived there. Five years later, he was living in his own million-dollar mansion and commanding $10 million per film.

"What have I got to lose?" is embedded in our universal unconscious for just that purpose—so that when all else fails, we'll take our boldest risks and end up with our best results.

> *There was a very cautious man. Who never danced or prayed.*
> *He never risked. He never cried. He never sang or played.*
> *And when he passed away one day, his insurance was denied.*
> *For since he never really lived, they claimed...he never died.*
>
> **Anonymous**

❦

Risk Success Stories

Decide that you want it more than
you are afraid of it.
Bill Cosby

No guts, no glory. No risk, no story. If fear wasn't a factor, our question moves from "What do I have to lose?" to "What do I have to gain?" Every adversity can make us bitter or better. We are the ones who get to decide.

The Three Greatest Risks

My eulogy will likely be filled with stories of the risks I took that worked out, but there have been many more that did not. Throughout all of my risking, I've found three kinds of risks that are the riskiest of all: believing, trusting, and setting boundaries.

1. Believing in our Dreams

Renna had been unhappy for years because her job had become more paperwork than people work. After eighteen years with a solid company, she told me she was leaving. Without another job lined up, she had decided to take some time off to figure out what she really wanted to do. Renna was a risk-taker!

It was a thrill to watch her adventure unfold. She'd always wanted to work in a bookstore, so for five months she worked part-time for $7.00 an hour and broke every sales record they had. But after awhile, she longed to return to a "career" and began applying for full-time jobs. Two months into that process, her self-confidence and faith in her ability to find that great job had begun to wane.

"I have a job interview today, but..." her voice trailed off during our phone conversation.

"But what?" I asked.

"But I'm probably not going to get it. There are so many people out there more qualified."

"Just curious," I said. "What have you got to lose by believing you'll get it?"

"I might be disappointed," she replied, but then realized that she'd been disappointed before and had survived. With that insight, Renna took the risk of believing, and the following week she was offered a great job.

2. Trusting

"I like you and I like most of what you're saying, but I can't work your program," said the young man sitting before me. "See, I don't have any dreams or goals, but I think that's okay. And there's no risk I can think of that I'd be afraid to take, so I can't do the homework."

I thanked him for his input and we chatted awhile. He told me he'd recently quit a job because of an unethical employer.

As he was explaining his decision he added, "One of my favorite phrases is to keep your enemies close but your friends at a distance."

I asked him to explain.

"Well, you know what your enemies are capable of, but you don't know what your friends are capable of."

"So why not expect them to be capable of wonderful things?" I asked. "I live a very different philosophy. Trust, trust, and when in doubt, trust. If you're betrayed, that's their issue, not yours."

> *You have to give up the life you have to get to the life that's waiting for you.*
>
> **James Hillman**

His eyes lit up as he said, "That's it! That's what I've been looking for!"

"What is?" I asked.

"That's the dream. That's the risk I need to take. I don't trust anybody right now. I want to learn how to trust. Thanks so much!"

3. Setting Boundaries

"I feel like I bite my tongue all day long. I just don't know what to do," shared a seventy-year-old woman who was in a fairly new relationship.

The one who takes a stand is often wrong. The one who never takes a stand is always wrong.

Anonymous

I asked her to explain.

"He's so good to me. When I'm not feeling well, he goes and gets my prescriptions and all sorts of things like that, so when he wants me to do something I don't want to do, I feel guilty if I say no. Yesterday he pointed out to me, 'I never say no to the things you ask me to do.' I can't tell what's healthy or loving at this point."

I reminded her of the formula for making every decision and knowing it's the right one for you: "If you had no fear..."

"If I had no fear, I'd tell him what I feel and let him sort out his feelings from there," she stated clearly. Thanks to the formula, her confusion and doubt disappeared. She acted with greater self-confidence. The relationship flourished.

Idling to Idoling

When I met him that July, Michael was eighteen and floundering. He'd just started singing in my choir on Sundays, but not much else was going on in his life. He'd considered going to the local community college, yet was anything but excited about it. Then in August, he lost his job because his car broke down. That next week, he called to say he couldn't make it to choir practice. I let him know that my car would work all the way to his house, and he reluctantly accepted my offer.

On the way to rehearsal, I asked him what I ask everyone when I get the chance: "Tell me about your dreams, Michael." Without hesitation, he told me he wanted to be a performer and singer. "Then you're auditioning for *American Idol* in Minneapolis in a couple of weeks!" He corrected me with a simple "no."

He explained that he'd "been there and done that" the year before and it hadn't worked out. "Well, eighteen is a good age to give up on your dreams," I replied, trying to egg him on.

He sat up straight and countered, "Did you forget why you're driving me to church today? How am I supposed to get there without a car or money?"

I challenged him with, "You're going to let a $120 round-trip bus fare stop you from reaching for your dream? Surely there's someone you could ask for help."

"Nope, my family is all asked out."

"Really? Well, I could pull over while you think of *someone* to ask." He finally got my hint.

"Well, I could ask you, but I hardly know you."

"True, and if you did, the worst thing that could happen is that I'd say no and you'd be a little disappointed. The best thing that could happen is you'd get the money to go and win a ticket to Hollywood."

Finally Michael got up his nerve and asked me. I wanted to see how serious he was, so I told him no, but that I had some ideas for how he could raise the money. That weekend he stood in front of a restaurant in ninety-five degree heat and handed out fliers offering to sing if someone would help him get to Minneapolis. He made a little money doing that, and my choir and the pastor pitched in for the rest the following Sunday.

That first big audition day in Minneapolis, as Michael entered a stadium with more than 17,000 other hopefuls, he took another risk and called me at 5:30 in the morning.

"I know even God isn't up yet and I'm sorry to bother you so early, but can you tell me that stuff you tell people? I could use a boost."

"I'm glad you called. Why are you there, Michael?"

He paused, and then said, "To claim what's mine."

"Then go do it."

Once in front of Randy, Paula, and Simon, Michael took his next risk.

When asked what song he was going to sing he replied, "Can you keep a secret?"

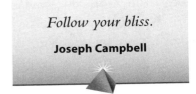

Follow your bliss.

Joseph Campbell

> *I want to stay as close to the edge as I can without going over. Out on the edge you see all kinds of things you can't see from the center.*
>
> **Kurt Vonnegut, Jr.**

The judges looked at each other and then told Michael they could.

"Meeeee and Mrs. Jones..." he began to croon. "We got a thing goin' on..."

They loved it and Michael was one of only sixteen people from Minneapolis that year who got a gold certificate and a week in Hollywood.

The first four days of that week, I got calls from California to tell me he'd made it through the next round of auditions—but on Friday, the last day before the top twenty-four, he was sent home. Even that didn't keep Michael from taking risks.

His conversation with a woman sitting next to him in the first-class section of the plane on the way home began with, "If you can smell rejection, that would be me."

"I beg your pardon?" she asked.

"If I start weeping, it's because I just got cut from *American Idol*," he said, tongue-in-cheek.

"Oh, my," she replied. "If you made it that far in Hollywood, you must be exceptional! My name is Nancy, and I run a talent agency. This is how I met Ashton Kutcher." (Ashton found stardom in *That 70's Show* and is the husband of actress Demi Moore.)

Before the plane landed, Michael was offered a $10,000 scholarship to study acting, modeling, and performance at Nancy's agency in Minneapolis. Six months later, the agency flew him to New York for a competition that included actors and performers from around the world. When all the votes were tallied, Michael had won seven awards, including Male Vocalist of the Year 2007, Best Duo Vocals of the Year 2007, and Entertainer of the Year 2007. He has since been featured on a music CD and has acted in six films, including *April Showers*, the story of the Columbine shootings. As Michael will tell you, he now takes risks every day.

Putting *Risk* into Practice

When you asked me what I would do if I had no fear,
I immediately thought—that's easy, I'd change the world.

Jaimee, a junior at an inner city high school

⋘

Take a moment to write down your answers to the following question: What are three risks you've taken that you're glad you did?

One woman's answers to this question were:

- ✔ I'm glad I risked having my baby even though I wasn't married.
- ✔ I'm glad I risked not marrying the baby's father.
- ✔ I'm glad I risked coming to this class today.

One man's answers were:

- ✔ I'm glad I risked walking up and talking to the woman who became my wife.
- ✔ I'm glad I risked following my weight loss program and losing the weight.
- ✔ I'm glad I risked getting another dog after ours died.

Next, write down three risks you'd like to take, but haven't yet.

Many people consider themselves poor risk-takers until they start to take their own *Risk Inventory*. We all take risks from time to time, and honoring that can help us expand our risk range and level of courage.

The First Step

Looking back over three risks you'd like to take, decide on the one you're going to take a step toward this week. Ask yourself how you could prepare yourself mentally and/or physically. Then do it.

> *Courage is the first of human qualities because it is the quality which guarantees the others.*
>
> **Aristotle**

With *Risk*, we all have to start where we are. By risking *small* things (like talking to a stranger on an elevator, singing karaoke, or learning yoga) we can become better at risking *big* things (like applying for a dream job or committing to run a half marathon). For every decision that presents itself this week, ask yourself the question:

"If I had no fear, what would I do?"

With each small risk, your courage and self-esteem will grow, no matter what the outcome may be. What you risk isn't important— only *that* you risk. Whether you're Bill Gates or Billy Jones, finding the edge of your comfort zone and crossing it will give you the confidence you need to follow your dreams.

Friendly Feedback

Finally, as you learn to take bigger and bigger risks, remember there's no such thing as failure. It's only Friendly Feedback, reminding you, "Don't stop here, keep looking." Can you recount the ups and downs in the lives of the people who inspire you? If not, go on the Internet or to the library and read the biographies of your heroes. Watch true-story movies like *Cinderella Man, Freedom Writers, Mother Teresa,* and *Pursuit of Happyness* to see risk in action. You'll find *yourself* in their stories.

Twenty years from now, you will be more disappointed
by the things that you didn't do
than by the ones you did do.
Dare. Dream. Discover.

Mark Twain

c∞ɔ

Q & A on *Risk*

The greatest risk is the risk of riskless living.
Stephen R. Covey

⌒∞⌒

Q: *Why does it always seem to be darkest before the dawn?*

A: What a great question. I've also heard this question asked as, "Why does every great achievement seem fraught with frustrations?"

There is a Divine Order to the universe, not some "whimsical" or "moody" deity who withholds good in order to teach us patience. My desires, prayers, and dreams sometimes put *each other* on hold while another is being answered, but they're answered in perfect time. Along that line, I don't believe we're being "tested" by setbacks. When we ask, "Why do I have to face trials before triumph?" we're asking the wrong question. Instead, let's ask, "Why is there so often great triumph *after trials*?"

When adversity hits us hard, we long for its opposite. If you forget something important, you immediately dream of your life as being more organized. If you overdraw at the bank, you instantly issue a silent cry for financial abundance. *Ask and you shall receive* is the truth of High-Way 1, and I've found that it's *in response to my greatest challenges* that I ask for and attract my greatest miracles.

The film *Miracle* is a perfect example. In 1980, the U. S. Olympic hockey team *came from behind* in every game they played. What if their being behind, and the resultant heightened

> *The Constitution only guarantees the American people the right to pursue happiness. You have to catch it yourself.*
>
> **Benjamin Franklin**

desire, was what elevated their clarity and caused them to win? To paraphrase an old Avis car rental adage: "We're number two, and we try harder!" Without the lows, it's more difficult to experience longing for the highs, and it's that *longing* that's the hallmark of every great achiever.

Q: *Can you expand on the "if I had no fear" concept?*

A: I recall being invited to speak to a group of high school juniors. Because I was feeling especially courageous, I sang them a song I'd written *that morning* entitled, "If I Had No Fear."

"I may never sing that song again," I told them, "but that's not important. I'm living a no-regrets life, and as a result I wake up every day excited about life. Would anyone here like to fill in the blank at the end of the phrase: If I had no fear...?"

> *The few who do are the envy of the many who watch.*
>
> **Jim Rohn**

Two students raised their hands. I called on a young woman first.

"I'd sing again," she began. "I used to sing in church, but my legs shook so badly that I could hardly stand up, so I quit. I want to start singing again." I thanked her for sharing.

Then a young man said, "I'd find a job outdoors this summer, but I'm not sure what I'd do."

I thanked him also, then added, "My brother once intended an outdoors summer job and ended up living on the side of a mountain shooing bears away from a fish pond for pay. If you'd like his phone number, I can give it to you."

"As for you, dear singer, I direct a choir and I'd like it very much if you'd join us this Sunday at 11:30."

She took my cell phone number and promised she'd call me—and she did.

Later that day I got a call from their teacher. More than half of the students wanted to buy my book.

"How can they get a dozen copies?" she asked.

Taking risks raises us from "surviving" to "thriving." Now I'm asking you: If you had no fear, what would *you* do?

Q: *Do we tend to take more risks if our parents did?*

A: Not necessarily. I'm an avid risk taker, yet both of my children went through periods where they weren't. I think at times they felt as if the sky was falling and that someone had to hold it up because Mom was so "out there." I do think it helps that I have supported them when they have taken risks—both those that worked out and those that didn't.

On that note, let me thank the two amazing risk-takers that raised me. When I was twelve, I asked if I could attend a "parents only" meeting at school concerning new school uniforms. As the only student in the hall that night, I remember waving my hand for some time before receiving permission to speak. At ten years old I argued for the uniform I thought was the most comfortable and easiest to play in. Although the one I suggested wasn't voted in, I'll always be grateful for my parents' love and support that evening. I can't help but believe experiences like that one helped mold the risk-taker I am today.

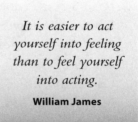

It is easier to act yourself into feeling than to feel yourself into acting.

William James

Q: *Why do so many people tell us to play it safe?*

A: I remember watching a scene in the true-story movie *Rudy* where the young man's dad meets him at the bus station and tries to talk him out of his dream. For many like his father, the pain of having one dream take a wrong turn can feel excruciating, almost life-threatening. Those well-intentioned people in our lives truly believe we'll die if we take a risk. Little do they know that we can die *inside* if we don't.

Q: *I feel like I'm in a rut these days. Help!*

A: Let me answer your plea for help with this powerful quote:

It's time for you to return to Nike's motto. *Whatever you've been doing, do something else!* Here are some possible risks to get you started:

Ask someone out
Climb a tree
Dye your hair red
Eat sushi
Rent a convertible
Ride a motorcycle
Go back to school
Go on a cruise
Go on the Chicago Ferris Wheel
Go to a nude beach
Go to a sweat lodge
Have a professional massage
Become a mentor for a student
Learn to play bridge
Learn sign language
Learn yoga
Ride a train
Ride in a hot air balloon
Ride a rollercoaster
Run in a race
Say no
Sleep under the stars
Take dance lessons
Take swimming lessons

Teeter totter
Travel abroad
Try out for a play
Visit a synagogue/Buddhist temple/church
Volunteer at a homeless shelter
Walk in the rain without your umbrella
Write a letter to the editor thanking someone

You know what you need to do next. Stop listening to what everyone *else* thinks you should do and do the thing that you know is right for you, even if it's to *stop* doing for awhile. Your stillness may birth your greatest miracle ever!

If there is one thing I would banish from earth, it is fear.
And the only way to do that is to see that there is nothing to fear,
nothing in all of life to be afraid of.

Henry Ford

∼∞∽

High-Way 3:
Full Responsibility
Life Is Your Mirror

Defining *Full Responsibility*

One thing to be grateful for each day is
that you are only responsible for you and no other person,
and only responsible for now and no other time.

Abraham-Hicks

⸙

Responsibility is defined in various dictionaries as "a duty; an obligation; a binding," which makes it sound somewhere between a burden and a prison. On the contrary, taking *Full Responsibility* for your life is one of the most freeing experiences you can have—but that freedom comes with a price. You must be able to accept the hard news in order to hear the good news.

First the Hard News

Once while speaking to a group of ninth grade girls in a small Midwestern community, I asked, "Why, out of all of the men I was dating in my twenties, did I decide to marry a man who would become physically abusive?"

One young woman in the front row quickly answered, "Because he treated you like you believed you deserved to be treated." I told her she could go to lunch because she obviously didn't need my presentation.

As the student pointed out, the hard news is that the greatest problem in our lives is, and always will be, *ourselves*. Until I become 100 percent *Fully Responsible* for my life, the world can feel unsafe.

We've all met people who believe they are victims. "Why even try?" they ask. They are the classic "5" on the **Power Pyramid**.

Now the Good News

Once we're ready to embrace the concepts of *Get the Picture*

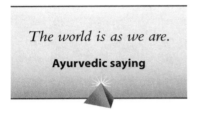

The world is as we are.

Ayurvedic saying

and "what we think about, we bring about," everything starts to change. When we understand that our thoughts attract and we are therefore responsible for our lives, we get everything we've ever wanted—peace, happiness, health, and a new sense of freedom.

When I see that my thoughts create my reality, I wake up to the unlimited potential before me and within me. It's an exhilarating experience. I remember my own wake-up call.

No Victims

At the age of thirty-four, I spent a month in a domestic violence shelter. I walked in believing I was a victim, but the first thing the counselor told me was that I couldn't so much as mention "his" name during the weeks ahead because *I was the only problem I needed to solve.* It was the best and the worst news I could have heard.

It was the worst news because I'd given up my job, my friends, and most of my self-esteem in an attempt to save my marriage. As a result, I was sick all the time and had become increasingly lonely and sad. In short, my life had fallen apart.

It was the best news because if I was the problem, I was also the solution. I began to take *Full Responsibility* for my life. To this day, working High-Way 3 continues to be one of my greatest challenges, but it yields many of my greatest rewards. When I stopped looking to others to "make" me happy, my relationships improved dramatically. When I accepted that my every thought was a request for more of the same and "reality" was malleable, I could no longer be imprisoned by despair. Now I see this High-Way's transformative power almost every day.

Let's start with a simple definition:

Full Responsibility is acknowledging that life is my mirror, every thought is a request, and the only thing I need to change in order to be happier is me.

When we aren't willing to take responsibility for ourselves, we give our power away by waiting for someone or something else to change *so that we can be happy.* This takes us down to a "5" on the **Power Pyramid.** While we're in a hopeless and helpless mindset, we can't possibly attract the life of our dreams. Fortunately, we can return to "95" by moving from *B.C.* to *A.D.*

From *B.C.* to *A.D.*

B.C. generally denotes "Before Christ," but in *8 to Great* it stands for *Blaming* and *Complaining.* Many of us get caught in the trap of *B.C.ing* about the aspects of our lives we don't like, but as we learned in High-Way 1, our lives are like they are because of *what we choose to think about and focus upon.* When we move into *Full Responsibility,* we realize there's no one to blame and complain about, since we are the architects of our lives.

An incident occurred in the late '90s in a Kohl's parking lot. The painful scene involved a young mother who was caught on camera beating her four-year-old in the backseat of her car. After she was turned in for doing so, she was questioned on TV as to her motivation. She said that she was enraged and lost control because Kohl's hadn't given her a cash refund for a return item. Are we to believe that if Kohl's had given her cash, the scene wouldn't have taken place? Kohl's was just the anger trigger (more about triggers in High-Way 4), but she was responsible.

Once we're ready to get out of *B.C.,* we can move into *A.D.* Rather than Anno Domini, in *8 to Great* the letter A stands for *Action* and/or *Acceptance* and the letter D stands for *Dreaming.* Sometimes there's an *Action* that I can and am willing to take. Other times, the frustration in someone else is there to remind me of what needs healing in *me* and I'm able to *Accept* the person or situation as they are. Either way, the next step is to *Dream*—to visualize being in a new place with the person or situation, whether that means releasing it/them or becoming closer to it/them.

We B.C.—Blame and Complain—when we feel like a victim.

We A.D.—Act/Accept and Dream—when we understand our power.

Unsuccessful people *B.C.* and stay stuck around "5." Successful people *A.D.* and float up around "95." We get to choose which category we fall into.

The Hurting Husband

I recall a coaching client who had challenges in two areas. He'd been out of a job for six months and his wife was threatening to divorce

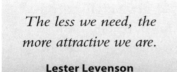

The less we need, the more attractive we are.

Lester Levenson

him. By helping him start daily *Gratitudes* and turn his focus to what he wanted rather than what he didn't want, within a week he was offered his dream job—for more pay than ever. He was ecstatic, but his wife didn't respond as he'd hoped.

He expected her to immediately forgive all the money problems and the less-than-desirable behavior he'd used to cope during his hard times. When that wasn't happening, he plunged into *B.C.* Even his daily Gratitudes became tainted with blaming and complaining:

- ✔ *I'm grateful for my new job. (I sensed he was truly grateful.)*
- ✔ *I'm grateful for my dogs, who kept me company all weekend. (Here were hints of "because she didn't.")*
- ✔ *I'd be grateful once she has seen that I'm not a bad person and that we should work through our problems. (He'd feel better when she changed.)*
- ✔ *I'd be grateful once she spends more time with me. (He'd feel better when she changed.)*
- ✔ *I'd be grateful for a long happy life together. (He'd feel better when she changed.)*

Full Responsibility is based on the premise that we get back what we send out—period. I coached him that his helpless and blaming mentality was pushing his wife away. It's hard to be attracted to someone who needs you in order to be happy. The missing component for his happiness was to take *Full Responsibility* for feeling good by focusing on all the gifts in his life, such as his new job, his health, and his ability to manifest his thoughts.

The Job Reprimand

A friend called me one evening very agitated.

"I've never received a verbal warning from my boss before. I can't believe it. Everyone else does what I did and they don't get warnings. It's so unfair."

I listened in silence. After awhile, she asked, "What should I do?"

When she requested coaching I asked, "Do you see yourself as responsible in any way?"

"How am I responsible?" she replied.

"You started mentally leaving this company three months ago. You've said nothing good about them during that time and that was when you started actively looking for another job. Now you're angry with them for starting to leave *you*. Not only do you *not* look like a victim, but in my eyes you look incredibly powerful. You're about to get the very thing you set into motion."

> *The truth that you are in charge of your life will set you free only after it really irritates you.*
>
> **Sky St. John**

Over time she'd fallen into a pattern of *B.C.ing* and focusing on what she didn't like rather than what she did. Once she saw the situation from the perspective of *Full Responsibility,* she had no trouble acknowledging the part she had played and shifting to a gratitude mindset. A year later, she was still working at the same job and loving it.

We often underestimate the power of our thoughts, thinking we can "get away" with blaming and complaining as long as it's just in our minds. Not true. As powerful as *Get the Picture* is for getting what we want, blaming and complaining are equally powerful in keeping it from us.

Who We're Not Responsible For

A key distinction of *Full Responsibility* is realizing who and what we're *not* responsible for. Byron Katie, my favorite author on this topic, defines this concept well:

> *There are only three kinds of business in the universe: mine, yours and God's. Suffering only occurs when we are in business other than our own.*

"Mind your own business" is a common reprimand today because we often go outside of our business. We go "out of business" when we find ourselves:

✔ *Complaining about the weather. Instead we could think, "It's cold. Nothing I can do about that. Glad I have an indoor job."*

✔ *Complaining about the way our spouse talks. Instead we could think, "She talks so loud. She's been doing it all her life, so there's not much I can do about that. Boy, am I grateful how many great friends she has and how she helps all of us laugh."*

✔ *Complaining that your teenager isn't getting good grades. Instead we could think, "I've reminded him about the effect his grades will have on scholarships so many times. Now I get to sit back and watch how he handles the events that will come his way. I'm grateful for the knowledge that like cats, we'll all (eventually) land on our feet!"*

One way to stay in your own business is to ask yourself, "If it's not within my ability to change it, how can it be my responsibility?" The only life we can live peacefully is our own.

> *People are just as happy as they*
> *make up their minds to be.*
> **Abraham Lincoln**

❧

The *Full Responsibility* Process:
B.C. to A.D.

My drug use was my fault. My time in prison was my fault.
But my successful business, my healthy relationships, my four years of
sobriety and the fact that I love my life today are also my fault.

Ryan S. (at twenty-four years old)

⚮

I recall talking to an old friend who'd just been reprimanded by his supervisor for something he didn't do.

"If they wouldn't have found that the error was made by somebody else, I could have been fired," he shared with me.

"And you would have been fine with that on many levels," I replied.

"What do you mean?"

We then talked about that fact that *nothing ever happens "to" us without happening "with" us, "by" us, and "for" us.* Life is our mirror. He admitted that he hated his job and was starting to think about leaving.

> *Freedom means responsibility. That's why most men dread it.*
>
> **George Bernard Shaw**

Until we take *Full Responsibility*, we can't enjoy freedom, and without feeling free, we'll never find happiness. When we understand that our happiness is ours to hold on to or throw away, we stop feeling like victims rafting on ocean waves that can capsize us at any moment.

Working with coaching clients, I have found that the first step toward accepting *Full Responsibility* for our happiness is to notice when we *don't*.

How We Avoid Responsibility

The primary ways we avoid responsibility are:

1. Believing we're helpless and not accepting our power.
2. Trying to control other people's business.

The first is a cycle that starts in our head with helpless or Blaming/Complaining thoughts.

Helpless Thoughts:

> *"I could never do that."*
> *"It's not my fault."*
> *"I can't stop worrying."*
> *"It's because of my childhood."*
> *"Must be nice."*
> *"My husband won't let me."*
> *"I'm too shy."*
> *"If only I felt better."*
> *"It's not that simple."*

Helpless thoughts center on "I'm wrong" or "I can't." We convince ourselves that we're defective and don't have what it takes to get the job done or to be happy. It blinds us to the multitude of possible opportunities that surround us. Then when we don't admit the power we have over our lives, we distract ourselves from feeling powerless by trying to change someone else. Soon after helpless thoughts arise, we find ourselves in *B.C.*, thinking or speaking phrases such as:

> *"How come you never…"*
> *"You're always so…"*
> *"You make me so angry."*
> *"I can't stand it when they…"*
> *"You should…"*
> *"People can't be trusted."*

I'm reminded of a story from my first book. For years my mom and dad were unhappy. Mom always seemed to be worried about something—my traveling for my job, her middle son climbing mountains, her youngest son being hurt in a game, and dozens of other things. She had lots of "shoulds" and shared them with us often. Once she and Dad separated (and months later reconciled in a very loving manner), her "shoulds" for us ceased. We still traveled, climbed mountains, and played sports, but because she was taking care of *her* business, she had no time to take care of ours.

As we love to say in *8 to Great*:

> *Happy and successful people don't "should" on themselves and don't "should" on other people.*

Dealing with "Shoulds"

When we tell people what they should do, we're trying to control them, and eventually they'll rebel. Throughout my life I've dealt with control issues, often letting people know that *I knew better*. I recall a time when I was replaced in a Christmas musical revue one week before the performance for making "too many suggestions," even though I thought I was just being helpful. Talk about the Queen of De-nial!

Giving advice that isn't solicited is codependent, unhealthy, and unpopular—even when it comes to our children. Giving instructions to small children is one thing, but giving advice to our young adults is something else. Sometimes we think that as parents and grandparents we're given a special pass that allows us to share endless opinions, but that's just an excuse for yielding to our addiction to control.

When we own *Full Responsibility* for our lives and release responsibility for the other adults in our lives, we acknowledge that we *don't know* how someone else should live their life better than they do. Releasing the need to change them frees us to come back into our own bodies and restores our sanity, well-being, and quality of life.

The best alternative to telling someone to change is to change *yourself*. Perhaps a job isn't a good fit for you. Rather than harping on someone about behavior that's uncomfortable to you, let them know what upsets you, and if it doesn't change, you can either *Accept* (let it go) or as I did in my violent marriage *Act* (go).

The next time you're upset or uncomfortable, ask yourself the following questions.

The Three Questions of Full Responsibility

1. Is there an action I can take?

2. Is there an action I can stop?

3. Is there a thought I can change?

1. Take an Action

The first option is to be proactive rather than reactive. Have you ever tried to tell a teenager what they *can't* do? You only get more of it. What we fear most, we attract to ourselves. Whatever we push against, we get more of. That's why nagging and begging don't work—because *what we resist persists.*

When you decide to take an action, look for one that *empowers you* rather than one you think will change someone else. Here are some examples of actions taken that brought greater peace and harmony to the individuals involved. (Note: Because I've been coaching for more than a decade and since the same issues reappear, some of these are composite stories, while others are condensed.)

The Rebellious Son

JM: I don't know what to do. I'm a single mom and my 6'3" son has gotten out of control. Things are going from bad to worse.

MK: Give me an example.

JM: I tried to ground him last week and said he couldn't use my car, but he took the keys out of my purse, got copies made, and waved them in my face.

MK: What action would a really powerful parent take in this situation?

JM: Stop him.

MK: How?

JM: Take the tires off the car!

MK: Do you know how to take the tires off a car?

JM: Yes! And I even have the friends to help me do it. Thank you!

The Broken Bones

By the time this female physician and I spoke, she'd had three employees go to the hospital with broken bones, all from falls in her icy parking lot within a thirty-day period.

MK: Talk to me about how you're feeling.

Dr. T: I'm furious and frustrated by all this chaos! How am I going to run my business with three people in the hospital? They should be here to help me!

MK: You're feeling out of control.

Dr. T: That's right. One person fell, then the other two thought about it, got afraid of it, and then it became a self-fulfilling prophecy.

MK: What was your fear?

Dr. T: Well, after the first one fell, I was afraid that someone else would, especially after one of them said, "What would happen if I fell at 7:00 in the morning and no one was around?" That's exactly when she fell the next morning!

MK: *Get the Picture* really works. So, if you're saying, "They should have known better," that's about them and gives them all the power. Try on *Full Responsibility* and move from "they should" to "I could." Change "they should have known better" to "I could have."

Dr. T: I could have known better. Yes, I can see that I helped attract this. I could have redirected their conversations and shifted my focus.

MK: It feels good to own your own power, doesn't it? Action-wise, how about the next time someone brings up broken bones, you listen, nod, and change the subject.

Dr. T: That will be a relief!

There were no more accidents of any kind that year at her office.

The Mother's Advice

CR: I feel like I'm suffocating. I've moved out but my mom is still giving me advice on my job, where I should go to church, and where my boyfriend and I should spend the holidays. It's driving me nuts!

MK: Are you fully responsible for yourself financially or is she still paying for some things? For example, who's paying for this appointment?

CR: She is, and she's still paying my car payment and insurance.

MK: Full freedom requires *Full Responsibility*. Is there an action you can take?

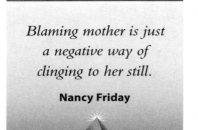

Blaming mother is just a negative way of clinging to her still.

Nancy Friday

CR: Yes. Even though it's going to be hard, I'm going to ask her to give me the car as a present for my birthday next month and I'll start paying my own car insurance.

At her next appointment, which she paid for, this young woman had nothing but great reports about her life and her relationships.

2. Stop an Action

The second option after taking an action is *stopping one*. When we overdo in a relationship, it almost always results in the other person *underdoing*. Here are some examples of how stopping an action was the fully responsible thing to do.

The Abusive Boyfriend

This woman had left her abusive boyfriend five times before she came to me.

RG: I miss him. Why do I love and hate him at the same time?

MK: You may never know why. You just do. What actions have you taken in the past?

RG: I leave after he has a fit, but then I always miss him and go back, and the whole cycle repeats.

MK: Is there something you can do or stop doing that will help you to find happiness?

RG: I could stop calling him.

MK: Yes you could. I recommend that you make one promise you feel capable of keeping. Only one. It has to become your #1 priority. Everything else will take second place.

Have you ever noticed that when there is a problem you are always there?

Ho'oponopono teaching

RG: I want to promise myself that I won't call him, no matter what.

MK: How can you support yourself in that resolution?

RG: It'll be hard, especially when other people tell me how he's doing.

MK: You can be clear with them that you no longer need or want that information.

RG: Yes I can. I think they'll actually be relieved.

The woman moved out of town two months later and was happily married to a new love two years later.

The Doughnuts and the Diet

PJ: I can't seem to lose weight because of all the doughnuts people bring to work. The snacks are right next to the restroom and I can walk past them once or twice, but the third time, I eat two or three doughnuts. What's wrong with me?

MK: Nothing. You like doughnuts. I do, too. Is there more than one bathroom at your workplace?

PJ: Yes, but it's on a different floor.

MK: Is there an action you can take or stop taking?

PJ: I could stop using that bathroom and use the third floor restroom instead.

MK: A little extra exercise and you'll only have to use it until you convince yourself you're strong enough to be around little, round, sugared circles without eating them.

He lost thirty pounds over the next four months.

There's Always Something I Can Do

When we release the helpless thoughts of "there's nothing I can do" and the blaming thoughts of "it's all their fault," we can more clearly see the next action to take. For those times when there is no action to take, it's time for a thought-based remedy—*acceptance*.

3. Change a Thought

Much of the time, the way to get back to "95" isn't by taking a new action or stopping an old one, it's simply changing a thought. When there's no action to be taken, it's time to release our "should" thoughts and exchange them for thoughts that feel better. We can go to a "higher" consciousness by confronting our problems, "getting *over* them," or "rising *above* them." As we *heighten* our awareness of the power of our minds, we move beyond our painful thoughts, observe them, and then discard or replace them as we see fit.

> *If even one person has to change so that you can feel better, you have no power.*
>
> **Abraham-Hicks**

For much of my life, living in *B.C.* drained me of energy, direction, and focus, limiting my creativity and joy. As I moved into *A.D.*, I began to feel a new peace, and once I calmed down, life got easier.

I invite you to "rethink" your most recent challenges using the definition of *Full Responsibility:* "Life is my mirror, every thought is a request, and the only thing I need to change in order to be happier is me." You'll know you're moving into the power of *Full Responsibility* when you feel a shift from within.

Life Is My Mirror

When I encounter a person or situation I can't change, I remember the power of acceptance. Acceptance of another person's "flaws" is easier when I remember *that I couldn't be irritated by this quality in others if it wasn't in me.* When we aren't willing to acknowledge our own shortcomings, we invariably find someone with the same core issue to criticize. When we don't honor our own gifts, we tend to find someone with those same gifts to put on a pedestal.

The Sorority Sister

HL: I've thought of quitting school three different times this week because I'm so tired of a couple of people I live with.

MK: Tell me about one of them.

HL: Where do I begin? Tori's always sticking her nose in other people's business. I've told her I don't need her advice, but she continues to do it. It's driving me nuts.

MK: And the other person?

HL: Katie's completely critical. I don't remember the last time I heard something positive come out of her mouth. All she can do is find fault with people. It's awful!

MK: Okay, thanks. Are you ready to feel better?

HL: Yes!

MK: You've found your judgment statements, so take a deep breath and remember that if these two traits weren't in you, you couldn't see them in anyone else. Can you accept that you sometimes stick your nose in other people's business? Tori's, for example?

HL: Oh, my gosh. I do!

MK: And are you sometimes critical of others?

HL: Yes, but not as often as—

MK: My teacher, Byron Katie, reminds me to let go of the "but" when I want to feel better.

HL: Yes, I'm sometimes critical of others.

MK: Of course you are. We all are. So instead of catching her doing it, you can focus on catching when *you* do it and changing the thought from "Katie should be more positive" to—

> *First take the plank out of your own eye and then you will see clearly to take the speck out of your brother's eye.*
>
> **Luke 6:42**

HL: I could be more positive.

MK: How does that feel?

HL [giggling]: Painful and lots better!

My Experiences with *Full Responsibility*

I had been practicing *Full Responsibility* in my own life for years when I came across Byron Katie's *The Work*. She broke the process of taking personal responsibility into four steps, and offers us easy-to-use phrases, such as "release the 'but'" and "Is that true?" I strongly recommend her books for those ready to live in the freedom of *Full Responsibility*.

I want to end this section with some examples of my own journey as I moved from *B.C.* to *A.D.* The thoughts below are written as a dialogue because that's often what they sound like in my head. It's as if my calmer, wiser Higher Self (HS) is speaking to the Me that wants to stay stuck in my anger or misery.

The Van Driver

I was dropping off my son at school on a beautiful spring day when a van ahead of me stopped right in front of the school door instead of moving to the designated area. When I tapped my horn, not only did the driver not move, but a student got out and gave me a "look," which irritated me greatly. Thankfully I was able to use Full Responsibility *to make an inner shift, and by the time I had driven out of the parking lot I was back to feeling free and peaceful.*

HS: Okay, you just fell from "95" to "5." Action (your honking) didn't work. Time to change your thoughts! What are you upset about?

Me: She was inconsiderate and irresponsible!

HS: That might be true or it might not be. Let's see, are *you* ever inconsiderate? For example, to her? She might have other things on her mind. Maybe she just put her mother into a care center or just got a diagnosis and was distracted.

Me: That's true.

HS: Can you take *Full Responsibility* here and do Byron Katie's turnaround?

Me: I was inconsiderate of her. I get that, but how was I irresponsible? I wasn't parking in the…oh, I wasn't taking responsibility for my attitude. OK, now I feel relieved. I almost gave that incident permission to ruin my day, but I caught myself. It was really about me. That feels great!

The Litterer

On a fall afternoon, I was stopped at a stoplight when I saw the driver in front of me flick his cigarette butt out the window.

Me: Who does he think he is? We don't need his garbage. Why are people littering public streets? Who's supposed to clean up their mess? How irresponsible!

HS: They're irresponsible. Could that be true about you?

Me: I don't litter, that's for sure. Let me think about it.

[Two hours later.]

Me: I figured it out. I have a whole lot of garbage I throw at people—mostly my judgments and unwanted advice. I sometimes make a mess and don't always clean it up.

As soon as I got that connection, I felt a shift.

A Final Thought on Trust

One of the complaints I hear most often is that "people (politicians, car salesmen, etc.) can't be trusted." I've grappled with my own versions of that belief, and offer this possibility:

When we trust too soon, we're trusting people to be us, and they never are.

> *It is not always easy to find happiness in ourselves, and it is impossible to find it elsewhere.*
>
> **Agnes Repplier**

When you fall in love too quickly, take the job without checking on the company, or sign on emotionally for a project where you end up doing all the work, it's time to take a step back to see if your pattern is fully responsible. When you don't take the time to find out who someone is (and it always takes time), you begin to assume that others are a carbon copy of you. Later, when you find out differently, you often feel stunned, disappointed, and angry.

The real question is, did they "let you down" or did you let *yourself* down by expecting something they could never give? Trusting people is healthy, but it needs to be tempered with trusting them to be uniquely themselves. Once we do that, we can't be disappointed.

The other factor in trusting is the Law of Attraction. We can only attract what we ourselves are sending out. If someone can't commit to us, we weren't ready to commit to ourselves or to them. If someone lies to us, we can look closer to see how we were lying to ourselves.

The day we wake up to *Full Responsibility* is the day we rebirth into our power. The more I work with pregnant teens, the more I see a version of the following journal entry from an eighteen-year-old: "I thought he'd be my knight in shining armor. Now I can see that I need to be that knight for myself. I'm ready to take *Full Responsibility* for me. I know I can do it."

Why We Don't Accept *Full Responsibility*

We have not passed that subtle line between childhood and adulthood
until we move from the passive voice to the active voice—
that is, until we stop saying "It got lost," and say "I lost it."
Sydney Harris

❦

The Choice to Grow Up

The aging process doesn't guarantee that we'll grow up. We grow up the day we take *Full Responsibility* for our lives. Many of us didn't have good modeling in this High-Way, but with all the self-help literature and empowering seminars available, we can unlearn and relearn. Business leaders, sports figures, and literary greats agree:

Ninety-nine percent of all failures come from people
who have a habit of making excuses.
George Washington Carver

The man who complains about the way the ball bounces
is likely to be the one who dropped it.
Lou Holtz

If you don't like something, change it.
If you can't change it, change your attitude.
Maya Angelou

I am in charge of my life. I am not in charge of yours. How simple, yet how challenging those concepts can be.

The Exceptional Excuse

One of the biggest culprits when individuals struggle with High-Way 3 is the belief that *our* situation is the lone exception to the rules. Excuses for getting involved in other people's business, such as "My daughter will be kicked out of school if I..." or "My boyfriend will lose his job if I don't..." start to sound unexceptional in the coaching business. Our love of the "just this once" clause makes *Full Responsibility* much easier to embrace in theory than in practice.

The Disease of Codependency

My classes at recovery shelters for thirteen years taught me that the biggest difference between that population and my other adult audiences was that early in their recovery, addicts tend to be in everyone's business but their own. I found myself regularly reminding them of the second half of the *Full Responsibility* equation—that they were not responsible for others and that pretending to be so endangered their sobriety.

Again and again I see parents in crisis because of the rescuing they've attempted with their adult children. At a time when the young adult needs to be learning from life, we too often coddle them by softening the blows of natural consequences. Little do these adult children know that there will be a price for their precious rescue— their freedom. If the rescue is successfully completed, the parents often shove "shoulds" down their throats for decades, believing they have proven their child "incapable" of handling their own affairs.

"Shoulding" on those close to us takes place when we're lacking either clear expectations or clear consequences. I've seen healthy parents establish the same clear boundaries found in successful businesses.

> *Once individuals in therapy recognize their role in creating their own life predicament, they realize that they, and only they, have the power to change that situation.*
>
> **Victor Frankl, former POW**

Clear Consequences

If an effective employer wanted her employees to be on time, she wouldn't respond to a second tardy with, "You really should be on time, you know!" Instead, she would set clear boundaries and consequences with a statement such as, "If this behavior continues, there will be a written warning, which could lead to your dismissal. I don't want to have to do that, so I look forward to your coming to work on time from now on." Clear consequences free up both parties to speak their truth and move on.

Likewise, my best discipline experiences with my children involved being clear before their choice was made. The arguments that occur from our lack of clarity are much harsher than the pain of being grounded for a week as a result of coming home late.

There are now theories that there's even a chemical "fix" we can get from *B.C.ing.* That may explain the person who each morning stops at every work station to tell the latest horror story before their first cup of coffee. For those of us ready to feel good and manifest our dreams, the excuses have run out. No matter what our reasons have been for staying in a less than fully responsible mindset, there will come a day when even *we* get tired of our tales of woe and yearn for the freedom of our own independence day.

Once we really "get" *Full Responsibility,* everything changes. We no longer bring up stories of what "they" did to us yesterday or ten years ago. We no longer rail against "unfairness" or "mean people," realizing that they're only reflections of the same qualities within us.

> *Tell everyone you know: "My happiness depends on me, so you're off the hook." And then demonstrate it. Be happy, no matter what.*
>
> **Abraham-Hicks**

The Good News

The good news here is that once we hit rock bottom and realize that happiness will elude us until we stop *B.C.ing*, our turnaround is usually swift and strong. It often takes a spouse leaving, a job ending, or an illness taking hold of our body, but thousands wake up every day to the fact that their life is as it is because of what they have chosen to think about and focus upon. I celebrate those of you who are making that shift today. May yours be the next success story.

Full Responsibility Success Stories

Our deepest fear is not that we are powerless.
Our deepest fear is that we are powerful beyond measure.
Marianne Williamson

c∞ɔ

As I've moved from *B.C.* to *A.D.* hundreds of times over the years, each time has brought a feeling of release into my own empowerment. Equally exciting is the shift I see in those I coach. Here are a few examples of how *Full Responsibility* frees us to own our power and find our peace.

Peace Unearthed

One of my all-time favorite e-mails from an educator was this one:

MK, I did as you suggested. The Full Responsibility work of "You spot it, you got it" wasn't a lot of fun. First I looked at four things that I don't like about one of the teachers at my school:

1. He blames others when things go bad, but when things go well he takes the credit.

2. He's always trying to "one up" somebody else for the kids' attention.

3. It's all about him.

4. He talks about people behind their backs, even though he's a friend to their faces.

OK, yes, I have these qualities too. Not all the time, but I do have these qualities when I get honest with myself. (This is really hard to admit.)

Examples of how I also do each of the above:

1. My wife and I both do this sometimes, not very often, but when the kids are fighting and we are tired, we want the other one to handle it and if it doesn't go well, we get upset with each other.

2. I've tried to "one up" more in the past than the present. Life isn't a competition, but sometimes I make it out to be. I always want to be "the person" my nephews want to play with when we all get together.

> *Things do not change, we change.*
>
> **Henry David Thoreau**

3. It's true. At times, I just focus on me and what I want. I'm a pretty caring person, but when I look at some things I do, I can also be selfish.

4. I'm embarrassed to admit this, but I used to do this sometimes with my wife at home.

Wow. I feel more liberated now because I am starting to be conscious of what I do. The lesson, I guess, is that people are what they are. They're not the problem, we are. It's great to know that you, by yourself, can make yourself feel better. Thanks so much for this **8 to Great** *program.*

The College Student

I recall the day I looked up to see a beautiful red-headed college student enter my classroom. As I got to know him, he became one of my favorites. I loved his openness and willingness to risk. As we worked our way through High-Ways 1 and 2, he shared that his best friend had committed suicide eight months earlier. When we got to the Full Responsibility *exercises, he bravely offered to talk about his deepest challenge.*

MK: Who has a "should" about someone they're willing to share?

RM: My friend should have been more open about his feelings.

MK: Thank you. When you take *Full Responsibility*, what does that sound like?

RM [beginning to cry]: I could be more open about my feelings... about his death. I've been holding a lot of my pain in. I get that now.

He finished the course with a new sense of energy and purpose.

The VP Who Was *Very* Perturbed

A female VP walked into our coaching session looking beaten down and tired.

VP: I have to get a different job. I'm working too hard and no one appreciates me. I feel stuck. The other day my boss asked if I minded if he missed a meeting. I told him I didn't, but the client really didn't get a great impression of our company when I was the only one who showed up. This happens over and over and I'm tired of it.

MK: Are you willing to try some new ways of being and thinking?

VP: Yes. Anything.

MK: Great. First, you're not ready for a new job yet. You're at "5" on the **Power Pyramid** where only 5 percent of your thoughts feel good. From there you can only attract another "5" employment situation. You need to move up to a better place before you make any changes or you'll take your "5-ness" with you. So start by describing your perfect job.

All blame is a waste of time. No matter how much fault you find with another, and regardless of how much you blame him, it will not change you.

Dr. Wayne Dyer

VP: I don't want a boss who—

MK: Can you tell me what you want, rather than what you don't want?

VP: I want respect, appreciation, honesty, clarity…not to have to take work home at night, and my evenings and weekends free for personal and family time.

MK: Wonderful! I wrote those down as you were talking. Now let's move to *Risk*. Real risk is when we run to, not from. Right now, quitting your job would be…

VP: Running from. I can see that.

MK: We call that an Escape, and it's a "5" behavior that can only attract more "5" jobs. Now let's move to *Full Responsibility*. Give me three "shoulds" that your boss should do or be.

VP: My boss should be more honest, affirm me more, and be more responsible.

MK: Great. So he should be more honest. Did you tell the truth when your boss asked your opinion about not coming to the meeting? Turn those phrases around to *Full Responsibility*—"I could"—and see if they're true.

VP: I could be more honest with my boss. That's true. And yes, I could affirm me more and I could affirm my boss more. I could be more responsible—Oh Wow!

MK: Fully Responsible, instead of *B.C.ing* about your boss. Remember, we can only see traits in others that are in ourselves. That truth works both ways. Your boss can only criticize you for making a stupid mistake if he's been beating himself up about the same thing.

VP: So I've been taking his criticisms personally when they were how he feels about himself?

MK: Yes. Until you forgive and get grateful for your boss, you can't feel good or attract what you really want. Once you've done your *Forgiveness of the Past* (High-Way 6) and *Gratitude for the Present* (High-Way 7) work, you'll be soaring at "95." Then you can stay or go. Either way, you will feel better.

VP: I feel like you've lifted 1,000 pounds off my shoulders. I've never thought of it like this before. Thank you!

My Parents Should Forgive Me

When I met James he was at an interim facility on his way to court and a more permanent placement. He signed up to work with me and asked for help to turn his life around.

MK: Thanks for taking the risk of working with me. Let's start with High-Way 3 today. James, who are some people you think should change?

> *At whatever point you judge another, it is you who do the very same thing.*
>
> **Romans 2:1**

JA: That's easy. My parents. They should forgive me. They should believe in me and give me another chance.

MK: How have you been feeling lately?

JA: Angry. Frustrated. Hopeless.

MK: Are you ready to feel better?

JA: Yes, ma'am.

MK: Then take a deep breath and start to take *Full Responsibility*. Keeping the same phrasing you used to say what your parents should do, move from "they should" to "I could" statements and see if they're true.

JA [after a few moments of silence]: I could forgive me. I could believe in me and give me another chance. [As he began to cry.] I deserve it. I do.

The Neglected Wife

This woman in her early 40s was extremely depressed when she came to my seminar.

FL: My husband doesn't treat me well. He should take better care of me and do nice things for me.

MK: Thank you. Now take *Full Responsibility*. You couldn't recognize these things in him if they weren't in you. Change "He should" to "I could."

FL: I could take better care of me and do nice things for me.

MK: Why haven't you taken care of yourself? It is about money?

FL: No there's plenty of that. I have a two-year-old son and I raised my first two children by myself. I thought I should be able to raise this one by myself, too. But I get so tired. I can see that I can ask for help and pamper myself once in awhile. I will.

She did take Full Responsibility, *and weeks later wrote me a thank you letter, saying her energy level and attitude toward her husband had shifted dramatically.*

My Son Should Get Help

This next father's challenge is a common one. Twelve-Step groups can be extremely powerful in situations involving addiction.

TW: My nineteen-year-old son has been a drug addict for three years. We've done everything we can and nothing seems to help.

MK: So you can't think of any new actions to take?

TW: No, but I'm open to your ideas.

MK: I can't think of any actions to take either. What about things you could stop doing?

TW: Well, I don't use drugs. I guess I could stop drinking beer. I have a couple on bowling night. Never more than that.

MK: Okay, that would help you understand how hard it is for people to change. That compassion might be good, yes?

TW: Yes, I suppose so.

MK: What about changing your thought from "he should" to the *Full Responsibility* of "I could." What are your shoulds about your son right now?

> *God, grant me the serenity to accept the things I cannot change, the courage to change the things I can, and the wisdom to know the difference.*
>
> **Serenity Prayer**

TW: He should get over his addiction. He should get help.

MK: Okay, and we can only see in other people what's in us, so where does that reside in you?

TW: Maybe I'm addicted to trying to get him to change? Maybe I could get help for that.

MK: Sounds like a fully responsible plan to me! Al-Anon and Coda 12-step groups might be a good place to start.

The Son Who Lost His Scholarship

Mother: My son flunked a class and now he's losing his scholarship. I'm furious.

MK: What are your thoughts?

Mother: He shouldn't have flunked. He's irresponsible! He said, "It just doesn't count if I'm not paying for it myself." Where did he come up with that?

MK: If that's what he believes, then he was responsible for bringing it about.

Mother: But now what will happen?

MK: Whose business is it—what happens in his life next?

Mother: His, but he's always been so cooperative and easy to raise.

MK: He's still cooperating with his own plan and now he's raising himself. Isn't that what you always wanted—that he be happy and on track with his own agenda?

Mother: Yes. Yes, it is.

MK: Move from "he should" to "I could" and see how it feels.

Mother: I could be more responsible for my own happiness and stop worrying about his.

MK: How's that feel?

Mother: Great!

The Story of the Two Snakes

Two snakes were having lunch one day, when one said to the other, "I sure hope I'm not poisonous."

"Why?" asked his friend.

"Because I just bit my tongue."

Whatever we send out to others will always come back to us. You can tell by how you feel if your own thoughts are loving or poisonous.

How Will We Know?

"I am in charge of my life." Say it over and over until you believe it. It will change everything. One evening while on a cruise with a group of friends, I listened to the cruise director share stories of the most ridiculous questions he'd ever been asked. My favorite was:

"When I go to the Photo Gallery, how do I know which pictures are mine?"

Many of us seem to ask the same question about our lives.

How do you know which life you're responsible for? The one you are in.

I am in charge of my life.

Putting *Full Responsibility* into Practice

No one can make you feel inferior
without your consent.
Eleanor Roosevelt

∽∞∾

I recall a beautiful young coaching client who tried to convince me that the problem in her life was her father not accepting her career choice. "This is really hard," she began. As we looked at the situation through the lens of *Full Responsibility*, her resistance softened.

First, I shared with her that the best person to take advice from about a job, a relationship, or a new car is one who isn't personally attached to whether or not you pursue it. Secondly, I reminded her that we attract people who mirror our own insecurities. As soon as we're completely comfortable with our choice, their comments won't bother us and will often cease. Finally, we used Byron Katie's wonderful turnaround and changed "He should accept my choice" to "I could accept my choice" or "I could accept his choice (not to accept mine)."

She wrote me a thank-you note the following week saying that she felt like a "95" on the **Power Pyramid**. We are free to enjoy happiness the day we stop needing from others what we can only give ourselves.

The Hero's Wish

I have spent much of my life helping people pull themselves out of pain. Sometimes I have crossed the line and found myself working harder than they did. Lately I've become more comfortable with pain—in my life or in the lives of my loved ones—and have even seen how challenge and adversity can be a response to our intentions.

Ever think about what heroes have in common? "Courage!" is likely our first thought, but an equally true response would be "challenge and adversity." There is nothing heroic about getting out of bed in the morning, but if you've been told you'll never walk again, as Olympic track star Wilma Rudolph was, then your effort in the face of pain makes you a hero.

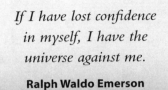

If I have lost confidence in myself, I have the universe against me.

Ralph Waldo Emerson

I saw this played out at a football game in November 2008. Nebraska was my team and this was going to be our comeback year. There was 1:43 left in the final game of the regular season and a decision had to be made. Down by a point, looking at 4th and 25, coach Bo Pelini decided to send in sophomore Alex Henery to try for a 57-yard field goal even though Henery had never kicked one longer than 52 yards.

While watching the young man run onto the field, I felt panic. I wanted to protect Alex from the "pressure" and said so to the football fans watching with me. "That's asking too much!" I remember yelling.

But it *wasn't* too much for the young kicker. He booted the ball through the goal posts with room to spare and sent the crowd into a frenzy.

After the game a very different picture came clear to me. It was of a young man growing up wanting to play football for the Nebraska Cornhuskers. He dreamed of being a difference maker, so as he practiced endless field goal kicks over the years, he had visualized that scene a hundred times. It was always a similar storyline: a big game was on the line and he's called in to save the day.

I wanted to "protect" Alex from being a hero and having a glorious moment of fame for his record-breaking kick. I now know that many times we need adversity to become better, and have become much "better" at sidelining my overprotective instincts.

Games for High-Way 3

It's possible and *important* to have fun while learning *Full Responsibility*. For example, the next time you're feeling "the weight of the world on your shoulders," have fun unloading your "shoulders" by ceasing to "should" on others. I guarantee that you'll have less of a shoulder ache when you take a "should-er" break!

Some simple games we offer in our curriculum for middle and high schools include:

The "Don't B-Lame" Game: Keep a note card in your pocket for one day. Every time you *B.C.*—Blame or Complain (even silently)—about someone or something, put a check mark on the card. At the end of the day, add up your marks. That's how many points down the **Power Pyramid** you moved, because it's how many times you gave away your power to feel good to something outside you.

The "Should to Want" Game: Start a new note card. Every time you use the word "should" or "shouldn't" or "need to" or "need you to," give yourself a check mark. This can be a hard one to break for my fellow teachers. I had one friend who had over fifty marks at the end of her teaching day. More empowering phrases that we use with adults are:

"I invite you now to…"
"Now I'm going to give you time to…"
"I'd like to move now into…"

> *Criticisms are like homing pigeons; they always return to their source.*
>
> **Dale Carnegie**

"Whose Business?" Cards: How much we enjoy the holidays is all…well, relatives. When you remember to take your "Whose Business?" cards with you, it can be *relatively* simple to deal with the challenges of in-laws.

First, find or make some blank business cards, and print on them the phrase "Whose Business?" Then put some in your pocket or wallet the next time you're leaving for a family reunion with fuming Aunt Freda and nosy Uncle Ned. If ever you think your relatives need to talk softer, drink less alcohol, or buy a more fuel efficient car, instead of "shoulding" on them with advice, pull out a card and read it silently, asking yourself, "Whose business am I in?"

The other fun part of this game is that whenever you want to give a "Whose Business?" card to someone so they'll stop shoulding, that means you are shoulding on them *not to should*. Simply pull one out and read it yourself. When you mind your *own* business, your business will earn you dividends of amazing comfort and joy.

Letting Go

From infancy on, we're all quite good at finding what makes us happy. As I finished this chapter, my son was a senior and it felt like I was cutting advice-giving umbilical cords daily. (It was even harder to keep my opinions to myself when he *asked* for my "words of wisdom.") I constantly reminded myself that in a few months he would be listening only to the voice in his head and that my silence gave that voice a chance to grow stronger. An anonymous poem that helped me through that time reads as follows:

Letting Go

To let go does not mean to stop caring,
it means I can't do it for someone else.
To let go is not to cut myself off,
it's the realization I can't control another.
To let go is not to enable,
but to allow learning from natural consequences.
To let go is to admit powerlessness,
which means the outcome is not in my hands, only my attitude is.
To let go is not to try to change or blame another,
it's to make the most of myself.
To let go is not to care for,
but to care about.
To let go is not to fix,
but to be supportive.
To let go is not to judge,
but to allow another to be a human being.
To let go is not to deny,
but to accept.
To let go is not to nag, scold or argue,
but instead to search out my own shortcomings and correct them.

To let go is not to criticize and regulate anybody,
but to try to become what I dream I can be.
To let go is not to regret the past,
but to be grateful for the present and have hope for the future.
To let go is to fear less,
and to love more.

⌒∞⌒

Q & A on *Full Responsibility*

Whatever you think is holding you back is not what is truly holding you back. What's holding you back is your thought that something is holding you back.

Ralph Marston

⁓∞⁓

Q: *If I'm fully responsible for the bad things in my life, that would mean I'm fully responsible for the good things, but I think God and a lot of people helped me get to where I am today. Doesn't that mean that a lot of people could have helped me go downhill, too?*

A: Let's go back to the **Power Pyramid**. Let's say today you're grateful to God and to all those people who have loved and supported you. You're soaring at a "95" and believe it's because they helped you, but it's really because you're focusing on the love and light around you. It's very possible to have the love of your Creator and those around you and still be miserable. I see it all the time.

Now let's imagine someone who comes along and is neither loving nor supportive. You allow their opinion of you to dash your self-esteem and good feelings and you bottom out at a "5," feeling worthless and hopeless. Whose responsibility was that?

Your level of happiness and your **Power Pyramid** "score" at any given moment are never dependent on what someone else does or says, but on what you focus upon and how that feels. Everyone has that freedom of choice.

Q: *I want to create a culture of Full Responsibility at my office. Where do I start?*

A: A manager I admire greatly shared with me something he learned while in the military. On his employees' first day, he hands them three envelopes with the instructions to only open them when things get rough and they need someone to blame. The trick is, they may only open the first envelope the first month, the second envelope the second month, and the third envelope their third month. The only other alternative is to rip them all up and hand them back to the manager.

Many curious employees open them the first day, of course. In the first envelope they find their predecessor's name. In the second they find their supervisor's name. In the third, their own name. He shared that 95 percent of his employees receive his message loud and clear and rip them up and hand them back immediately. If this manager's success is any indication, setting the tone of *Full Responsibility* builds an extremely dedicated and empowered team!

Q: *In High-Way 1, you say to have high expectations, but my counselor says my expectations are too high because I expect to be treated with respect. I expect people to be responsible and do what they promise me they'll do.*

A: Those are wonderful visions for the environment you want to live in. Now you just have to let go of the Who, What, When, Where, and How. If you continue to work this process, you'll have the life you describe, in which you and those around you act responsibly the majority of the time, but right now, life is your mirror. You're getting back what you put out because you're acting irresponsibly. How? You aren't taking responsibility for your own attitude.

Just as others are using a car breaking down or a poor memory as an excuse not to act as they said they would, you're using someone's actions or attitudes as excuses for not feeling good. What if you respected yourself and took *Full Responsibility* for feeling good, no matter what happened or who was late or who forgot to call you back?

Q: *I'm trying to teach responsibility to the teenagers who work at my shop, but haven't had any luck yet. Do I need to buy them your book?*

A: That might help. Here are some areas to look at. First, do you expect them to succeed? Pull them aside, one by one, ask what their dreams are, and then refer to them as if they've already achieved them such as, "Dr. Bryce, how's it going?" Let them know you believe in them. Listen to their input and give them special responsibilities. At the same time, be clear about your expectations and ramifications.

Teens respond amazingly well to clear expectations. One of my favorite restaurant owners recently revealed his secret weapon for hiring and keeping good high school help. When they apply, he warns them, "If your mother calls me, you're fired!"

Q: *I'm afraid that if I start believing I'm fully responsible, I'll feel so ashamed that I won't get out of bed.*

A: You're playing the "I should have known better" tape in your head. The fact is that you *didn't* know better. You'll learn more about that in High-Way 6. Meanwhile, in High-Way 4, you'll see how you can move from shame to anger, from anger to hope, and from hope to joy. Shame is based on inaccurate assessments (lies) about your past. Keep reading. You're on the right track.

High–Way 4:

Feel All Your Feelings

Allow Emotional Freedom

∾

Defining *Feel All Your Feelings*

The fastest way to freedom is to feel your feelings.

Gita Bellin

⌘

In the world I grew up in, talking about or feeling your feelings was for young girls and "sissies." In the world I live in now, the healers I respect most understand that the primary cure for addiction, illness, rage, depression, and destructive behavior can be summed up in one word: *feel*.

Feelings wield amazing power. They can motivate us to greatness or plunge us into despair. They're catalysts for everything from weddings to wars. We do what we do with one primary intention— *to feel good*. But in order to feel good, we must feel.

The alternative to feeling is to *run from*. Some of us avoid feelings through addiction to food, others through perfectionism, drinking, drugs, computer solitaire, or pornography. Even a seemingly benign act like volunteering for every church function can be an attempt to escape from dealing with feelings. But running *from* is always running in circles. Eventually, our feelings find us.

Pain is required, suffering is optional.

The Problem

For many of us, *growing up* meant *shutting down*. "Children should be seen and not heard" thinking has long labeled the quiet child as "good" or "easy." We've forgotten to give ourselves permission to feel the "noisy" and "messy" feelings. Politeness and peace-at-any-price have often replaced happiness and joy as our ultimate goals. Do any of these sound familiar?

> *"Please don't cry. I hate it when you cry."*
>
> *"You shouldn't be angry about that."*
>
> *"Stop crying or I'll give you something to cry about."*
>
> *"Don't raise your voice to me, young lady."*
>
> *"Don't cry. You'll upset the little ones."*
>
> *"You can't be mad at them, they're family."*

Children often receive more of these messages when they enter the classroom. "I don't like your attitude, young man" is often thinly disguised disapproval of a student's anger. One large Midwest school system recently published their definition of positive attitude as "staying pleasant in times of adversity," an alarming implication that anger and grief aren't healthy and must be suppressed. My objective in this chapter is to invite you to consider that *there is no such thing as a negative feeling. Feelings just are.*

The Day Feelings Died

I recall a teacher telling me the story of the day she shut down to her feelings. The year was 1998. In her rural school system, most of the eighth graders rode the same bus to school. One fall morning, they drove by the scene of an accident and saw a classmate receiving CPR from his mother.

When they reached the classroom, a distraught young girl voiced the fears of the class when she choked through her tears, "Is he dead?"

The teacher, grieving deeply herself, had been given a directive by the principal to keep everything as normal as possible "for the children's own good."

"We don't have word yet," the teacher said softly. "Please sit down and open your books so we can get started with class."

Word came later that morning that the young man *had* died in the accident and counselors quickly flooded the classroom. The following day classes were held as usual. Life simply "went on."

The teacher wept as she shared the rest of the story with me.

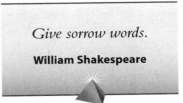

Give sorrow words.

William Shakespeare

"We didn't know how to deal with the students' feelings—or our own, for that matter—so we didn't even try. The following evening, during parent-teacher conferences, the best friend of the student who'd been killed took his own life."

Workplace Woes

Meanwhile, in many of today's workplaces, there is a continued assault on the natural flow of emotions. The person in the office or cubicle next to yours could be dealing with challenges ranging from divorce to downsizing, credit card debt to defiant teens, heart palpitations to ailing parents, yet sharing feelings at work is often discouraged.

I once spoke to a Minnesota IT firm and during a break after teaching *Feel All Your Feelings*, I was confronted by a supervisor.

"I don't want you talking about emotions anymore. Someone could have had a...breakdown!" he said louder than was necessary.

I realized that he meant someone could have cried. Tears are common among my audiences and I am grateful for this healthy release. In fact, rather than a breakdown, I call tears a *breakthrough*. I was able to listen to the manager and he was able to allow me to continue to teach the process. The evaluations were their "best ever."

The Price We Pay

The suppression of emotions exacts a high price. Addictions, illness, accidents, and destructive behavior against ourselves and others are just some of the symptoms that surface.

1. Addictions

The "Just Say No" anti-drug campaign of the '90s fascinated me with its lack of understanding about why people use drugs. Drug addiction is never the result of peer pressure alone. Whether in a child or an adult, substance abuse is a desperate attempt to *run from* our feelings.

I recall a conversation with a thirty-something recovering alcoholic who was new to the homeless shelter where I was speaking.

When I asked how she was doing, she quietly replied, "I've been shot three times, but the pain of having to face my feelings this past week has been worse than all of them put together."

She'd been using alcohol to avoid her emotional pain, but now she was processing a lifetime of stored up anger and sadness. No wonder it was hard.

2. Illness

Another price we pay for stuffing our feelings is illness. Years ago, I realized that I'd stopped getting colds. Back in my high school teaching days, I used to get three or four a year. When I saw that it had been nine or ten years since I'd had more than a scratchy throat for an hour, someone gave me a book entitled *You Can Heal Your Life*. Author Louise Hay studied indigenous cultures and found that lifetimes of wellness were as common for them as doctor appointments are in this culture. Hay's book helped me make the connection that colds and crying have the exact same physical symptoms.

> *It's what they've been asking us all our lives. "How are you feeling today?" You're either feeling all the feelings or not feeling well and stuffing them.*
>
> **Dr. John Meister**

"If you do not allow yourself to release the toxins in the natural way, through crying, you'll have to release them in a more painful way, through a cold," she writes. Now when I get a scratchy throat, I journal, take a hot bath, or rent a three-Kleenex movie to help me cry.

3. Accidents

I remember the night my babysitter walked in the door crying. When I asked what was wrong, she told me she'd been in another car accident—her fourth that year—and she was afraid she was going to lose her license.

> *If you bring forth what is within you, what you bring forth will save you. If you do not bring forth what is within you, what you do not bring forth will destroy you.*
>
> **Gospel of Thomas**

After she finished, I asked, "What are you so angry about that it makes you keep running into people? What is it you want that you're not getting?"

It turned out this Midwestern girl wanted to move to California but was afraid her mother would disapprove. As she admitted that she really wanted to make the change, she calmed down and got very clear. She confronted her mom the next day and California has been her home for more than a decade now. Last I heard, she was still accident free!

4. Destructive behavior against ourselves and others

When young Reggie's parents divorced, he assumed that it was their driving him to so many sports practices and games that had been the cause. As a result, he quit most of the sports that he loved so much and with nowhere to release his pent up anger and sadness, turned them back on himself. The result was severe depression and suicidal thoughts.

Once out of high school, the pain continued and drugs became his best friend. When he was kicked out of college for selling narcotics he moved back home. When I met him, at the request of his mom, he wasn't sleeping and was shut down emotionally, but he still had hope, and was open to whatever I could offer. Today this handsome and talented athlete is right on track with following his dreams to be a professional basketball coach.

I could tell dozens more similar stories. The *underlying cause* of all addiction is the suppression and repression of feelings. Healing can only take place when we allow ourselves to *Feel All Our Feelings*.

The Energy of E-Motion

What are emotions, where do they come from, and why do they often overwhelm us? The word *emotion* stands for "energy in motion." Emotions are the energy that "moves" us, so the worst thing we can do is try and stop them. Getting stuck in a feeling is a sign of resistance and always brings suffering. The two emotions that we *"should"* on (refer to as negative) the most are the ones we most often get *stuck* in: mad and sad. Once we realize that there's no such thing as a negative emotion, we can accept mad and sad as natural and healthy "energy in motion."

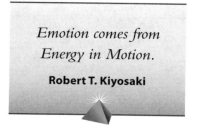

Emotion comes from Energy in Motion.

Robert T. Kiyosaki

The Mad/Sad Balance

It is becoming evident to those who study our emotional makeup that we always feel mad and sad *at the same time and in the same amount* because we need them both to balance each other. These normal and natural feelings only become a problem when one is suppressed and the balance is disrupted.

When teaching this concept to young children, I use the images of fire and water. Mad (fire) is a good thing, but too much of it is not. When there is too much fire, we need water to keep it in balance. Similarly, sad (water) is a good thing, but when there is too much of it, we need fire and heat to dry it up.

Where does the suppression begin? As small children, we often heard phrases like "Dad's in a bad mood." We knew Dad was angry, so at a young age we made the inference that anger was "bad." In our efforts to be "good," we tried to stifle our normal frustrations, but it never worked and we ended up even angrier as a result.

Similarly, hearing "Leave Mom alone because she's feeling bad right now" was interpreted as "sadness is bad," so we went off by ourselves and either cried quietly in our pillows or just stuffed our tears completely.

In my first book, I shared a story about the time in my childhood when I saw my kitten get run over by a car. I was rushed into the house, but was told not to cry so I wouldn't upset my younger brothers and sister. I can see now that my loving and well-meaning parents were part of a culture that wasn't taught about the powerful nature of feelings. They were doing the best they could with the information they had—doing as they'd been taught—but now it's time we teach and model emotional acceptance.

No Such Thing as a Negative Feeling

It amazes me that many popular self-help books today still refer to mad and sad as "negative feelings." *8 to Great* does not label any emotion as positive or negative. Some feelings are more pleasant to experience, but as you'll see, they all have potential benefits. The healthiest and most positive people on the planet regularly feel both their *sads* and *mads* because they understand the power of feeling *all* their feelings.

Dr. Martin Luther King, Jr. felt all his feelings and even credited his angriest moment as a youth for inspiring his civil rights work. Regarding that first racially-charged incident as a boy, King wrote: "Riding the bus that day was the angriest I have ever been in my life."

> *The truth is that our finest moments are most likely to occur when we are feeling deeply uncomfortable, unhappy, or unfulfilled, for it is only in such moments, propelled by our discomfort, that we are likely to step out of our ruts and start searching for truer answers.*
>
> **M. Scott Peck**

Mother Teresa was also known for her anger, which she used to fuel her passion to work with the poor. It's often a characteristic of our greatest leaders and saints. They remind us that feelings of anger aren't synonymous with acts of violence. Anger is energy for change.

Defining Anger as "Angergy"

When we talk about anger, we're referring to the energy/adrenaline rush we experience when we encounter a real or supposed injury or insult. From a lioness protecting her cubs to an employee upset at unethical behavior in a workplace, anger pulses through us to give us the energy to take action.

As we start to see anger in a more positive light, we can more easily give ourselves permission to feel it. To remind us of how anger energizes us into action, I blended the words anger and energy and refer to it now as *angergy*. Angergy is a byproduct of passion—that wonderful life juice that tells us what we want to co-create next, whether it's an art piece, a winning team, a loving relationship, or a political reformation.

> *I never work better than when I am inspired by anger; for when I am angry, my whole temperament is quickened, my understanding sharpened, and all temptations depart.*
>
> **Martin Luther**

"I'm Angry" Is Not True

We are *not* our feelings. To say "I *am* angry" is inaccurate and not in our best interest because the way the mind hears it, we have taken on our anger as our identity. The reality is much less dramatic. Anger is something we feel, like we feel the drops of a spring rain on our face or the heat of a winter's fireplace on our hands. We would never say that we are the rain or we are the heat. Similarly, we are not our emotions.

Instead, we can start to reframe our relationship to emotions with phrases such as, "Right now I'm feeling a little (angry, scared, sad, excited) about what just happened." It's similar to saying, "Right now I'm feeling a little warm from the sun shining through the window." See yourself as separate from the emotions that move through you. You are not your feelings.

Defining Sadness as "Release"

The other emotion we often get stuck in is *sadness,* which shows up with anger because it's the perfect release valve for our excess *angergy.* Just as the heart brings blood in through the veins and takes it out through the arteries (or as I call them, the *outeries*), *angergy* builds up energy for change and sadness releases the extra we don't use. A blockage of anger/angergy *or* sadness/release will cause physical or emotional problems, just as a blockage in the veins *or* the arteries will cause physical problems.

The Mad/Sad Diagram

When we're experiencing an upsetting incident, our natural tendency (like that of a small child) is to feel and express our anger and sadness at the same time. Mad and sad are like two sides of the same coin, so I use the following diagram to demonstrate their relationship:

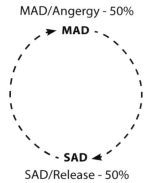

MAD/Angergy - 50%

MAD

SAD

SAD/Release - 50%

When there is deep grief, such as at the death of a loved one, there is also strong anger—anger that they "left" us, anger at the disease, or anger at ourselves for not having done more for them or appreciated them more while they were alive.

The Benefits of Sad and Mad

Many of us grew up in homes where there was a lot of shaming anger. As a result, we may have come to the conclusion that all angry people were "mean," therefore cutting ourselves off from feeling and expressing our own angergy/fire. What we didn't realize was that when we cut ourselves off from our fire energy—mad, we will eventually experience an overflow of water energy—sad. The most common name for too much sadness is depression.

> *Only through emotions can you encounter the force field of your own soul.*
>
> **Gary Zukav**

How much energy do you have when you're depressed? None. Why? Because you've cut yourself off from your angergy. By telling yourself that anger isn't appropriate and that only mean people get angry, you end up with all release/water and no angergy/fire.

No Angergy/fire = Too much release/water

MAD/Angergy - 0%

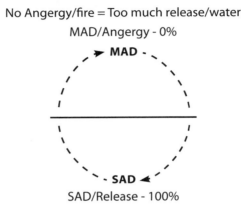

SAD/Release - 100%

Too much release/water = Depression

Others of us may have grown up in homes where a parent was sad a lot and didn't stand up for themselves or ask for what they needed. They looked "weak," so we decided that no one would ever see *us* as weak! The result was that without our sadness/water, we got stuck in our anger/fire, which then ignited into rage. When you cut yourself off from your sadness, telling yourself that only weak people cry, you end up with all angergy and no release.

No release/water = Too much Angergy/fire

Too much Angergy = Rage

MAD/Angergy - 100%

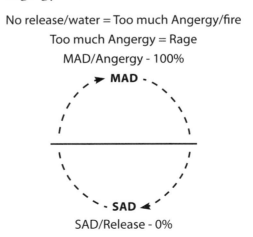

SAD/Release - 0%

We need both the *Angergy* of our anger and the *Release* of our sadness to stay in a healthy balance. When we don't feel them, they "go to the dark side" and turn into their shadow opposites: depression and rage. Therefore, the way to diminish our rage and depression isn't to stop feeling so much, but to fully experience both our mads *and* our sads.

We can learn to befriend all our feelings. There's no need to get depressed about our depression or angry about our anger. I've come to a place in my emotional life where depression is a rare visitor, but when it comes, I now "watch it," knowing it will only be with me for awhile. When I observe it without judgment, it goes on its way more quickly. The last thing depression wants is acceptance.

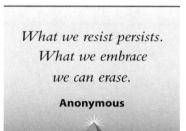

What we resist persists. What we embrace we can erase.

Anonymous

The Mad/Sad Bowl Theory

What happens when we don't allow or express our emotions and bottle them up instead?

"Honey," I said to my unusually quiet seven-year-old son in the back seat. "You're usually singing on the way to school, but it's pretty quiet back there. Is anything wrong?"

"No, Mom," he said mournfully.

"Are you sure? Remember, we don't keep secrets about feelings in our family."

"I don't want to tell you 'cuz I don't want to make you feel bad."

His statement startled me. I'd never realized my kids were suppressing their feelings because they wanted to "protect" me from feeling them. I pulled over and stopped the car so we could get out and talk a bit.

"Oh, the great news, sweetheart, is that you can't make me feel anything. Not sad or mad or glad. You can't *make* me feel, but you might be able to *help* me feel sad," I told him.

"What does that mean, Mom?"

"Well, honey, it's as if everyone has two bowls inside of them, a sad bowl and a mad bowl. If we let ourselves cry when we want to cry about something, our sadness bowl is empty. But if we don't let ourselves release our tears, like when Grandpa died or when our neighbors moved away, they get stored in our sadness bowl. Then, when someone we care about cries, it can *help us* pour out our tears by crying too. That's how you'd help *me* cry by allowing yourself to cry."

"So what about the *mad* bowl?"

"Well, it works the same way. When something upsets me, I can talk it out, walk it out, or write it out, *or* I can store it inside. If I keep it inside, it will start to fill my mad bowl, not with tears like the sad bowl, but with *kerosene!* If I keep putting kerosene in my mad bowl, someday, someone with a match is gonna walk by—"

"And there'll be a big explosion!" Zach spouted.

"That's right, sweetheart, but an explosion is *never about the match.*"

Little did I realize that this story I made up for my son would bring me such insight. The more I reflected on it, the more clearly I saw that when we explode in rage at someone, it is never about them, but about the kerosene we've been carrying. It is an insight that changed my life.

> *Emotions are the next frontier to be understood and conquered. To manage our emotions is not to drug them or suppress them, but to understand them so that we can direct our emotional energies and intentions...*
>
> **Doc Childre**

The *Feel All Your Feelings* Process:
The Mad-Sad Balance

In the last decade, researchers have found that even more than IQ, your emotional awareness and abilities to handle feelings will determine your success and happiness...

John Gottman

⌘

The process for feeling our feelings is as natural as breathing. We've been doing it all our lives. The key is to do it with *every* feeling, not just the ones that feel the best. The benefits of becoming aware and accepting of all our emotional states are as numerous as the emotions themselves. We not only decrease the likelihood of disabling addictions, illness, and accidents, but we also have:

✔ *more energy*
✔ *more clarity and focus*
✔ *clearer boundaries*
✔ *more insight and access to our intuition*
✔ *more assertiveness*
✔ *more compassion for others*

To put it in the simplest terms, when we feel more, *we feel better!*

Awareness vs. Denial

"I'm not angry!" a young mother yelled at her children, unaware of how ridiculous her denial sounded to everyone in the store.

It reminded me of this acronym for DENIAL:

Don't
Even
Know
I
Am
Lying

> *Acceptance means you allow yourself to feel whatever you are feeling at the moment.*
>
> **Eckhart Tolle**

Denial is a tool we use to cover up something we've been trained to believe is "bad." Most of us grow up hearing that anger is harmful and that we should be ashamed of such feelings. That's why we try to cover them up. The truth, however, is that suppression of anger causes much more harm than expressing it.

Honoring the Balance

I recall a day many years ago when a co-worker was mocking me because he thought a question I had asked was naïve and stupid. I felt a gut punch, reminded myself that only those who've been wounded can wound, and then found a quiet place to get in touch with my anger. I didn't have to look very hard into my past before remembering being mocked by my teachers when I asked questions they thought trivial.

Once I acknowledged feeling sad and hurt, I was also able to get in touch with the anger I had suppressed years ago over those incidents. I did my anger work (see the options below) and eventually my *Forgiveness* work, which we'll cover in High-Way 6.

We sometimes need to take an action to regain our emotional freedom. If you're feeling stuck emotionally, my favorite ways to get in touch with feelings are:

1. Walk 'em out
2. Talk 'em out
3. Write 'em out
4. Movie night 'em out
5. Art and music 'em out

1. Walk 'em out could include:

✔ *a workout at the gym*
✔ *hitting a pillow (yelling, "It's not okay!" is optional)*
✔ *throwing ice cubes at sidewalks*

✔ dancing

✔ mopping floors or digging a garden

✔ hitting a punching bag

The above options could include anything that gets you breathing deeply.

2. **Talk 'em out could include:**

✔ with your spouse

✔ with a friend on the phone or in person

✔ with a counselor or pastor

✔ with a teacher or coach

✔ with a hotline or support group

✔ with your higher power

(Note: I do not recommend using Internet chat rooms for sharing strong feelings.)

> *There is no feeling, except extreme fear and grief, that does not find relief in music.*
>
> **T.S. Eliot**

3. **Write 'em out could include:**

✔ in a journal (online or on paper)

✔ on a napkin

✔ as a short story or a poem

✔ in a letter that you burn

✔ writing one phrase over and over

If privacy is an issue, throwing the pages away or burning them can bring great relief.

4. **Movie night 'em out could include:**

✔ renting a movie

✔ going to a movie with a friend or by yourself

✔ going to a play or musical

5. **Art and Music 'em out could include:**

✔ going to a concert

✔ playing a song

✔ drawing or painting a picture

✔ creating a sculpture

✔ listening to music

✔ visiting an art gallery

> *Even if you're not at ease right now, being aware that you're not at ease embraces that unease and dissipates it. Learn to be with and accept what is.*
>
> **Eckhart Tolle**

No matter what you're going through, you're not alone in how you feel. Emotions are a universal language we *all* share. Whether by talking with someone or watching a movie, it's comforting to relate to another human being or character on the screen who is experiencing similar challenges.

Why We Don't *Feel All Our Feelings*

One of the deepest truths about the cry of the human heart is that it is so often muted. It is strange that members of a species renowned for communicative gifts should leave unexpressed some of their smoldering resentments, their secret hopes, their longings to serve a higher purpose.

John W. Gardner

⟡

Ultimately, there's only one reason that we, who began life screaming and kicking through all of our feelings, shut down emotionally. Fear is the culprit, but F.E.A.R. is nothing more than *False Evidence Appearing Real*. What makes fear even more interesting is that some of us are so frozen emotionally that we fear even admitting that we're afraid.

The alternative is awareness and acceptance of our emotions. Then, with our new perspective, we can make new decisions about how we will start *feeling better* from here on out.

Scrooging

One reason we don't *Feel All Our Feelings* is because we've been hurt in the past. In Charles Dickens' *A Christmas Carol*, Scrooge wasn't born bitter. He became that way when he shut down emotionally. He was enjoying life and connecting with those around him until his fiancé left him. In order to protect himself from ever feeling that intense pain again, he decided to shut down his heart.

We have all "scrooged" to some extent, closing off our hearts by degrees after this or that painful incident. But when we cannot feel our sads and mads, we cannot feel our glads. Thank heavens there are alternatives other than being visited by ghosts in order to learn how to feel joy, hope, and love again!

Myths Around Emotions

Many of us don't feel our feelings because we carry so many misconceptions about emotions. Some believe that anger isn't feminine, others that crying isn't masculine. While some have been told that getting emotional is a sign of losing control, others believe that people who display emotions are only doing so to manipulate others. Meanwhile, some expect their loved ones to be able to explain why they feel a certain way and others believe that emotions are optional and therefore taking time to feel or express them is a complete waste of time.

> *If we do not transform our pain, we will most assuredly transmit it.*
>
> **Richard Rohr**

I have heard each of these sentiments from my coaching clients. Recognizing them as false is necessary to the "unlearning" process that paves the way for knowing the truth about how and why we feel.

One morning I heard from a friend who had just dropped her daughter off at a college out of state.

"I'll bet you had a good cry over that experience," I shared.

"No, not really. On the way to the campus, my nine-year-old son said, 'You're not gonna cry are you, Mom?' and I promised I wouldn't."

I asked her if she would like permission to break that pledge. In response she began to weep.

"Real Men" *Do* Cry

When asked by a fellow actor how she cried so easily on set, Meryl Streep was once reported to have answered, "How can you not?"

Unfortunately, tears from men in films have been longer in coming. Another reason we don't *Feel All Our Feelings* is that we've bought into cultural stereotypes from our cinematic heroes. On a Hollywood set in 1995, while Clint Eastwood and Meryl were filming *The Bridges of Madison County*, the actress noticed during one particularly moving take that there were tears in Clint's eyes.

According to sources on the scene, Meryl begged him to use that take, but he wouldn't do it.

"I don't cry," he said.

A decade later, things had changed. As anyone who has seen the Academy Award winning film *Million Dollar Baby* knows, Eastwood's character was required to get in touch with deep levels of grief. Al Ruddy, the film's producer, recalled the day they shot the film's climactic sequence:

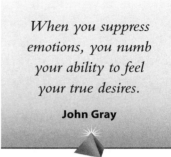

When you suppress emotions, you numb your ability to feel your true desires.

John Gray

> "Everyone was standing around the set crying. The makeup girl was crying. Hilary Swank was crying. Clint was crying. It was amazing."

Feelings at Work

A woman came up to me after a seminar crying uncontrollably. Between sobs, I discovered that her job had transferred her four times in three years. Recently, she had been held back from a promotion because she was overheard crying in her cubicle. The report said: "has trouble handling stress." As I honored her tears and urged her to take deep breaths, I reminded her that the person who had trouble feeling and dealing with stress was the person who wrote that report. We only try to suppress those emotions in others that we have practiced suppressing in ourselves.

Medicating Our Pain

The *GQ* man of the '80s and '90s was famous for his expressionless face. One reason many people shut down is because our culture is full of the message that feelings are not "cool." We don't want the pain or the stigma of being "emotional," so we often turn to prescription drugs to "Band-Aid" our feelings. According to a 2003 *Boston Globe* article, the use of stimulants, antidepressants, and antipsychotics among people under eighteen have more than tripled since 1989—a staggering statistic.

When my mother was grieving the loss of my father, a psychiatrist put her on a strong antidepressant because she was "crying too much." When she complained that she didn't feel any better, he doubled the dose—without even scheduling an appointment.

In the past few decades, the use of prescription drugs has skyrocketed as we attempt to medicate our pain away. When we hear a fire alarm, our first impulse isn't to turn off the annoying noise, but to get to safety and call someone to deal with the fire—yet our medicine cabinets are full of substances that only "turn off the alarm." Numbing ourselves with medication is the equivalent of ignoring a warning signal that says we're out of balance physically, mentally, or emotionally. Taking a pill without allowing yourself to *Feel All Your Feelings* is a sure prescription for more visits to the doctor and pharmacist.

> *All addictive behaviors are attempts to suppress and avoid feeling what we feel.*
>
> **John Gray**

When my mother lost my father, she was crying not only for her loss, but also for missed opportunities in the past. I was delighted when she chose to stop medicating her pain. She found a new doctor, a new support group, and, eventually, a new *love* to share her life with.

Feel All Your Feelings Success Stories

To feel is to heal.

Eddie Buchanan

∝∞๑

Recently, a psychologist came up after a seminar and told me, "Last time I heard you speak, I made a shift in my life. I had just lost my pet of twelve years. I was totally incapacitated and overwhelmed by grief, and your stories enabled me to get closure on an old wound. Years ago, my father accidentally shot one of my dogs in a hunting accident. In order to protect him from feeling any worse than he already did, I didn't grieve my beloved pet. I realized that my intense pain was due to the fact that I was grieving both dogs at once."

The Secret Vows

Bill and Paulette were in their sixties when I met them. They were separated when Bill wandered into my seminar in a small Nebraska town. We talked for an hour afterward over a cup of coffee. I recognized his story. He'd been raised by a German farmer who had no time for feelings. Bill's mom passed away when he was young and in his words, "the family went silent." He hadn't allowed himself to cry for years.

"So you were always raging at Paulette and she did all the crying for you?" I asked.

"Exactly."

I've seen it many times. It's as though some couples add to their wedding vows: "I'll do all the anger if you'll do all the sadness." When you are ready to feel better, you can change your relationship dynamics by *Feeling All Your Feelings*. Over the next few months Bill and I worked through the High-Ways together and the couple reunited. Bill wrote to me that on his sixty-fifth birthday he felt such immense gratitude that his tears saturated his piece of cake.

Seven Freshmen

I got a call a few years back from a private school saying that they had a dilemma and didn't know who else to call. Seven of their freshmen were flunking *every course* and the school didn't know how to get through to them. They requested that I come and present my material.

No surprise to me, all seven were boys, full of more *angergy* and dreams than they knew what to do with. At our first meeting, I asked them to *Get the Picture* of what they wanted for themselves and their futures. Unfortunately, I asked them to do it aloud. (I've since learned to do this in journaling.) All their anger would let them admit was that they wanted fast cars and "hot chicks." The angriest young man said he just wanted out of the school so he could become a professional dirt bike racer.

As the bell rang at the end of that first session, they all ran out of class. I wasn't sure how I was going to help them because they all had so much fear of feeling that their dreams were being kept at a safe distance. After class, Charlie, the dirt biker, walked back into the room and asked if I had a minute to talk.

"Of course," I said.

"I lied, Ms. Mueller, and you don't deserve to have people lie to you when you came here just for us. I want something. I want it bad, but I didn't have the guts to say it in front of the guys."

"What is it?" I asked.

> *Feelings only come to pass, never to stay.*
>
> **Kaylene Smith**

"I want to make honor roll," he said, his eyes brimming with tears, "but I was afraid I'd start crying if I said it out loud. Thanks for listening."

The following semester, Charlie went from all F's to the honor roll.

Physician Prescriptions for Health

Studies show that an inordinate number of heart attacks occur between 7:00 and 9:00 on Monday mornings, when many people are heading to jobs they hate but have stuffed their feelings about. The medical community is becoming aware that having emotional outlets and allowing yourself to *Feel All Your Feelings* is a vital part of the healing process.

> *I teach kids that tears that do not flow will make other organs weep inside us. We get sick if we try to hold all that pain in. Then, the unaddressed grief turns to anger, and the anger to rage.*
>
> **Michael Pritchard**

Once we regain our emotional freedom, we start to "feel" better physically! After feeling both their mads and sads at our *8 to Great* training weekends, people's migraines have stopped, their blood pressure has dropped, and they have reported sleeping better.

A few years back, as I addressed a group of physicians, I asked them to list "the real cause of their patients' problems." After that, I asked them to write a corresponding list of "real cures."

Most of the "real problems" of their patients fell into these categories:

✔ *Fear and anxiety*
✔ *Depression and despair*
✔ *Lack of emotional stability*
✔ *Low self-esteem*
✔ *Inability to deal with stress; feeling out of control*
✔ *Lack of self-care*
✔ *Loneliness*
✔ *Repressed anger*
✔ *Not knowing how to say no*

I was amazed that not one doctor in the audience wrote that drugs and surgery were the "real cure." Instead, they wrote that the most effective remedies included:

✔ *Education*
✔ *Positive attitude*
✔ *Healthy relationships*
✔ *Learning to get angry*

✔ *Having someone listen to their feelings*
✔ *Finding hope*
✔ *Assertiveness*

Lamonte's Story

I met Lamonte when he was in college. He inspired me, and we became good friends. When I offered to host his graduation party at my home, he shared that he had never had a party with cake and decorations. I wanted to share part of his amazing story to open our eyes to the pain and powerful emotions that many carry silently inside.

> *When a nurse in the cancer ward tells me we have a cantankerous patient in Room 214, I respond, 'Good, they'll live longer.'*
>
> **Dr. Bernie Siegel**

I grew up in a rough part of Chicago in the '90's. When I was in elementary school, there was never enough to eat. Because my mother did not have her high school diploma, there weren't many decent paying jobs for her. So instead of being gone all the time to make enough money for us, she went on welfare.

We lived with my Grandma and my uncles in a small home. The problem was that there were seven of us in a house that was really meant for two. The noise level was something else. Outside there were people shouting and the constant sirens, while inside there were TV's going in every room. Add to that the fact that my Grandma loved to have the police scanner on all the time so she could hear the police reports of where the criminal activity was, and you can imagine how loud it was.

In order to study, sometimes I'd take the bus to Barnes and Noble. I also really liked it when it rained, because then I could walk in the rain and it would be quiet because everyone else was inside.

As I said, we never had enough to eat. I'm sometimes asked why I didn't reach out for help during those grade school years. That's easy. The one time in second grade when one of my teachers asked if I had eaten supper the night before and I said I hadn't, we had the child welfare services threatening to come and search our home and put my mom in jail.

Let's see, lie or watch my family get split up? That was an easy decision. I got really good at making up stories about how much we had to eat.

Because we didn't have any food at home, I also got really good at figuring out ways to find it or make money to buy it. I joined choir because they gave out bagels and juice every morning. I joined violin because they had coffeecake. I'd shoot hoops with anybody dumb enough to compete with me and win a quarter. That would pay for my reduced lunch the next day.

But I also needed money for things like tennis shoes for me and my little brothers. In 4th grade I figured out a new plan. I'd get a Sports Illustrated *magazine—back in those days there were always stories about the Bulls or Notre Dame—and then I'd rent it to the kids in my homeroom. They could keep it all homeroom period for a quarter, and then they had to give it back. We had homeroom twice a day so that really added up.*

Pretty soon, with back issues, I was renting out ten issues a day twice a day, so I was able to buy stuff like socks, underwear and toothpaste. I sold the old magazines for a dollar when they were done. It helped out a lot.

By 7th grade I was a mess of rage and depression. I'd do anything to make a dollar, shoveling snow people for who hadn't asked me to do it just so I could get a tip, raking leaves, walking dogs...but it still wasn't enough to really change anything.

I looked around and noticed that none of the kids in my neighborhood who were going to the local high school were making anything of themselves, so I decided to go for my dreams big time. I got out a phone book and started calling every private school I could find.

I'd talk to anyone, coaches, counselors, principals, or deans. My Ma said I was using too much phone time, but I knew this was my only way out. Then I'd write them letters, on cardboard or notepads, whatever I could find to tell people my situation and ask for a scholarship.

I decided to ask one of my teachers for help, so I told my 7th grade teacher that I wanted to go to a university and needed to figure out a way to get into a good high school. I remember she laughed at me and said, "Oh, that's ridiculous. The local high school will do just fine." I'm glad

I didn't let people like that get me down. My anger movtivated me to just keep writing.

Unfortunately, even though I established lots of relationships with my letters, I still didn't have my scholarship. Finally, during my 8th grade summer, I did get an invitation to attend a summer basketball camp at Notre Dame High School, 90 minutes away by bus.

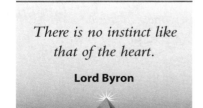

There is no instinct like that of the heart.

Lord Byron

I knew I had to get their attention and help them know I could be "one of them," so every morning I dressed up in the suit and tie I bought at Goodwill. Then I rode the bus the 90 minutes to practice, walked into the locker room, changed into my gym clothes, practiced, then changed back into my shirt and tie and rode the bus back home.

It got their attention. The last day of camp the coach asked me why I came in a suit and tie every day and I told him. He asked me to wait a minute and he walked down the hall to the principal's office to try and get me a scholarship.

When he came back he apologized and said they didn't have any-thing right now, but that he'd keep trying. I didn't hear anything for a week. Then at 6:15 the morning I was supposed to start at my neigh-borhood school, the phone rang. "We've got an anonymous donor that's going to fund you for four years," they said. I was ecstatic. Two days later, the first day of school at Notre Dame High School, I was enrolled as a student.

I graduated with lots of honors and two trips to the state basketball championships. I also got a scholarship to a great university. But I still had to be resourceful because the scholarship didn't cover food or books. The first semester I had to choose between food and sheets and blankets for my bed, but after that it got easier.

Through all this, Feeling All My Feelings *has been really impor-tant. For example, when the movie* **Pursuit of Happyness** *came out in 2007, I went to it with a couple of my buddies.*

The entire movie I could feel myself holding back, almost shutting down at the emotional parts of the film. It totally reminded me of my experiences, but I didn't feel comfortable crying around my guy friends.

So right after it was over, I drove them home, turned around, and went back to watch it again—this time with lots of tears and cheers. There was no way I could tap into the passion and power of that film if I didn't allow my emotions to be felt.

Now I have my finance degree and a really good job. One of my dreams is that I will sell the old house my Ma and Grandma and uncles still live in and buy them a nicer one. Life is what you make it. I'm glad I took the high road.

Allowing the Feelings of Children

When my daughter was getting ready to move out, I had a discussion with my eleven-year-old son about the fact that when young adults prepare to leave home, they often get angry at their parents for every little thing.

"Why?" he asked.

"I imagine because they're afraid if they don't stay angry, they'll cry," I said.

That led to a good talk about sadness, during which I reminded him of the importance of tears when we experience the loss of someone or something we love.

"If you died, Mom, I'd probably cry a whole week."

"Wow!"

I am Me. In all the world, there is no one else exactly like me... However I look and sound, whatever I say and do, and whatever I think and feel at a given moment in time is authentically me... I own me, and therefore, I can engineer me. I am me, and I am Okay.

Virginia Satir

"Or maybe even more." Then he added, "But I'd be crying happy tears, too, because I'd be so glad you're in heaven."

His comments, of course, helped me cry happy tears as we hugged. Allowing our kids' feelings, both mads and sads, can help us heal the future. Learning to feel all our feelings in their presence can heal the present.

Putting *Feel All Your Feelings* into Practice

Journaling can write your childhood wrongs.
Catherine L. Taylor

⌒∞⌒

Journaling

I have found that journaling feelings is the best entry into the world of accepting them. This kind of writing has no rules. The only guidelines are that you don't share it with anyone and you refrain from *editing* your writing. Whatever comes out, comes out, spelling errors and all.

A middle-aged woman credited my class with giving her "a ton of energy." A week later, I discovered the only thing she'd done differently was journal her feelings.

"Wow!" I said. "If you're having that much more energy, you must be journaling a lot."

"Not always," she replied. "On Wednesday I just wrote one word, *Damn!*"

Feelings are often just underneath the surface, patiently awaiting our permission to come forth and free us.

One Rung at a Time

Below is a list of feelings from the phenomenal book *Ask and It Is Given* by Jerry and Esther Hicks. The feelings at the top of the list are how we feel when we *remember our power*. The further down the list, the more *powerless* the feelings. In other words, you could say this is where the emotions would be placed on the **Power Pyramid**.

Joy, Empowerment, Gratitude, Love
Passion, Eager Enthusiasm
Optimism, Hope
Contentment
Boredom
Pessimism

Frustration, Impatience
Disappointment
Doubt
Worry
Blame, Anger
Hatred, Revenge, Jealousy
Guilt, Shame
Fear, Depression, Despair

What I have learned from these wonderful teachers is beyond measure. Two of their most important insights concern emotions.

1. Anger is not at the bottom of the emotions/power list; it is one-third of the way up. In other words, we might assume that an angry teenager has "fallen down" from joy and gratitude when he has actually "climbed up" from depression and despair. A despondent young person is much more of a concern than one expressing anger.

2. We cannot ascend this ladder of emotions in one large leap. What we can do, and encourage others to do, is move up one or two feelings (rungs) at a time. For example, when I am feeling depressed, revenge is two steps higher and therefore would actually be a positive and feasible step. Likewise, when I am able to choose thoughts that move me from guilt to anger, I am making important progress up the **Power Pyramid** toward the empowered feelings of joy, gratitude, and love.

No one lives at the top of the **Power Pyramid**. We all experience a range of emotions in a day, a week, or a year. But as we've seen, embracing and honoring each of them for their unique gifts can weave a wonderful tapestry of a fully-lived life.

This being human is a guest house. Every morning a new arrival.
A joy, a depression, a meanness, some momentary awareness comes as
an unexpected visitor. Welcome and entertain them all!

Rumi

⟋∞⟍

Q & A on *Feel All Your Feelings*

This topic can be heavy, so I thought we'd start with something light.

A friend of mine is a mortician, and he says one of the questions he's asked most frequently is, "Are you sad a lot?"

His answer is always, "Sure, I'm sad, but then someone dies and I perk right up!"

Okay, now let's get to some wonderful questions about feelings.

Q: *How do I know if I'm feeling all my feelings or if I'm just poor-pity-me-ing?*

A: I've asked myself this question in the past. Am I crying for attention or for release? My litmus test is whether or not I *want* people to see me cry. If I want them to see me, it's likely I'm tearing up for attention or pity. If I don't want them to see me or don't care, I am more comfortable that I am feeling in order to release, with no hidden agenda.

Q: *Where do apathy and laziness fit into the feelings equation?*

A: This is an interesting question. First, does anyone care about *everything*? Heck, no. That isn't healthy or realistic, but if someone contends that they don't care about *anything,* that's another issue. There's always a deeper truth underlying their seeming ennui.

When a family, company, or organization doesn't want to deal with anger in their midst, they'll soon be dealing with apathy. When teens or spouses get angry but are shut down by those who don't want to listen to their "emotional outbursts," they'll move forward in one of two ways: exploding into rage or imploding into depression or boredom.

As for laziness, I get agitated when I hear people talk about "lazy" teenagers. I've never met one. The only teens I've met who are referred to in that way are those who set such high goals for themselves that they've given up any hope of attaining them. They're not under-motivated as much as they're *over-motivated*.

No one wants to be a couch potato. It happens as a result of having really big dreams with no one to coach them through the success process. *8 to Great* is the perfect solution for turning couch potatoes into powerhouses!

Q: *I want to call this guy who just broke up with me. Is that stupid?*

A: No. What I hear you saying is: "I'm not quite over him. I have lots of unresolved feelings." The only thing *not* to do in that situation is to stay stuck. Go ahead and call him. Get mad, get scared of being alone, feel jealous, or whatever you want to—just don't stay stuck in *sad*. Calling him may bring you two closer or it may help you realize the distance between you is too great. One angry woman, after an unpleasant call to her ex, joined two singles groups the same day. Action is often the result of feeling our *angergy*. You go, girl!

Q: *I cry all the time. What's that about?*

A: Crying is healthy, but if it's all the time, you're feeling helpless and powerless. Repeat over and over to yourself this week, "I'm in charge of my life." Journal about the things that make you angry. Unleash your *angergy*. Own your power. If you're suicidal or find yourself nearing a "9" out of "10" on the sadness scale, let someone know immediately.

Q: *Lately I've been kind of frozen, not wanting to work or talk or cry or be angry—just numb.*

A: When we feel frozen, it's because a big feeling is ready for healing. It's usually to heal something from the past. If you're frozen, you're in survival mode. With feelings, the best way to a new one is through the one you're having. Journal about it with phrases like "right now I'm feeling frozen" and let the pen take you from there to places like, "The good thing about being frozen is..."

Q: *How can I get my daughter angry enough to leave her abusive relationship?*

A: Take a deep breath. I'm going to coach you in a skill that will take you out of your comfort zone. You're feeling anger *for* your daughter, thereby robbing her of the *angergy* she needs in order to start over. We're all half-jerk, half-jewel, and I'm assuming that when you talk to her, you've been bringing up all of his bad points, which has forced her to defend him.

The next time you talk, focus on his jewel points. Mention that he's in great shape, that he holds the door open for you, or that he's knowledgeable on a particular subject. This will almost always angergize her into action—and then she'll take care of the rest.

Q: *What would an educational setting that encouraged healthy awareness and expression of emotions look like?*

A: When my son was eight years old, he was extremely sad over a death in our extended family. As I drove him to school one morning, I noticed his grey mood and offered to let him stay home. He declined and after a half-hearted hug, walked slowly into his Montessori school. Later in the day, I was relieved to hear how his grief was honored.

According to his teacher, that morning during reading time he asked to sit in a quiet corner. With a book on his lap, he sobbed for nearly an hour amid occasional tissues and hugs from his instructor. When I picked him up at the end of the day, the little boy who got in my car laughing and asking questions was one who'd been shown that it was acceptable to *Feel All Your Feelings*.

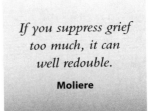

If you suppress grief too much, it can well redouble.

Moliere

Q: *How do I tell people I'm getting a divorce? I hate how awkward it makes them feel and the downer discussion that follows. I even had a friend start to cry yesterday.*

A: When I was in the process of getting divorced, I just said, "I've been meaning to tell you we're getting a divorce."

I'm not sure there's a softer way. Yes, people will cry, but their tears will be more about them than about you. It's like when you get to the sad part in a movie and you have tears come up about some completely different issue that you haven't cried about. I cried for two hours solid after watching the movie *ET*. Remember, tears are *good*. You're not *making* anyone cry. You're helping them cry.

Q: *Why do you only mention mad and sad? What about all the other feelings?*

A: These are the two feelings we *should on* and *shut down from* most in our society. They're neither more nor less important than the others. Joy, fear, confusion, elation—everyone of them is part of a healthy life.

Q: *When I started out working the High-Ways, it was the highest high I'd ever experienced, but now when I have a day that's not as "up," I get worried that I'm doing something wrong. Why do the grey days come?*

A: Thank you for reminding us all that the road to success is bumpy for *everyone*. Oprah's been working these concepts for decades, yet she is open in her articles and interviews about how she gets discouraged and angry and sometimes uses food for comfort. Many TV talk show hosts and guests wept at the election of Barack Obama. There are many good models for healthy emotional expression.

Let's say you have a "blue" day—low energy, sad, and un-enthusiastic about upcoming events. First, realize that you may have these feelings for many reasons. For example, there's a phenomenon known as "anniversary grief." It may be the day your dog died when you were five. Although you don't recall the date with your left brain, you remember the sadness with your right brain.

Maybe you're highly sensitive and pick up on the sadness of others. One day I was immediately saddened as I entered a room where I was to speak. Halfway through the talk (when we got to this Feelings High-Way), I discovered that their leader, who had retired a year before, had abruptly died the previous day.

When we learn to *allow* feelings rather than judge or analyze them, it lessens their impact and helps move them through us with greater ease.

Q: *You've told us that anger is healthy and that we should allow ourselves to feel it, but you're also telling us to be grateful every day. How can I do both?*

A: Let me first express my gratitude for the great question. It shows that you're digesting and integrating the information.

There's always *trouble in River City*. No matter where you live or who you are, life has its challenges. You may choose to see them as a curse or realize that each difficulty offers opportunities for hidden blessings.

Recently I had a driver cut me off on the highway. I was angry at first, jolted into awareness. Then, for the first time in years, I became aware of the hundreds of cars around me driving safely and courteously—and immediately felt immense gratitude. My anger at the driver was followed by a pull into the present moment, and I felt gratitude for my wake-up call.

One way to look at a day in the life of our emotions is to compare it to riding bumper cars. When we hit a wall—feel anger at what we do *not* want—it helps us be clear and focused on what we *do* want and we can turn ourselves around. All our dreams come from our desires, which come from our adversities. And who isn't grateful for a ride on the bumper cars?

The best and most beautiful things in the world
cannot be seen or even touched.
They must be felt with the heart.

Helen Keller

⚬∞⚬

High-Way 5:

Honest Communication

*Send and Receive
the Highest Truth*

∽⚬∾

Defining *Honest Communication*

*Happiness is when what you think, what you say,
and what you do are in harmony.*

Gandhi

⌒∞⌒

Honesty is essential for a well-lived life, yet in many environ-
ments, open and honest communication bucks the system.
We tell our kids, "Don't tell Dad—it will just upset him."

At school, we hear, "Come on, everybody cheats on tests."

Studies tell us that one out of every ten people has an alcohol or
sexual abuse secret they've been warned to keep.

As a result, hiding the truth can become the norm and we can
find ourselves living in a prison of lies we've built for ourselves. What
we can't lie about is our longing for the peace we know only truth
can bring. When I ask audience members to complete the phrase: "If
I had no fear I would..." the most common response among all age
groups is, "I'd tell people what I really think/feel."

Despite the risks, the rewards of honesty are among life's greatest
gifts—but how do we reclaim our integrity? The good news is that by
the time you've traveled the High-Ways of *Risk, Full Responsibility*
and *Feel All Your Feelings,* you're well prepared for this next segment of your High-Ways journey.

The River of Life

Think of the abundance life offers as a river of love/grace/energy.
When we have integrity with ourselves and others, we *grow* with the

> *I was angry with my friend: I told my wrath, my wrath did end. I was angry with my foe: I told it not, my wrath did grow.*
>
> **William Blake**

flow and the current is strong, carrying us swiftly to our next dream destination.

Each time we lie, it's as if we come to a fork in the river where a large portion of the water is siphoned off to a stream. One lie always requires another to cover it up and another stream veers off to feed that new untruth. With each falsehood, the river grows weaker and is slower in carrying us forward.

We have a choice. When we choose truth, the current in our lives remains strong and we are in the flow of all things good.

The End of the Cold War

Communication comes from two words: *common* and *union*. When we honestly communicate, we unite with our highest selves and feel closer to those around us—even when we don't agree. Two figures from recent chapters in history who didn't agree, though they were phenomenal communicators, were Ronald Reagan and Mikhail Gorbachev.

Margaret Thatcher once referred to President Reagan as "the man who beat communism." Many historians contend that it was Ronald Reagan's honesty and openness in his *personal conversations* with Russia's top leader that brought an end to the Cold War.

It's worth noting that Reagan didn't soften his truth to find peace. On the contrary, he publicly confronted Gorbachev before the two met privately. In 1987, against the counsel of his top advisors, Reagan spoke the following words in front of the Berlin Wall:

"General Secretary Gorbachev, if you seek peace, if you seek prosperity for the Soviet Union and Eastern Europe, if you seek liberalization, come here to this gate! Mr. Gorbachev, open this gate! Mr. Gorbachev, tear down this wall!"

That same year, the two leaders were talking across a table and referring to each other as friends. Decades later, former first lady Nancy Reagan, put it this way: "From the moment they first sat down with each other there was a connection. You could see it. You could feel it. When they left [the bargaining table] they would go down to the little place where the fire was going and stay there for about an hour. All the others were getting worried. What is he doing? What is he giving away? But taking that time turned out to be very, very successful."

> *We are each of us angels with only one wing, and we can only fly by embracing one another.*
>
> **Luciano de Crescenzo**

That success not only earned Reagan *Time* magazine's "Man of the Year" and Gorbachev the Nobel Peace Prize, but personal victories as well. When Reagan died in 2004, Gorbachev attended his funeral, openly weeping as he embraced the first lady.

"In terms of human qualities," he later told reporters, "he and I had, you would say, communicativeness, and this helped us carry on. I take the death of Ronald Reagan very hard."

In this High-Way we'll define *Honest Communication* as *speaking your truth* in a fully responsible and respectful way, and *listening with respect and compassion* to the thoughts and feelings of others. It's a High-Way that can bring peace to *your* world.

Honesty with Self

Honestly? I've known for years that I get major heartburn over the dishonesty of others. Unfortunately, because of High-Way 3, I have to assume *Full Responsibility* and constantly look to see where I can be more honest with *myself*. What I've discovered over the years is that the more honest we become with ourselves, the more we recognize when we're being *less* than completely honest with others.

One example of my little white lies cited in my first book was when I heard myself say things like, "Oh, the kids and I would *love* to come over for dinner on Friday." (And watch your TV while we eat? No thanks!)

Another concerned becoming conscious of my food choices. When I first joined the weight loss program that worked best for me, my counselor encouraged me to write down everything I ate.

Although I didn't think I needed to, I promised I would. I was soon amazed at all the food I'd "forgotten" until I started charting my intake. I continued charting for the next six months and eventually reached my goal—and I credit *honesty* for my new waistline. In fact, I've never seen anyone write down what they ate week after week and *not* achieve their weight goal.

Honesty with others starts with honesty with ourselves, and that can start anywhere. In High-Way 4 we looked at the biggest hurdle—facing and allowing our feelings—but it can also begin with:

✔ *balancing our checkbook*

✔ *opening our mail and cleaning our living or working areas to face what's in those piles*

✔ *acknowledging our age*

✔ *facing the fact that we over-scheduled ourselves to avoid intimacy or commitments we don't want to keep*

✔ *stating our opinion in a calm way, even when it's unpopular*

✔ *admitting we need help*

Once we start to see ourselves more clearly, we're ready to be honest with others.

Honesty and Love

> *Be who you are and say what you feel because those who mind don't matter and those who matter don't mind.*
>
> **Dr. Seuss**

How does honesty interface with being loving? Prior to my experience in a domestic violence shelter, I might have said something like: "Love is feeling connection and affection, demonstrated through acts of kindness." However, spending time there, I redefined it as: "Love is being authentically myself with you and encouraging you to be authentically yourself with me." One of my favorite authors once put it this way:

> *Love is the process of my leading you back to yourself.*
>
> **Antoine de Saint-Exupery**

When I moved away from defining love as doing things for others, I was freed. I began to see that so much of what I was doing for others wasn't in their best interest and often not even on their wish list. My efforts were really attempts to manipulate them into connecting with me. When I became more honest in my dealings with others, I found greater peace.

One year on Valentine's Day as I was addressing a group of couples, I separated them by gender and asked, "How important is honest communication to a healthy marriage?"

> *Honesty is the first chapter in the book of wisdom.*
>
> **Thomas Jefferson**

The women took less than thirty seconds to respond: "100 percent."

The men took three minutes to come up with, "94.5 percent."

As we had a good laugh about the differences between men and women, one thing was clear—they all considered honest communication one of their highest values! So what keeps us from being more honest, and what would living with greater honesty look like?

The goal of this chapter isn't to give an overview of the rudiments of good communication. Instead, we'll focus on seven common areas that prevent loving connection and then offer processes for each:

Process 1: The AVA Formula for Deep Listening

Process 2: Sharing Fully Responsible Feelings

Process 3: Learning to Say No

Process 4: Asking for What You Want

Process 5: Constructive vs. Destructive Criticism

Process 6: Ending Third Party Communication

Process 7: Stopping Sarcasm

Any *one* of these processes can quiet your mind and open your heart to the power and good feelings that honesty brings.

The *Honest Communication Process:*
Telling Your Truth and Open-Hearted Listening

Truth and a lie went swimming.
The lie got out and put on truth's clothes.
The good news? Whenever there's a lie coming toward you,
the buck naked truth is not far behind.

Keith Brown

Learning to Listen

In our hectic world, there are endless things vying for our attention. Whether it's the television blaring, three people talking at once, or someone texting you, it takes effort to move beyond just hearing to really *listening*. Add to that the fact that we listen three times as much as we talk, and it's clear that learning to listen is vital for successful communication.

After working with men and women in various stages of anger over the years, it's become clear to me that the main cause of anger on the planet is *feeling disrespected*. Understanding that, it's important to ask what is the most *respectful* thing we can do for another human being? The answer is to *listen*. No matter what triggered the anger in the first place, listening *from the heart* is the balm that calms.

What kind of listening has such a healing effect? *Open-hearted attention*—hearing and honoring the thoughts and feelings of the person who is speaking. Most of us are pretty good listeners when someone is telling us good news or talking about *us*, but once someone starts sharing a painful emotion, we're tempted to want to fix it, talk them out of it, or just ignore it. I often use this poem by Ralph Roughton to draw a picture of open-hearted attention:

> *Listen long enough and the person will generally come up with an adequate solution.*
>
> **Mary Kay Ash**

Please Listen

When I ask you to listen to me and you start giving me advice,
you have not done what I've asked.
When I ask you to listen to me and you begin to tell me why I
shouldn't feel that way, you are trampling on my feelings.
When I ask you to listen to me and you feel you have to do some-
thing to solve my problem, you have failed me,
strange as that may seem.
Listen! All I ask is that you listen.
Don't talk or do—just hear me.
Advice is cheap; I can do for myself; I am not helpless.
Maybe discouraged and faltering, but not helpless.
When you do something for me that I can and need to do for my-
self, you contribute to my fear and weakness.
But when you accept as a simple fact that I feel what I feel, no
matter how irrational, then I can stop trying to convince you and start
understanding what's behind my irrational feelings.
And when that's clear, the answers are obvious and
I don't need advice. Irrational feelings make sense
when we understand what's behind them.
So, please listen, and just hear me.
And if you want to talk, wait a minute for your turn—
and I will listen to you.

As we see in this poem, we can dismiss feelings as "irrational." That's because when we feel strong feelings our brain sometimes exaggerates the facts to heighten the emotion. Learning to listen from the heart can help a person feeling strong emotions gain clarity and feel validated.

Defensiveness vs. Deep Listening

When I speak to parents and their teens, I ask, "What's wrong?" Parents answer, "They won't talk!" Teens respond, "They won't listen!"

> *It takes courage to stand up and speak. It also takes courage to sit down and listen.*
>
> **Winston Churchill**

The same scenario often happens when I ask women and men what's wrong. People will only talk when there's someone who will truly listen.

One of the most common and damaging errors we make as listeners is becoming defensive during an argument. Think back to the last time you got defensive in a discussion. Did it help? Of course not. The reason *why* it didn't help is because you couldn't hear what the other person was saying. You may have been listening to their words, but you weren't hearing what they needed you to hear—their *feelings*.

Process 1: The AVA Formula for Deep Listening

We call this initial process for *Honest Communication* Deep Listening. I first learned to listen instead of defend from Harville Hendrix, author of many enlightening books on relationships, such as *Getting the Love You Want* and *Keeping the Love You Have*. I've seen relationships transformed by the following AVA formula.

When to Use the AVA Formula

It's always counterproductive to defend yourself against accusations during an argument. When there's anger that's dangerous or physically threatening, the best option is to remove yourself to safety until the other person calms down. However, when only angry *words* are being hurled around the room, the AVA formula can help.

You'll know that AVA is needed when a speaker uses one or more of the three *Rage Phrases:* "you always," "you never," and "you are such a…" Remember, it's not about you—you're just the "match" that set the fire. The AVA formula offers a powerful alternative to defensiveness.

A. Acknowledge, and if appropriate, Apologize.

Although this will feel awkward at first, encourage the person who is using "You always" or "You never" to keep talking. Rather than correcting their "facts" (which are exaggerated), let the person know you hear their feelings. Use phrases such as, "Uh huh," "Go on," "Is there more?" or "I can see you're upset" to signal your respect. An apology may be helpful for healing as it acknowledges that something has happened that you want to avoid happening again.

One phrase to avoid in acknowledging is "I'm sorry you feel that way." It infers that a "normal" person *wouldn't* feel that way and that their emotional response was invalid. This ignites more *angergy* as they feel even more disrespected. Keep reminding yourself that the angry person is ultimately looking for validation and respect, whether they're your parent, sibling, boss, customer, or teenager. When they sense that you're sincerely open to what they're sharing, they'll calm down, often immediately.

V. Validate their feelings.

Once you've acknowledged their feelings, speaking a phrase such as, "You have every right to every one of your feelings" soothes and calms the person who's hurting.

> *We are never angry for the reason we think.*
>
> **A Course in Miracles**

Don't we have a right to all our feelings? Even though some of their statements will sound illogical because their facts are distorted, just let the facts *be* for now and remember that they simply need you to hear their feelings.

A. Ask the million-dollar question: "Does this remind you of anyone or anything else?"

This optional final phrase helps them get in touch with feelings that may have been stored in their mad bowl for many years. It can help them touch the root of their anger and heal it.

"You Never"

When Kelsey, my coaching client, started dating Kyle, she noticed two idiosyncrasies about him. First, he hated it when she got up from the table while they were eating. Secondly, he ate slowly, at least compared to Kelsey.

> *Defensiveness is the first act of war.*
>
> **Marianne Williamson**

One Tuesday afternoon, Kyle called to say he was getting off work early and asked if she was free for supper.

Kelsey was delighted to reply, "I have a meeting tonight, but 4:30 would be perfect!"

They decided on a restaurant close to his work and not far from her meeting.

As soon as they sat down, they started chatting, not even noticing that the waitress didn't ask for their order for twenty minutes. After ordering, they continued their lively discussion, unaware that the food took another thirty minutes to get to the table. At 6:10, Kelsey noticed that although she'd finished her meal, Kyle hadn't. At 6:20, she told him she had to go.

"I'm sorry, but I need to get to my meeting—"

"I thought your meeting was at 7:00! I'm not finished yet!"

"I forgot to tell you that it was at 6:30, and I've got to give a treasurer's report. I'm so sorry. Call me tonight so we can talk, will you?"

He didn't respond as she headed out the door.

The AVA Phone Call

That evening, knowing he'd be upset, Kelsey was determined not to take his anger personally and to use the AVA process and just listen. She was grateful when the phone rang and it was Kyle.

"I just can't believe you did that today," he began.

She acknowledged him. "I can tell you're really upset. Tell me about it."

"I'll tell you about it, all right. Every time we're together, whether we're out to eat or you're jumping up to get something out of the refrigerator at your house, it's the same thing. It's ridiculous that you can't stay seated until I'm finished!"

"I hear you. Go on."

Go on, he did. For the next five minutes, she heard many "every," "always," and "never" statements, reminding her that she was just the match.

Finally, when she asked, "Is there more?" his answer was, "No."

Now it was time to move to Step 2: Validating.

"I'm sorry I upset you, Kyle. You have every right to every one of your feelings," she said. She truly meant it.

Immediately the conversation changed tone. In a softer voice, he thanked her for being such a great listener. She decided to move to the third and final part of the process.

She thanked him and asked, "I'm just curious. Does this possibly remind you of anyone or anything else?"

"Of course!" He went on for five more minutes about the fact that he'd regularly had to sit alone at the table as punishment when he was a child. He watched as his older brothers got to go out and play baseball while he sat there. "I should be over it, but I'm not."

> *It is not our purpose to become each other; It is to recognize each other, To learn to see the other and honor him for what he is.*
>
> **Hermann Hesse**

Kelsey thanked him for sharing and promised to be more aware. Over the next few dates, things changed and Kyle started noticing. She made a real effort to stay seated, but one day, a month later, she forgot—and Kyle didn't even notice. Her deep listening had dried up the kerosene in his mad bowl.

Hearing Unspoken Feelings

By the time Shelley and Don came to me for coaching, they'd been to many counselors, but nothing had helped. They were walking through their lives in silence, hardly speaking. That was because when they did speak, no one was listening. Here was a typical defensive exchange:

"Honey, I have good news. While you were gone on your fishing trip, I had a garage sale and sold your old gear."

"You what?"

"I sold your rusty old fishing gear and I got $75 for it!"

"You what?"

"You told me you liked the new stuff I bought you for your birthday. Were you lying?"

Shelley was doing the *Defensive Dance*, trying to argue her point from her *head* with fact after fact, but Don didn't care about facts. His *heart* was hurting from losing his precious mementos, so when he walked out of the room yelling, "You're not listening. You never listen," what he was really talking about was listening to his feelings.

I was able to coach Shelly to respond differently when she heard Don's strong emotions. She learned to acknowledge his feelings using phrases such as: "Go on, I'm listening" and then move to, "I can tell how much this upsets you. I'm sorry, I had no idea it was so important to you." Soon their arguments were rare and short-lived.

Displaced Anger

One of the greatest gifts we can give another person is the permission to speak their feelings. A couple who'd been married for ten years was suddenly faced with a rush of deep emotions the year after the husband's mother died. He started to feel his anger about his mother's drinking—something he'd suppressed for thirty years. At first, it came out against his wife.

When she came to me for coaching, she was angry that he was lashing out at her instead of his mother. As we talked, she began to see that feeling *any* anger is a first step toward expressing feelings about the original wound. By allowing him to express his anger, she gave him permission to do the powerful work ahead, which involved speaking his deeper truths.

We *Don't* Understand

I steered her away from the overused phrase, "I understand." We don't. Each person's experience is unique. She realized how the phrase could sound disrespectful, and together we made a list of optional phrases:

You're upset.

I can tell how upset you are.

I didn't mean to upset you.

You have every right to be angry.

Go on, tell me more.

Thanks for sharing how this affected you. It's good to know.

I care about you and I care about your feelings. Thank you for sharing them.

Whenever someone starts using one of the *Rage Phrases*, think of it as an open door to their heart. You have the ability to help them heal a deep wound. That's what happens each week in twelve-step groups around the country. Millions of people come together to speak their unedited yet fully responsible truth to open-hearted listeners. As a result, lifelong addictions are healed. There's truly no substitute for hearing with our hearts.

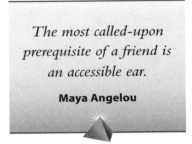

The most called-upon prerequisite of a friend is an accessible ear.

Maya Angelou

Process 2: Sharing *Fully Responsible* Feelings

B.C.ing when we feel angry or hurt is as common as it is destructive. Instead we can learn to take *Full Responsibility* when we're communicating strong feelings. Which of the following are you more likely to say:

A. *"You make me so mad."*

B. *"I'm really mad."*

C. *"I'm feeling mad and hurt right now."*

D. *"Something has triggered a lot of anger and sadness in me right now. I'd like to talk about it."*

Notice the increased responsibility and objectivity in the above phrases.

Statement A isn't owning any responsibility and is trying to blame the other person for how they feel. This victim mentality is at "5" on the **Power Pyramid** and can lead to staying stuck in *miserable*.

Statement B, while an improvement, tells our brains we *are* our feelings. That can prevent us from stepping back and looking at our emotions objectively, which means we can feel engulfed and over-whelmed by them.

Statement C moves us to a healthier place in two ways. First, moving to "I'm *feeling*" from "I *am my feeling*" gains a distance that helps us become more aware and accepting of our feelings. Also, we admit that we're feeling *both* mad and hurt, which can help calm us. (Remember, sadness releases excess angergy.)

Statement D is the most empowered way to communicate. It takes *Full Responsibility* while admitting that we're not even sure of all the triggers or the emotions we're feeling. It asks the listener to help sort them out, rather than accusing that person of *creating* them, thus minimizing the chances of the listener getting defensive.

Fully Responsible communication doesn't come naturally for most of us, but it's a skill we can learn and practice until it does—and the rewards of fewer and shorter arguments are well worth the effort.

Process 3: Learning to Say *No*

Have you ever noticed how the healthiest and happiest people are really good at saying *no*? They use phrases such as, "No, I won't be doing that, but thank you for asking." Try saying that right now, out loud. Don't you love it? It's a slam dunk for ending a discussion because *you don't give a reason* for your answer. As soon as you *do* give a reason, an argument could break out about the reason.

Learning to say no is powerful, but it can be so foreign that sometimes we have to warm up to it. If you're not quite ready for the big *NO-NO*, here are some possible alternatives:

> *Let your "yes" mean "yes" and your "no" mean "no."*
>
> **Matthew 5:37**

"I'll consider that in the future, but right now, no."

"Ask me later. I need to think about it."

"I won't be able to. I'm busy that evening." (Reading a book or relaxing in the tub!)

Another favorite for beginners: "Oops! Gotta go (because you're uncomfortable). We'll have to talk about this later." That phrase gives you time to work up the nerve to say you're not interested.

Face it. You're going to pay a bigger price for saying yes than the momentary discomfort of disappointing someone. Make no your friend and you'll be surrounded by yeses, including the most important: "Yes, I respect myself."

Meanwhile, when someone offers you unsolicited advice, you can set clear boundaries with a phrase such as, "Thanks for sharing. When that decision comes up for review, I'll let you know."

> *It's hard for people to understand that you can not agree with them—and not be against them. That you could be for something without being against something else.*
>
> **Abraham-Hicks**

Process 4: Asking for What You Want

In the next few pages, I'm going to share a powerful skill for getting what you want. So why do only 10 percent of the adults and students I coach use this skill after they learn it? I'm told, "It's new," "It's a risk," or "I might do it wrong." The fact is that of the 10 percent who use it, 95 percent say it works wonders.

Pre-step: Have you got a minute?

This preparation step is crucial in today's fast-paced society. I use it to begin almost every phone conversation because I never know what I've caught someone in the middle of. Inviting someone to sit down with you for a minute or to go for a short walk signals that you need their undivided attention.

Step 1: "When _____ (describe one time and one place)..."

Oftentimes this will start out with something like, "When I didn't hear from you last night" or "When you interrupted me." Be sure to stay as calm as possible. Most importantly, steer clear of "you always" or "you never" phrases or insinuations. One example from the past forty-eight hours of the thing that upset you will get your point across the best.

Step 2: "I felt (a little)…"

The temptation when we're upset is to use phrases like, "I felt like" or "I felt that," but neither of those are *feeling* statements. They're judgments, exactly what you don't need if you want someone to keep listening. Using the phrase "a little" after you state your feeling will keep you from veering into *opinion* territory, such as, "I felt you were making a huge mistake." The truth is, you *thought* that they were making a mistake. Instead, say something like, "I'm feeling a little concerned about your decision." Their ears and heart are more likely to stay open.

Step 3: "Because…"

In this step, explain what your perception of the situation is, and remember, it's only *your perception*. It usually works best to use a phrase such as "because it seems like" or "because it looks to me" to remind yourself (and them) that you're only checking out the facts.

> *If you don't ask, you don't get.*
>
> **Gandhi**

Step 4: "Therefore…"

This fourth step isn't always necessary, but sometimes we need to be clear as to what behavior would work better for us. A new spouse might say, "Therefore, if you can focus on a few things you liked about the meal I fixed, it'll help my confidence." A friend might say, "Therefore, if you can drive every other time, I'd feel more comfortable." A parent might say, "Therefore, if you'd like to go to the game tomorrow night, you'll need all your chores and homework caught up."

Always end with "Thanks for listening."

Process 5: Constructive vs. Destructive Criticism

There are two kinds of criticism: one is respectful, the other isn't. One is constructive, the other is destructive.

C is about **B:** Constructive criticism is about a *Behavior*
D is about **C:** Destructive criticism is about *Character*

Destructive criticism is always disrespectful. When you scream and holler statements such as "You always," "You never," or "You are such a..." they're *never* true statements about the person you're berating—and when they hurl such phrases toward you, they're never true about you.

Constructive criticism, however, can be wonderful. After completing a three-month twelve-step program, one young mother would often ask her children, "Is there anything Mommy could be doing differently?" Their answer was usually, "No," but at her birthday dinner, as her children went around the table sharing one thing they appreciated about their mom, her six-year-old blurted out, "Mommy, one thing I don't like is that you lie down too much."

The woman's husband tried to shush the little one and encourage her to say something nice, but that amazing Mom immediately said, "She's right."

Tears ran down her cheeks as she relished her daughter's honest communication and admitted to herself that she often slept to avoid dealing with life. She remembered it as a turning point in her recovery.

I'm grateful for those people in my life who have offered *constructive* criticism. Other than counselors, it's a short list. Cindy Osterloh, a high school principal from a nearby community who helped make this book possible, was one. I'll never forget her e-mail one morning as we were launching **8 to Great** at her school:

MK,

I wanted you to know that when you said on the phone yesterday, "You need to get the mayor or superintendent to introduce the assembly on Friday," it didn't work as well for me as "What do you think about" or *"Do you think this would this work?"* Yesterday, it felt like I was being told what to do. You're the expert on this program, but I know the people in this town. Thanks for listening.

Cindy

I replied:

Cindy,

Thank you. My apologies. Please help me catch this when I come across as demanding like that. Your honesty with me is perhaps the greatest gift you have given me so far. I feel blessed by your courage to speak your truth.

MK

Her constructive criticism was clear, but not shaming. She told me what I *did* wrong, rather than that I *was* wrong. She also gave me a picture of what would work better, and finally, she said it didn't work as well "for her," taking *Full Responsibility* for her feelings. She's a master communicator in that regard.

Process 6: Ending Third Party Communication

How destructive is Third Party (XYZ) Communication? I've seen it take down marriages, extended families, church choirs, businesses, and even small towns! If you've been bothered by XYZ games recently, you were a participant. The good news is that if you're a participant, you have the power to step out, and once you get out of the game, it can only topple to the ground.

The big misunderstanding in Third Party Communication (also called *gossip* or *triangulation*) is who the real culprit is. When X has a problem with Z and goes to Y with her complaint and then Y runs to Z to tell her what X thinks, the biggest troublemaker is Y, who will do her level best to convince Z that the problem is X. Don't believe it.

How to Avoid the XYZ Game

When you find yourself in an XYZ situation, there are easy ways out, depending on which part you're playing. Here are guidelines for never getting caught in XYZ again:

1. If you're X, just go talk to Z. You have the skills: "When you," "I felt a little," "Because," and "Therefore." Share your *feelings* rather than your *judgments*. Chances are Z will be more open than you think.

2. If you're Y and X comes to you *B.C.ing* about something Z did, simply tell X, "You need to go talk to Z about this." If they protest, say something like, "No, really. You're making good points and I'm sure Z will benefit from hearing your concerns." When you make it clear that the ball is in their court, they'll never come back to you whining about that situation again.

3. If you are Z and Y comes to you saying, "Do you know what X said about you?" Simply smile and say something like, "Thank you, but if X really had an issue about that, I know she'll come and talk to me herself" or "You must have just caught X on a bad day. I appreciate the thought, but you never need to carry X's messages to me again."

Then I love to add, "By the way, do you agree with X?" Y never carries a message she/he doesn't agree with. In fact, whenever Y tells you about X's problem with you, *it's almost always Y's agenda*. Oftentimes, Y feels more passionate about it than X, who was just letting off steam and forgot about it the next day. Don't give Y any encouragement for their behavior or you'll get a lot more of it.

> *A lie gets halfway around the world before the truth has a chance to put its pants on.*
>
> **Winston Churchill**

To summarize: If you're X, go to Z with a "When you, I feel" statement. If you're Y, encourage X to go to Z. If you're Z, ask Y, "Do you agree?" and watch them do a dance while backing out the door.

And one final thing: don't feel bad if you are Z. I've found that in life, *either you will talk about others because their lives are more interesting or they will talk about you because yours is.* Aren't you glad it's the latter?

Process 7: Stopping Sarcasm

Sarcasm: *A cutting remark intended to wound or demean. Often thought of as "witty" by the user, sarcasm can be poisonous and can cause permanent relationship damage.*

The first few times I encountered sarcasm I was tricked into thinking that the person using it was witty and intelligent because they could wordsmith their jabs to perfection, often adding sneers or a shake of the head at the "stupidity" of their prey. Over time I came to realize that sarcasm is nothing more than a desperate attempt by a frightened individual to gain attention at any cost.

Examples of sarcasm could be:

"Right. You didn't say that. I was hallucinating."

"Oh, did I step on your teensy weensy feelings again?"

"No, it's not my real name. I'm just breaking it in for a friend."

According to Dr. Richard L. Williams, "A person who regularly uses sarcasm is nothing more than a verbal bully. The sarcastic bully uses words rather than physical threats to try to gain an advantage over the other person."

Those who use sarcasm fight a losing battle. Looking for more power through their cleverness, their sarcasm results in less. Looking to be "one up" in social stature by putting someone else down with verbal barbs, the perpetrator ultimately loses the admiration and trust of others along with lowering their own self-esteem.

The "butt" of the sarcasm also loses. The mockery can make us feel inferior if we don't respond and sorry if we do. We often feel helpless at first and infuriated later. We eventually withdraw from the perpetrator, leaving that person more alone, lonely, and frightened than ever.

Being around someone who uses sarcasm is like trying to walk through a war zone. You never know when the sniper is going to jump out of the bushes and fire an insult in your direction. It may be that their main goal is to get you to respond angrily to keep the game going. Remember that people would rather be unlovable than invisible.

How to Stop the Sarcasm

If you're ever the recipient of sarcasm, you have options. Start by observing how and when it's used and what feelings it brings up for you. Once you have at least two clear-cut examples of someone's sarcasm, sit down with that person when you're both fairly calm. Use the "When you, I feel" process noted earlier in this chapter.

For example:

"Have you got a minute?"

"When you interrupted what I was saying a few minutes ago with 'don't you have anyone else you'd like to bother right now?' I felt very uncomfortable because it seemed a harsh way to say you wanted alone time. Therefore, I'd like to talk about taking sarcasm off the options list when you're communicating with me."

If you're the one who's been using sarcasm, start your healing by becoming aware of your tendency to judge. For example, how often do you find yourself talking about the incompetence or inabilities of others? Then once you see what you're doing, look at how you're feeling. Judging looks like arrogance but is always rooted in low self-esteem. With time and patience, we can all learn to love ourselves again.

Find a counselor, friend, or sponsor to work with you to rebuild your faith in yourself. It will take humility to admit that the know-it-all the world sees in you is just a cover for your insecurities. It will take patience to discover how loveable you are, and it will take courage to admit how hard you've been running from your pain. But no matter how challenging it is to release sarcasm and judgment, doing so will allow trust and loving relationships back into your life.

Why We Don't *Honestly Communicate*

Honest communication means responding with what is true to you,
regardless of how someone may react to your answer.

Byron Katie

❧

Secret Keeping

Years ago, I spoke with a friend who was learning Russian. When she learned the word "journal" she got into a deep discussion with her instructor about journaling. She discovered that the English word "journaling" didn't exist in that language. Her instructor made it clear that no one in Russia would ever do such a dangerous thing as to write down their true thoughts and feelings on a sheet of paper.

We don't have to live in the Ukraine to keep secrets. I've seen similar patterns in the relationships of those around me.

✔ *A young woman who was deeply ashamed of her anger at her alcoholic parents went into denial by cleaning the entire house regularly, often into the wee hours of the morning.*

✔ *A wife who kept hundreds of secrets from her husband while she "did nice things" for him was eventually served with divorce papers.*

✔ *A man who worked extra hard while becoming more and more upset with his boss one day just up and quit, later regretting it.*

Over-Promising

One way we're dishonest with ourselves comes back to High-Way 3: *Full Responsibility*. We make bigger promises than we can keep.

> *We are as sick as our secrets.*
>
> **AA Member**

Living with integrity means *doing what you say you'll do when you say you'll do it* to the best of your ability. When you can't follow through on a promise you've made, you can usually make it right. (More on this in High-Way 6: *Forgiveness of the Past*.)

It's like a child learning not to take more on his plate than he'll eat. If we find ourselves in an over-committing pattern, we need to stop and take *Full Responsibility* and make amends. When I over-commit, I do my best to make the amends that are costly to me. For example, "The next meal is on me" at a very nice restaurant, or "I'll drive the document over myself this afternoon." That pain wakes me up—and makes me promise *myself* to be more honest by not taking on so much the next time.

The Approval Addiction

Another reason we hide our truth is *Fear of Rejection*. We want people to like us, but we forget that we only like people we respect, and everyone respects a person of *integrity*. No matter how much we want to impress others with the number of balls we can juggle, our reputation can come crashing down after a few broken promises.

Another piece of the Approval Addiction is a penchant for perfectionism. When this sort of striving takes over, a person is unable to feel satisfaction and joy because in their own eyes they never do things well enough to warrant feeling good. At their worst, perfectionists set impossible goals and then measure their worth in terms of productivity and accomplishments.

> I was always fearful of failing. It seemed no matter what I did right, I always saw something I was doing wrong. I never felt good enough, no matter what I did. I felt God was displeased with me. I was deceived!
>
> **Joyce Meyer**

Since perfectionists tend to be "all or nothing" thinkers, they often put too much effort and attention on small details and miss the larger picture.

A wonderful story about the challenges of all or nothing thinking is described in Robert Pirig's *Zen and the Art of Motorcycle Maintenance*. It's known as the "South Indian Monkey Trap." The story tells of villagers who were desperately trying to curb a growing monkey population. One day someone came up with the idea of placing rice grains inside a long narrow hole that had been widened at the bottom. The thinking was that the monkeys would grab the grains of rice, and since the hole was just big enough for them to put their hands in but too small for a fist full of rice to come out, the monkeys would be trapped. It worked. Like the perfectionist, the monkeys hung onto something insignificant while losing something precious—their freedom.

Other powerful antidotes for perfectionism are yet to come: High-Way 6 (*Forgiveness of the Past*) and High-Way 7 (*Gratitude for the Present*).

Nice vs. Kind

On the other side of the honesty fence are those who have trouble admitting when something doesn't feel good. Some of us were brought up hearing, "If you can't say something nice, don't say anything at all." In doing so, we lost our voice. We could no longer speak our truth because the truth might hurt. Little did we realize that lies hurt much more.

In our *8 to Great* trainings, we refer to the overly "nice" person as one who is "on-ice." My theory on Overly Nice (O.N.) people can be described as follows:

1. O.N. people have had all the passion squished out of them. Because I've been there myself, I can easily spot those who have to know how you feel before they can figure out how they feel. The danger for O.N. people is that they wear a mask so long they *become* their mask and lose touch with who they really are.

2. O.N. people are scared. They will say they agree with you when they don't because they're frightened—of rejection, of hurting someone's feelings, or of being seen.

3. O.N. people will break promises. Sooner or later, it's not nice to be around O.N. people. Because they have no "no" in their vocabulary, their "yes" means nothing. Friends of O.N. people have to work hard to figure out what they really mean and they get tired of it, so they eventually leave, which is one reason that...

4. O.N. people are lonely. O.N.'s do too much for others while never asking for what they need. Therefore, other people assume they don't need anything, leaving O.N.'s high and dry. This can lead to a final characteristic...

5. O.N. people are angry. Because they smile when they're angry or hurting, O.N.'s have to push their pain down—but it eventually erupts. They're angry that they're alone, that they've had to swallow their truth, and that all they do is give. Because they've been quiet for so long, their anger all comes out at once. When that happens, the O.N. feels ashamed, which leads to more dishonesty, which leads to more shame.

> *Compulsively proper and generous people predominate among cancer patients because they put the needs of others in front of their own.*
>
> **Dr. Bernie Siegel**

I find it interesting that some of my friends who are the most active in church work tend toward O.N. behavior. I'm not sure why. Jesus wasn't afraid of calling a Pharisee "a white-washed sepulcher" or telling Peter to "get thee behind me, Satan." He was passionate, fearless, and he got angry.

I thank God for the friends and counselors over the years who knocked the O.N. out of me. They may have saved my life. I know they gave me back my serenity.

Honest Communication Success Stories

If I lose mine honor, I lose myself.

William Shakespeare

⁓∞⁓

She Faced Her Fears

Laura's mom noticed that something was wrong with her. Lately she'd been coming home from her part-time job calling people "stupid." Her mom had never heard that level of blaming and name-calling from her daughter so she asked for a time to talk about it. When they sat down, she asked Laura if anything had changed with the job she had loved when she started a year before. Why the *B.C.ing*?

After Laura had finished telling her how frustrated she was at the paltry effort most of her co-workers put forth, her mom asked, "Is it possible you want to quit and just don't feel comfortable telling your boss?"

To Laura's credit, she thought for a minute and then admitted that she felt she'd be letting everyone down if she quit. Together, mother and daughter looked up statistics on how many jobs the average person holds in a lifetime and agreed that learning to bring honest closure to a job was a life skill worth learning. Laura gave her notice the next day and sat down to write a letter of thanks to her employer.

The first time I shared that story with young adults, I was amazed at the response. *One-fourth* of those in the session had experienced a similar challenge, but rather than admitting their discomfort, had gotten themselves *fired* for absenteeism or tardiness! Leaving a job with ill feelings drags us down to a "5" on the **Power Pyramid** and makes attracting our next "95" job much harder. It pays, in both emotional and financial ways, to tell the truth.

If you tell the truth, you don't have to remember anything.

Mark Twain

No Longer Living a Lie

I'll always remember the high school senior who took the risk of writing on the anonymous feedback form after our first class: "I lie all the time. I lie so much that I can't even tell when I'm lying. Can you help me?"

The next time that class met, I unfolded the paper and read the comment aloud to the group. Holding it up I said, "Whoever wrote this, you just told the truth. You must feel a lot better. Congratulations! You're right on track." A few classes later the author introduced himself and thanked me for starting him on a new path to a more honest and happy life.

The Courage to Claim Our Truth

We don't have to read the newspaper to find honest heroes. I recall training my first class of high school seniors to teach *8 to Great* to the freshmen at their school. As we ended the second day, I asked students if they'd be willing to share what they were going to take with them from the training.

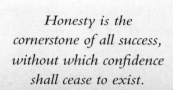

Honesty is the cornerstone of all success, without which confidence shall cease to exist.

Mary Kay Ash

A beautiful young woman looked at me with misty eyes and said, "I'm ready to tell my mom the truth. I have a scholarship to Julliard in clarinet, but I've known for awhile it's not where my passion lies. I want to play the guitar professionally. I know it will be hard, but *8 to Great* has helped me see that taking the risk of being honest with myself and her will ultimately turn out for the best."

Can you imagine the kind of guitarist her truth will unleash?

The $20,000 Error

Another example of the rewards of honesty involved a friend who worked as an administrative assistant to a successful CEO. She had many responsibilities and some of them included working with large sums of money. One day she realized she'd made a $20,000 error. It took days to get up the courage to tell her boss, but she finally walked into his office and shared the painful truth. Crying, she said she understood that she'd have to be fired, but he stopped her mid-sentence.

"Fire you? Why would I do that? I just spent $20,000 training you!"

Honest Communication is worth its weight in gold to bosses, co-workers, friends, and family members. It's a High-Way that can *truly* take you where you want to go.

Putting *Honest Communication* into Practice

If honest communication between two people isn't extended to the point of resolution and peace, the energy will appear again as wounding in another relationship.

Marianne Williamson

෴

The Honesty Workout

"I hope this one works out," a new friend shared at the end of our conversation, referring to her latest romantic relationship.

The reality is that every relationship *works out*. They give our hearts and minds a workout like nothing else can. The goal is not to "win" him or keep from "losing" her, but rather to do the real workout of intimacy and love—*integrity*.

Integrity is when we share who we truly are with another human being; when we're the same person in and out of that person's presence. It's a risk that requires a high level of courage, but when encountered, is deeply healing. Perhaps the most beautiful part about the love-work of integrity is that its success rate has *nothing to do with the other person's response to us*.

Holding another person while *withholding* from them isn't loving, but many people have never allowed themselves to be emotionally naked with another human being because they've never been fully honest with themselves. The great news is that we can learn to release attachment to another person's response. As we do, we can allow them the gift of "in-to-me-see."

We all fear abandonment on some level, but as Marianne Williamson reminds us, no one can "leave" anyone. We're all *one* on this playground called life, together for an eternity. You can't even be untrue to yourself for any length of time—your truth will come oozing out when you least expect it.

The Three Questions

I learned a wonderfully heart-opening process from Quantum Learning Network, an education and training corporation based out of Oceanside, California. In order to enjoy it, first select a partner for the exercise. Then ask your partner three questions, one at a time, waiting for them to answer until you continue.

1. Tell me something I don't know about you.
2. Tell me something you like about me.
3. Tell me something we agree on.

Then you and the speaker will trade places, with them asking you the questions. I have used this with my son when our schedules were not allowing much together time. I have also used it with new and old friends and shared it with thousands of couples. It's amazing how open-hearted attention heals. It "makes" love on the deepest level. *Have you told the truth in love today?*

Because It Doesn't Feel Good

Perhaps the best reason for us to tell the truth is that it feels better—worlds better—than the alternative. If "when we feel good, good things happen," obviously when we *don't* feel good, we're attracting and manifesting things we *don't* want. Lying feels awful, and because lying always requires more lying, the cycle continues itself until a radical shift is made.

If you are in need of such a cleansing, I suggest watching the film *As Good As It Gets*. Jack Nicholson's character has been dishonest with himself and with women for decades. At first, he can't imagine ever coming clean, since it would require too great a change. Yet, after a massive heart attack and a glorious week with a woman who is completely honest, he decides to face the truth and find peace and joy. You will find, as he did, that honesty is as good as it gets.

Teaching a class to recovering addicts for more than twelve years, it's been my blessing to watch men and women step out of the dungeon of despair into the light of day by simply telling the truth.

The first truth is usually that they're angry. Once they find out that they're not struck by lightning for sharing painful feelings, they move toward telling the ultimate truth, being honest about their gifts, their unlimited potential, and the profound goodness of life.

I was recently informed by a good friend that we do not measure cold, only the absence of heat. Later I heard a speaker remind us that there is no "dark switch" when you enter a room, only a switch for light. As I wrote the words below, I was comforted that you and I do not need to battle the cold, dark elements of life. Instead we can choose to let our warmth and light shine through.

> *If there is no cold, only the absence of heat,*
> *and there is no dark, only the absence of light,*
> *and there is no despair, only the absence of hope,*
> *Then there is no hate, only the absence of love.*

The Pen Is Mightier Than...

Finally, if you have not discovered the power of writing to your spouse, friend, teenager, or sibling, let me make one final appeal. Whenever you are having a hard time communicating with them, write them a letter. Tell them what's on your mind. Tell them what you are grateful for about them. Share your dreams for your relationship. They will often write you back, but even when they don't, the door is open for greater integrity and intimacy.

"I decided not to join the gang because of my teacher," said the young Latino student after he completed the **8 to Great** course at his high school. His teacher, Danelle, was indeed exceptional. When she first gave her freshmen time to write in their journals, most used it to share their innermost thoughts and feelings, but some, she could sense, were holding back.

"So one day I decided it wasn't fair that I was reading what they were opening up about, but they weren't getting to read my thoughts and feelings. I began doing my journaling on the board. It was very hard at first because it was around the anniversary of my father's death. But I knew openness and honesty were the best gifts I could give those kids."

I have had hundreds of teachers tell me of students who wrote what they could not say.

- ✔ *"My parents are both dying of AIDS. I'm an only child and have never told anyone…"*
- ✔ *"My mom and I are getting kicked out of our house on Friday and don't know where we'll live…"*
- ✔ *"My grandpa is dying and I'm the only one home at night to care for him. I'm scared that…"*

I beg of every teacher, parent, or youth minister reading this: give your students a half sheet of paper, some instrumental music, and five minutes to write once a week. We cannot meet the needs of our youth when we don't know what their needs are. Journaling helps us hear their needs and then find ways to help meet them.

Likewise, wonderful movements like World Wide Marriage Encounter (WWME) report divorce rates *under 5 percent* when couples use their ten-minute writing technique at the end of the day to communicate their love and/or concerns. Writing is a positively powerful way to break down barriers and strengthen connection.

Finally, let me add a lesson I have learned the hard way. Writing a letter is very different from writing an e-mail. Whereas the old rule of thumb: criticize (constructively) privately and compliment publicly is solid and true, so I would add: compliment in e-mail but never criticize using that medium.

I once had one of our team ask in an e-mail how I thought he could improve. I mistakenly answered in an e-mail. Although I did not write anything close to "You always," or "You never," even constructive criticism can sound like yelling through the Internet. The next time I saw him, the pain in his eyes was my wake-up call. I have never done it again.

Truly Grateful

Let me conclude with a personal story. While writing this chapter, I faced the challenge of my teenager acting out. I watched as he decided to be honest about his dishonesty. I gave him stiff consequences, which triggered intense anger and sadness. He learned to communicate his feelings to me, and I processed my intense feelings as best I could.

As I watched him make the decisions that go with starting over, I knew that working my program involved doing *less* for him, not more. I was often scared, sometimes for his physical safety, while realizing we have to each face our fears to find greater enlightenment. For my part, I did my best to stay open and honest with him, even when he had no response.

> *Be honest to those who are honest, and be also honest to those who are not honest. Thus honesty is attained.*
>
> **Lao Tzu**

Because we were able to both talk and listen as we worked through our feelings and concerns we survived those challenging months, and today our lives are richer, our relationship deeper, and his former habits are no longer an issue. I'm truly grateful for re-learning these lessons in a new way with him— and for the power of *Honest Communication*.

Q & A on *Honest Communication*

Q: *I want to improve my relationship with my mom, but she doesn't trust me when I tell the truth because I used to lie a lot. What can I do?*

> *Being straight with people will get you in the best circles.*
>
> **Anonymous**

A: You've dug a pit with your lying, Dear One, and now you'll have to re-earn her trust. It's good that she doesn't trust you right now—you haven't earned it. Have you made amends for your past mistakes? You can start by telling her the *truth* about being sorry for what you've done. You may want to write her a letter of apology, offer to make amends, and show your appreciation. You probably won't get all of your privileges back right away, but once you do, you'll be able to appreciate how good it feels to tell the truth!

Q: *I want to join the military, but my parents would rather I go to college right away. The military will pay for my tuition, books, and lab fees after I've served my time. I've used* Honest Communication *to tell my parents what I want. Should I do what I want to do and ignore what they're saying?*

A: Let's look at "what you want." I always encourage young adults to follow their dreams, but I don't hear your dream. I hear your fears about not having enough money for college. If someone offered to pay for all your tuition, books, and lab fees, would you still be passionate about joining the military?

I recall a young man of twenty-two who couldn't decide between joining the priesthood and marrying his sweetheart. When I asked what appealed most about both options, he told me he wasn't sure where he'd ever get a teaching job. In other words, the life of a priest had more job security!

This is a case of discerning between running *from* and running *to*. The military and the priesthood are looking for men and women who are running to their calling. What will your decision-making process look like?

Q: *I sometimes feel hopeless around stories like presidential candidate John Edwards having an affair on his wife. Why do so many leaders lie?*

A: I've met both ethical and unethical people at the top, but the more successful a leader is perceived to be, the higher their perceived "cost of failure." They begin to fear being seen as human, so some stop taking risks, including the risk of telling the truth.

If what we think about we bring about, we can turn our focus to the brave truth-tellers at the top. If "we spot it, we got it," each time we point a finger at a liar, we need to see that we're pointing three fingers back at ourselves. When we come clean and admit that we too have lied, the sting loses its poison.

> *Honesty is not so much a credit as an absolute prerequisite to service to the public. Unless a man is honest, we have no right to keep him in public life; it matters not how brilliant his capacity.*
>
> **Teddy Roosevelt**

One story during the 2008 presidential campaign that didn't make front page headlines involved Mark McKinnon, chief strategist for Republican candidate John McCain. When it became clear that Barack Obama would be the Democratic nominee, Mark resigned from the campaign.

In an interview, McKinnon said that although he had policy differences with Obama and believed McCain was best suited for the presidency, "I just don't want to work against an Obama candidacy. I believe he is honest. Obama's election would send a great message to the country and the world."

It was heartening to know that Mark McKinnon, one of America's most respected political masterminds, valued his integrity above all else. He turned down a five-million-dollar paycheck that campaign year, but it was a price he was willing to pay in order to be true to himself. There are thousands of people in politics we can all be extremely proud of.

Q: *I often feel like I don't belong. Is that because I don't know how to communicate? Do other people feel this way sometimes?*

A: Members of every group I've ever asked have told me that they feel that way often. We feel like we don't belong because we look at people's outsides rather than insides. People use religion, race, money, power, age, and IQ to try and separate themselves, but at our core we're all connected. That was one of the messages of September 11, 2001. When everyone had grey dust from the towers on them, from executives to sewer workers, they were all the same.

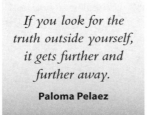

If you look for the truth outside yourself, it gets further and further away.

Paloma Pelaez

It could be that you feel like you don't belong because you're not sharing who you *really* are with others, or not listening to who they are. Do more of the courageous risk-taking you did when asking this question and you'll find out just how alike we all are.

Q: *How do you get a friend to open up when you know he has problems?*

A: People aren't like cans. We can't just open them at will. First we have to earn their trust. Keep reminding your friend that you care and that he can count on you to be there for him.

Consider writing a letter saying you've noticed some things and that you're concerned. Invite him to write back or remind him you have time to listen if he wants to talk. If he doesn't respond, do the most loving thing we can ever do for a friend. Honor his choices.

Q: *I was recently asked to lunch by an old friend who said she wanted to get together to catch up. I was shocked when she then made a multi-level marketing sales pitch. I felt very disrespected. Should I call or write and tell her?*

A: It sounds like this is the first time it's happened to you. The good news is that you learned your lesson quickly. Take responsibility for the fact that you didn't ask her clearly about the goal of the lunch. Let it go as a lesson learned, and the next time a friend asks you to coffee or lunch, get clear about their intentions before you make your decision.

Q: *What if I'm being criticized so much by someone that it's affecting my life?*

A: First, remember that everyone who has ever communicated anything to you has only been saying one of two things: "I love you," or "I'm scared and hurting, please help me." This will give you more compassion.

Second, remember that they have no power over you. None. We are like Dorothys in *The Wizard of Oz,* running from the wicked witches of our fears. If we just turn and face them, we see that the meaner people are, the more desperate and lonely they are.

I remember a time when one of my eleven-year-old son's friends came over to play while I was speaking across town. When I got home to relieve the sitter, my son was crying.

"He said awful things to me, Mom. He even said awful things about you—he said you were a bad Mom."

"Look who he's talking about, honey," I said as we hugged. "He lives with his grandmother because he hasn't seen his own Mom for years."

My son was then able to see the boy through new eyes.

Finally, realize that they're continuing to criticize you because it's achieving its desired effect of upsetting you. I challenge you to claim your power. We think that a word spoken (or not spoken) can deal us a fatal blow, but it can't. We're *so* much bigger than that.

> *This pity, insecurity, and self-indulgence is*
> *unbecoming of the Great Soul that you are.*
>
> **Bhagavad Gita**

⌒∞⌒

FGH

The World's Simplest Positive Attitude Formula

High-Way 6:

FGH: Forgiveness of the Past

The Power of Release

❧

Defining *Forgiveness of the Past*

*Unforgiveness is like taking poison and hoping
the other person dies.*

Anonymous

⌦

Forgiveness is the ultimate remedy for what ails us. As Marianne Williamson writes: "The practice of forgiveness is our most important contribution to the healing of the world." In her powerful statement lies another truth: like all the High-Ways, *Forgiveness of the Past* is a skill that can be learned through *practice*. A simple definition:

*Forgiveness is releasing regret, resentment,
and the desire for revenge.*

Releasing Resentment

The Aramaic root word for forgive means: "let go." *Forgiveness* isn't an admission that what someone else did was acceptable. It's a decision to release the weight of resentment and the desire for restitution.

What does the alternative look like? In 2008, a Cambodian couple who separated after forty years of marriage took things literally when it came to "splitting" their assets: The husband cut their house in two and moved his half to his parents' property. When we decide to hold onto bitterness, it can take on a life of its own and, like the monsters of horror films, one day will have us in its grip.

Why We Forgive

We have all been there. We became angry and hurt about being lied to or disrespected. At first we were confused. Then, once the initial shock registered, we had to make a decision whether to go *inward* and find our peace or move *outward* into bitterness because of a belief that forgiveness might "let them off the hook." Unfortunately, in the latter state *we* were the ones who got "hooked" as our vengeful thoughts consumed us.

The alternative is release. It is forgiving them for *our* sake, not theirs. The harm they did to us can't begin to compare with the harm *we inflict on ourselves* every day when we hold onto judgment. Whether it's the physical and mental drain of living in the past or the inability to function in the present moment, the only person who pays a price for unforgiveness is you, and that price is your *life energy.*

> *We are not held back by the love we didn't receive in the past, but by the love we're not extending in the present.*
>
> **Marianne Williamson**

We only have so many thoughts and so much energy to invest in each day. If we choose to invest, say, 40 percent of that precious resource in thoughts of regret ("I should have") or bitterness ("they should have"), we'll find ourselves waking up tired, with not enough energy to build our futures.

Just as the other person isn't harmed by our harboring resentments, we won't be doing them a favor by forgiving them, either. Most if not all of those people have already moved on. Some may never even admit that anything bad happened. Because their feelings are completely out of your control, all you can do (as High-Way 3: *Full Responsibility* reminds us) is stay in *your business* and forgive.

Your business is to *feel good*, and that requires making peace with the past so that we can come home to the power of the present.

How to Forgive

"All right," a female client asked me. "I want to forgive him for what he did to me years ago, but where do I begin?"

I recommend beginning with a simple formula:

The *Forgiveness* Formula
We were all doing the best we could at the time with the information we had.

How can we absolutely know that we were doing the best we could at the time? Think back to an incident you feel regret about. Then ask yourself: "If I would have known then what I know now, would I have acted the same way?" Of course not. It's not that you were a bad person *then* and you're a good person *now*. You were a good person then as now. You just needed more information. You're reading this book because you are seeking more information. You're right on track.

Who to Forgive

When I ask my audiences, "Who is the hardest person to forgive?" they all respond in one voice, "Yourself."

We can go one step further and remind ourselves we're the *only* person to forgive, because as we learned in High-Way 3, what we despise in others are those things we despise in ourselves. Whatever upsets us most in others is a reflection of those pockets of pain within ourselves that we haven't yet forgiven. Once we accept *Full Responsibility*, it's easier to move into forgiveness of our "in-a-me"—ourselves. The more we understand this universal truth, the more it shines light on our darkest memories. We were doing the best we could.

I've been lied to and betrayed, just like you, but I was always able to go back and see that I had lied to and betrayed myself *first* through denial. We're not victims. In telling and owning the truth now, we move to a new place on the **Power Pyramid** and therefore attract different types of people and experiences into our lives.

> *We have met the enemy and he is us.*
>
> **Pogo**

Who else do you need to forgive? That person (living or deceased) or group of people you consider hardest to forgive is the best place to start. It has taken me years to forgive teachers who put test scores before the needs of children. On my best days, I see them as scared and hurting children *themselves*, and that fills me with compassion. However, on my worst days, I realize it's time to use a *Forgiveness* process.

Why Forgive? The Mary Read Story

Mary Read was born in South Korea in 1988. Her parents, retired Air Force Lt. Col. Peter Read and Yon Son Zhang of Palisades Park, New Jersey, had met in Korea when Col. Read was stationed there. Mary was a "fun-loving nineteen-year-old" who had just graduated from Fairfax's Annandale High School, where she had played clarinet in the band, was on the lacrosse team, and had gotten good grades.

In 2007, her aunt shared the following story with the *Washington Post*:

"The last time I saw her, a year ago Thanksgiving here at my house, she kept disappearing. I finally said, 'Mary, what are you up to? Are you reading a good book or something?' She was knitting a beautiful scarf—a multicolored fluffy scarf like the girls wear—for her grandmother for Christmas. My mother still wears it. She often did thoughtful things like that."

On the evening of April 15, 2007, as Mary was sitting in her dorm room, she got out a red notebook and journaled some of her thoughts about life.

In a section where she kept her favorite quotes, she wrote: "When a deep injury is done to us, we can never recover until we forgive."

The next day, Mary was gunned down in her Virginia Tech classroom, along with thirty-one others.

The more we love, the greater the temptation to hate when what we love is taken from us—but as Mary reminded us, we must forgive, because hate kills love. Hate killed Mary Read. Forgiveness is the path to the peace we seek.

Research on *Forgiveness*

According to Dr. Fred Luskin of the Stanford University Forgiveness Project, there are dozens of reasons to forgive, including many for our own health and well-being: Forgiveness...

- ✔ *can help you enjoy the present by freeing you from the past.*
- ✔ *can help you concentrate on work or school.*
- ✔ *can help you distinguish between bitterness and resentment about old issues and anger and sadness about current events.*
- ✔ *can help you make better decisions (choosing to run to rather than from).*
- ✔ *can improve your relationships with others.*
- ✔ *can restore the energy drained by bitterness and resentment, thereby helping you accomplish your goals and dreams.*

Meanwhile, Dr. Luskin writes, those who make a practice of forgiving on a regular basis report improved health:

- ✔ *fewer incidences of heart disease*
- ✔ *better, deeper sleep*
- ✔ *fewer incidences of cancer*
- ✔ *lower blood pressure*
- ✔ *stronger immune systems*
- ✔ *less muscle tension and disorders such as TMJ*

What researchers all agree on is that whatever you're missing in your life can be recovered more quickly when you forgive.

When to Forgive

The time to forgive and allow the flow of good feelings back into your life is always *now*. Signs that you still have *Forgiveness* work to do include:

- ✔ *you have angry outbursts over small incidents*
- ✔ *you avoid family gatherings*

> *Forgiveness is a dramatic action we can all take to improve our health.*
>
> **Dr. Joan Borysenko**

✔ *you warn people not to trust others*

✔ *you feel depressed or anxious most of the time*

✔ *you use food, drugs and/or smoking to try and ease your emotional pain*

The Power in *Forgiveness*

Her name was not Lucille, but that is what I shall call her. She came for coaching and told me things were "fine," but her body language told another story. I asked her what she was grateful for and the closest she could get to gratitude was, "Grateful I only have to work four days this week!"

As her feelings found words, I heard her passion for a new job, but needed to remind her that from where she was on the **Power Pyramid**, she couldn't attract a new position that would fulfill her. I invited her to think of one thing she *could* be grateful for about her present situation. After a long silence, she said, "I really can't think of anything."

If you had not suffered as you have, there would be no depth to you, no humility, no compassion.

Eckhart Tolle

"Not even the regular paycheck?"

"No. I'm a really good saver. I don't really need the paycheck. No, not even that."

"Then why haven't you quit?"

"Oh, I'd never hear the end of it from my father."

I asked her if her use of the word "father" indicated of a lack of warmth in their relationship. Theirs, according to this young woman, was frozen shut.

The more I listened to her story, the more curious I became. "Have you ever wondered why he gives you so much advice?" I asked. She shook her head. "Perhaps it's because he thinks you waffle and are unsure of yourself."

"That's true enough."

"So what might happen once you stand your ground, look him in the eye, and let him know you're quitting no matter what he thinks?"

She couldn't imagine doing any of those things, so we got out some paper and envelopes. First she sat and wrote an angry feelings letter to him using the strongest language she could muster. When she was finished, we placed it in an envelope and burned it.

"Now I invite you to write a *Forgiveness Letter.*" Her tears flowed as she wrote her long letter forgiving her father for not being the kind of Dad she'd dreamed of having. As she sealed that letter and walked with me to the fire pit, there was a new purpose in her posture. She told her father of her plans the following week and was able to find gratitude for lessons learned at the job she left.

What to Forgive

It's important to distinguish between *forgiving* something and *dismissing* it. In our humanity, we forget things, break things, and step on an occasional toe, but not all of those things need forgiving. When a child spills milk at the dinner table while company is present, for example, it certainly doesn't require forgiveness, just acceptance.

"But on the other end of the spectrum, aren't there things I *shouldn't* forgive?" I am sometimes asked, most often by a woman married to a philanderer. I take her back through the first three High-Ways: 1) I ask her to *Get the Picture* of the life she wants. 2) I ask her what she would do if she had no fear. 3) I encourage her to do the *Full Responsibility* work of Byron Katie (www.thework.com).

By the time she's completed those steps, her original question has been answered.

The *Forgiveness* Challenge

I congratulate you on making it this far into the High-Ways. Now that it's time for forgiveness, don't give in to thoughts of "this is too hard" or "I can't do it." You're the most *powerful* being you know. Claim that power to get you through this transforming step and join the thousands of us on the other side in gratitude!

> *Everything can be taken from a person but one thing: It is the last of human freedoms—to choose one's attitude in any circumstances, to choose one's way.*
>
> **Victor Frankl**

The *Forgiveness of the Past* **Process:**
Face it, Feel it, Forgive it

An eye for an eye leaves the whole world blind.

Gandhi

During my stay at the domestic violence shelter, one day my counselor leaned forward and asked, "Why are you smiling? You're describing awful things, yet you're sitting here smiling."

"Am I?" I asked. My naïveté was wide and deep. "It must be because I've forgiven him."

"Hardly!" she replied. "You haven't even faced what's happened to you. You certainly aren't ready to forgive it. I want you to go to your room, write down every abusive incident over the past six years, and show me the list tomorrow."

Eleven and a half single-spaced pages later, I was no longer smiling, and began to face my feelings, feel them, and eventually, forgive.

The Three Steps to Forgiveness

It was then that I saw that the process of *Forgiveness* had three distinct steps:

1. Face it
2. Feel it
3. Forgive it

It's often tempting to *run from* the first two steps. *Forgiveness* is a risk, and when we don't want to face it, we can make ourselves extremely busy or create new crises that keep us from dealing with our feelings and healing our pain.

Unfortunately, if we can't face it and don't feel it, we can't forgive it. *Forgiveness* is heart-work, as is the entire **FGH** formula. It can't be done in the head. That's why *Forgiveness of the Past* comes *after*

High-Way 4: *Feel All Your Feelings.* We must be in touch with our feelings to truly forgive.

If you haven't yet faced your pain and given yourself time to feel your *mads* and *sads* about what has happened to you, go back and review High-Way 4. Soon you'll see that the more you practice the three steps of *Forgiveness*, the quicker you'll be able to work through new painful issues as they arise.

How *Forgiveness of the Past* Works

Forgiveness of the Past frees us not only from our past, but also from the unhealthy connection with those we have held in judgment. There's a poem that circulates around the Internet every so often that starts: "Some people are in our lives for a reason, others for a season." Once you've forgiven someone, you're free to stay or go. Until you forgive them, however, that person has a hold on you. Do you want an energetic leash connecting you to someone who has hurt you?

> *Enlightenment is putting down a burden and not picking it up again.*
>
> **Peter McWilliams**

Remember, the goal of forgiveness is to get to a place of detaching with love and releasing resentment. One way to describe it is that we're forgiving them for *not being the way we wanted them to be.* That brings us to the final "peace" of the *Forgiveness of the Past* process.

How to Know if You've Forgiven Someone

The test I've used over the years to see if I've fully forgiven some-one is as follows:

> *If good things happen to them and you celebrate,*
> *and bad things happen to them and you commiserate, you've forgiven them.*
> *If bad things happen to them and you celebrate, you have not.*

I don't believe the axiom "time heals all wounds" because I've seen too many people who've wasted decades of bitterness and regret over a word spoken in haste or a solitary painful event. I do believe that *forgiveness heals*. I've experienced it hundreds of times in my own life and I've seen it in the lives of my coaching clients. Take the test for yourself. If you still have *Forgiveness* work to do, this chapter will show you the way.

Appropriate vs. Inappropriate Guilt

I'm one of those who believe that discomfort or guilt over wrongdoings is okay. Do you have moral values? Of course you do. Imagine a circle around where you're sitting right now that's four feet in diameter. Think of that circle as your "moral boundaries." If you step outside of that circle, it's okay if you feel remorse.

My son stole some things in his middle school years. My greatest concern was that he didn't seem to feel guilt or remorse, and therefore his apologies to me and others were shallow.

One day he came to me and had a good cry. He could clearly see the person he wanted to be and the life he wanted to live, and he felt bad about his behavior. It was the first day of the "best" of his life and allowed him to stop stealing. That's healthy guilt.

I sometimes joke about my "Catholic" guilt, but the truth is that I continue to discover layers of guilt I've heaped upon myself and must continue to release. When the big G of Guilt loomed over me, I reminded myself that anger is a better feeling than guilt (higher on the **Power Pyramid**). I tried to think of who else I could be angry at besides myself to spread the blame around.

All of a sudden it hit me. We attract our experiences—ALL of our experiences. That meant that the man I let down by forgetting to e-mail him a rehearsal schedule was attracting that kind of experience. I just happened to be the person who showed up to act it out. It was truly liberating. Practice "we both attracted each other" thinking to relieve yourself of any remnant guilt after you've done the rest of your *Forgiveness* work.

> *It feels like forgiveness is about what somebody else did, but it's not.*
> *It's always about letting yourself be who you are.*
>
> **Abraham-Hicks**

Why We Don't Practice *Forgiveness of the Past*

When one door closes, another one opens,
but we often look so long and so regretfully upon the closed door
that we do not see the ones which open for us.

Alexander Graham Bell

Over the years I've heard a litany of paltry reasons not to forgive someone. I call them:

Forgiveness Fallacies

People say they can't forgive someone because

✔ *that person hasn't apologized or isn't remorseful.*
✔ *then the other person will "win".*
✔ *that person has died.*
✔ *justice must be served.*
✔ *if they're forgiven they'll do it again.*
✔ *forgiveness is a sign of weakness.*
✔ *they have to understand why it happened first.*
✔ *it needs to stops hurting first.*
✔ *others don't hurt as much as they do.*
✔ *there is too much to forgive to ever work through it all.*

These are all excuses to stay stuck in our misery. We can replace them whenever we're ready with:

Forgiveness Truths

✔ *Forgiveness is something you do for you, not for the other person.*
✔ *Forgiveness is a proactive decision to take your power back.*
✔ *Forgiveness is refusing to live in the past.*
✔ *Forgiveness is a skill you can learn.*
✔ *Forgiveness is freedom from the burdens of the past.*
✔ *Forgiveness is refusing to give the offender power over the present.*
✔ *Forgiveness is a choice.*

- ✔ *Forgiveness is running* to *rather than running* from.
- ✔ *Forgiveness is caring about your quality of life more than theirs.*
- ✔ *Forgiveness is a process. Once you begin, it gets easier and easier.*

> *Bitterness is like cancer.*
> *It eats upon the host.*
> *But anger and forgiveness*
> *are like fire.*
> *They burn all clean.*
>
> **Maya Angelou**

When You're Not Ready to Forgive

As I was speaking at a young women's rehab center, sixteen-year-old Shawna was sullen and resistant to my message, and when we got to the *Forgiveness of the Past* High-Way, her emotions boiled to the surface.

"There's no way I'm forgiving him!" she said firmly. "He left us with no warning. We lost the house and we had to be split up! He used to beat my mom and was drunk all the time. There's no way I'm forgiving him!"

As tears spilled onto her desk, I knelt down and thanked her for being so honest. Then I reminded her that she didn't need to forgive him now and that her feelings were completely valid. Shawna was clearly working through High-Ways 4, *Feel All Your Feelings*, and 5, *Honest Communication*, and was exactly where she needed to be. While the rest of the young women wrote *Forgiveness Letters* later that afternoon, I asked Shawna to write a letter expressing her feelings to her father. Although she would never send it, it would be a huge release for her. She eventually went on to complete the *8 to Great* program and make peace with the choices her father and mother had made.

Your Pain Isn't Special

A middle-aged woman in a homeless shelter helped me understand that our pain is never unique. At the completion of her recovery program, she stood to give a testimonial.

"I walked into this shelter believing no one had ever been hurt as much as I had. Therefore, I gave myself permission to wallow in my misery and continue using. My greatest insight, for which I have all of you to thank, is that my pain is not special."

When we release our excuses, we're the ones who are released.

Forgiveness of the Past Success Stories

Forgiveness is not an occasional act; it is a permanent attitude.
Dr. Martin Luther King, Jr.

When we learn to forgive, life gets easier. Our dreams can manifest more quickly because much more of our energy is in the present moment. We are "95-ing" more often, and what goes around comes around effortlessly. Classroom teachers who come to my **8 to Great** Institute to learn our program are often surprised by the level of healing they personally receive along the way.

> *Happiness is nothing more than good health and a bad memory.*
>
> **Albert Schweitzer**

Forgiving Her Ex-Husband

After one of our **8 to Great** training weekends, I received this beautiful testimonial to the power of forgiveness:

MK,

After the wonderful weekend, I had a very personal experience with forgiveness. I'd been struggling for years with forgiving an old debt (money owed me from years of past due child support). I felt like I should forgive and move on, since both of my children are grown and married with families of their own, but I didn't want to. After the training weekend, I knew that I'd be a happier person if I released that part of my past, so I wrote a Forgiveness Letter to him, burned it, and then did the legal paperwork required.

The very next day, not only did I feel happy and freed from a heavy burden from the past (more than just money) but in less than twenty-four hours my (second) husband and I received word of an inheritance totaling $1,500 more than the debt and the interest combined! It was just as you described. Forgiveness gets us back in the flow! I am so grateful for that amazing weekend and the 8 High-Ways!

Janice

The Tired Twin

I was privileged to coach a middle-aged farmer who was at his wit's end. Even though he had been financially abundant, in recent years his finances had been declining and he couldn't seem to turn them around. After listening to his concerns I asked about his relationships and discovered that he hated his twin sister and had never forgiven her for a number of things.

After working on *Get the Picture* and not seeing any progress, I focused on forgiveness. When he wasn't able to answer all my questions, I suggested that he go to someone to be muscle tested. (The process is called NET—Neuro-Emotional Technique—and is akin to a lie detector test to determine your body's path to healing.)

Although skeptical, his emotional and financial pain prompted him to make an appointment with a woman in a nearby community. She immediately picked up on his need for forgiveness. She was able to help him discover that since he and his twin were about the same birth weight, they had fought fiercely for dominion in the womb, which they had then carried into their lives.

He called me after his session with her, sobbing and telling me that he'd never felt so free. He'd finally forgiven his sister and himself for all the years of bitterness—and his good fortune returned soon thereafter.

Wouldn't it be lovely if we could always find out why someone treated us badly? However, the reality is that such insights are rare. That leaves us with two choices: choose not to forgive unless we find out "why they did it"—or just choose to forgive.

> *Judge not,*
> *lest you be judged.*
>
> **Matthew 7: 1**

The Sins of Others

A Catholic priest I know usually chooses not to wear his clerical garb when traveling. He found himself on a plane sitting next to a well-known radio commentator who casually made comments about the Catholic author

Andrew Greeley. He concluded with, "Father Greeley is a good man, not like those other priests who mess with kids."

My friend later remarked, "I felt like I had a target on me for the next two days. No matter what was going on, my thoughts seemed to return to that judgment, which had felt very personally about me. I realized that I needed to forgive that man in order to regain peace with myself."

How powerful is forgiveness? On the flight back home, my friend had a very different experience. A woman walked down the aisle mid-flight and stopped at his seat.

"Excuse me, but did I overhear that you're a Catholic priest?"

When he replied that he was, she told him she'd made a promise to herself never to encounter a priest or nun without stopping to thank them for the wonderful education she'd received in Catholic schools while growing up.

> *If her past were your past, her pain your pain, her level of consciousness your level of consciousness, you would think and act exactly as she does. With this realization comes forgiveness, compassion, peace.*
>
> **Eckhart Tolle**

What many people don't realize is that the Roman Catholic Church hasn't just been in great *need* of forgiveness, but it has also been a great *model* of forgiveness over the centuries. In 1984, Pope John Paul walked into the cell of Rebibbia prison in Rome to meet Mehmet Ali Agca, the man who had tried to kill him just months before. The pope took the hand of the man who had fired a bullet at his heart and forgave him.

Years later, when news came that the pope had died, the press reported that his would-be assassin wept.

"They had declared brotherhood when the pope visited him in prison," Adnan Agca said of his brother's 1984 meeting with the Holy Father. "The pope was Mehmet's brother; wouldn't you be sad if you had lost your brother?"

My Father

My father was a very good man. He worked hard, loved his family, was honest to a fault, and generous to all he met. However, forgiveness didn't come easily for him. There were times I remember him holding grudges and not speaking to people for years at a time. In fact, he didn't speak to his own father for *fifteen years*. It was just accepted in our home as "the way it was," and no one ever questioned it.

Just after Dad turned seventy, he was told he had lung cancer and had only a few months to live. We were all devastated. Because he lived in Florida and the kids were sprinkled around the United States, we alternated weeks to be with him, flying to Florida when it was our turn.

The second time I flew there, Dad was hospitalized. I remember one difficult day very clearly. He was coughing hard for long spells, so I kept calling the nurse for help. She finally pulled me aside and explained that his lungs were filling up with fluid. She was sorry, but there was nothing she could do. The next time Dad went into a coughing spell, I just held him in my arms.

When it was finally over, he looked up at me and asked, "Am I going to die today?"

"I don't know, Dad," I replied. "I don't understand this disease, but if this *is* the big day, you're ready, and I'll be right here with you."

Just then the phone rang. It was my sister in North Carolina calling to talk to him.

As I held the phone to Dad's ear, all he could say was, "I love you, I love you, I love you."

> *There is no revenge so complete as forgiveness.*
>
> **Josh Billings**

As soon as I hung up the phone, it rang again. This time it was my brother in Seattle. Again their conversation was short and full of "I love you's" from Dad. Then it rang again—my brother in Iowa.

Tears ran down Dad's cheeks as he said again and again, "I love you, I love you, I love you."

When I hung up the phone after that conversation, I knew there was one more phone call to make—to a family member Dad hadn't spoken to for years—but I also knew I'd have to dial the number, and I did.

As soon as Dad heard who was on the line, he began to sob, "I'm so sorry. Please forgive me. I love you, I love you, I love you."

When that phone call ended, Dad was quiet for a moment, and then asked, "Why did you do that?"

"Dad, do you remember Jacob Marley in *A Christmas Carol*, carrying around all those chains? You don't want to carry those chains any longer."

He thanked me and cried some more, this time from relief. From that day on, there was a new peace about him.

One month later he was gone, but I'll never forget the lessons he taught me in those final weeks. Forgiveness frees us to love and be loved. Although he wasn't cured, I believe Dad was healed. I know I was.

> *What could you want that forgiveness cannot give?*
> *Do you want peace? Forgiveness offers it.*
> *Do you want happiness, a quiet mind,*
> *A certainty of purpose,*
> *and a sense of worth and beauty that transcends the world?*
> *Do you want care and safety and warmth of sure protection always?*
> *Do you want a quietness that cannot be disturbed,*
> *A gentleness that cannot be hurt,*
> *A deep abiding comfort and a rest so perfect it can never be upset?*
> *All this forgiveness offers you.*
> *You who want peace can find it only by complete forgiveness.*

A Course in Miracles

❦

Putting *Forgiveness of the Past* into Practice

One secret of a long and fruitful life is to forgive everybody,
everything, every night before you go to bed.
Ann Landers

❦

At the beginning of this chapter, we defined *Forgiveness* as *releasing regret, resentment, and the desire for revenge.*

Just as we asked in High-Way 2, *Risk*: "If you had no fear, what would you do?" we ask in this High-Way: "If you had no regret or bitterness, who would you be?"

The *Forgiveness Letter*

When you're ready to do the physical process of forgiveness, get out a journal and write down the names of those you haven't forgiven—including yourself, God, or anyone else, living or deceased. Then decide who to write your initial *Forgiveness Letter* to.

You won't be sending it. This ritual is for *you*, not them. After you complete it, you'll burn it to signify that you've released the person or event and are free to live more fully in the present. You may want to put on some quiet music to get you started.

1. Take a few moments to think about the things you haven't yet forgiven.

2. When you're ready, begin your forgiveness or "release" letter. It can say things like, "I don't know why you did it and may never know, but I don't care. I'm releasing the past and moving on."

3. When you're finished, sign it, fold it, put it in an envelope, and seal it.

4. Write a big "F" on the front of the sealed envelope, which stands for: "I Faced it, Felt it, Forgave it, it's going into the Fire, and now I am Free."

5. Burn it and feel the release as you do.

One of the most common questions I hear in my seminars is, "If I forgive them, will I forget?" The answer is yes and no. No, not right away, but as the *Forgiveness of the Past* process becomes more natural to you, painful thoughts will begin to fade, making room for more joy and appreciation of the present. Occasional memories may still arise from time to time, but they'll have less power to diminish your power or your peace. If you're still having painful memories weeks and months after writing your *Forgiveness Letter*, you may want to consider writing *another Forgiveness Letter*.

"Thank You For-giving Me..."

A common benefit from doing your *Forgiveness* work is that many find themselves moving into *Gratitude* for the event that previously brought them pain. There are lessons to be learned from every adversity, and forgiveness frees us to find them. Author Michael Beckwith describe the forgiveness blessing this way, "Thank you *for-giving* me this opportunity to grow."

We might also say it this way: "Thank you for being my mirror." It's so hard, yet healing, to remember that people treat us the way we believe we deserve to be treated. As we learn to take *Full Responsibility* for our lives, the tone of our *Forgiveness* will move toward an increased self-awareness, self-forgiveness, and self-love.

> *Relationships do not cause pain and unhappiness. They bring out the pain and unhappiness that is already in us.*
>
> **Eckhart Tolle**

It's possible to become grateful for *every* event. Each challenge has helped make you the **WISE** person you are today:

Wonderful
Insightful
Strong
Empowered

One Woman's Light

Would you be reading this book right now if you'd never experienced adversity? I recall a wise woman at one of my seminars who lit up the room.

I saw her coming toward me and before she could speak I asked her, "What is your secret? You're absolutely glowing and radiant. What is it I'm sensing?"

"Many people make comments like that," she replied. "I guess it all started the year we lost the twins."

She shared that her only two children were gone in the blink of an eye because the young man driving their car was drunk.

All things work to good...

Romans 8:28

"Tell me more," I asked her in that crowded room.

"I cried and cried, of course, for weeks that turned into months. Then one day I looked outside and noticed that the sun had come up again. I walked out of the house looking for a new reason to live. Today my husband and I have a huge ministry to parents who have lost children. Our girls live on in our hearts and in our work. We're so grateful we had them for that time."

Four Letters for Ending a Relationship

Romantic relationships don't end—but they often transform. When the latter happens, there can be pain, either before the breakup or afterward. But just because our feelings are hurt doesn't mean we have to suffer or make the other person suffer. Although ending a relationship is one of the most joy-challenging experiences you can face, no matter who initiates the breakup, writing four letters can help you close the door and move on. After writing each one, burn it.

1. A letter of anger

2. A letter of sadness

3. A letter forgiving the other person and yourself (these are often separate letters)

4. A letter of gratitude for all the good times, which you may send or burn, depending upon the situation (this is often the longest letter)

When my coaching clients see this list, they sometimes ask, "Will letter #4 make me want to get back together with the person?" There's a chance that it will, but for most people, it just reminds them that there *were* good times and that they weren't fools to have stayed in the relationship until now.

"I Can Be So Controlling"

I still have trouble forgiving myself when I catch myself being bossy and controlling. One day my question to a good friend was, "How come I get micro-manage-y at certain times and other times I'm fine?"

Her reply described exactly what was going on inside of me, "In your childhood you were unpleasantly surprised more than once. You then went on 'alert' and decided that if you were always on your toes you could prevent catastrophe. When you have the most to lose, you go into hyper-drive, just like the rest of us who have experienced such incidents."

"But I've heard all this before," I protested.

"You could only process so much of it at the time, but the seeds were planted then and now they're sprouting into a new level of awareness."

Her gentle words about a part of myself I have always had trouble loving helped me tremendously.

The Price of Judgment

I've worked with many women who were grieving an abortion years after the fact. In almost every instance, they had gotten pregnant while unmarried and had aborted the baby because they thought it would "kill" their parents to be so disgraced, "kill" their relationship, or that their parents would "kill" *them* if they found out. The result of those judgments was that those young women felt as if they had many lives to save and were pulled between them. It is one of the most powerful experiences I have had watching these women forgive themselves for doing the best they could at the time with the information they had.

Forgiving My Daughter's Stalker

One afternoon years ago, my twelve-year-old was offered a ride by a stranger on her way home from school. She ran crying all the way home. We filed police reports and alerted the school. We hoped it was a one-time event, but he showed up again three mornings later.

It was traumatic—for her and for us all. That entire week I felt paralyzed—choiceless. I had trouble working the High-Ways and became a raving robot to my fight-or-flight instincts.

"Should we move?" "Why aren't the police doing more?" "I should have…" "It's my fault…." "If only…" I felt caught on a merry-go-round of negative, fear-based thinking.

Then, on the fifth day, I saw what was happening and got off the carousel. I calmed down and breathed deeply again. I returned to my *Gratitudes*. That day I even laughed at a joke. Although we hadn't yet identified him, I realized I could choose to find peace *inside* me, if not *around* me.

I reminded myself that the definition of peace isn't the absence of war, but the absence of fear. When I released my judgment of the situation, I was able to do my *Full Responsibility* work, accepting it as "how things are." I *forgave* the present circumstances for being painful. I went back to my **FGH** formula and became grateful for the excellent police team that was assigned to her case, for her safety, and for her courage. I regained my hope for our future.

> *Forgiveness is the key to freedom.*
>
> **Hannah Arendt**

The police contacted me the day before the final day of school to tell me, "We think he's going to show up tomorrow. We'll have six armed officers in hiding along the way—but we need you to let your daughter walk to school alone."

Watching her walk out the door that morning was one of the hardest things I've ever done as a Mom. I still remember it clearly. The night before she had told me she wanted that man found so the chaos could end. I was in awe of her bravery.

As predicted, two blocks into her five-block walk, he appeared. When apprehended, it was discovered that he was carrying a loaded gun.

Fast forward to his court date. I went with a friend to hear them set a date for the hearing and to look at his face for the first time. After the short proceedings, we began to file out of the room and I saw him glance at a couple as he was taken away by police.

> *When you make it a habit not to take anything personally, your anger, jealousy and envy, even your sadness will simply disappear.*
>
> **Don Miguel Ruiz**

Once in the hallway, I decided to approach them and introduced myself quickly with, "I'm Joanna's mother. I just want you to know that we mean him no harm. We only want everyone to be safe."

The woman almost collapsed in her husband's arms as she exploded in tears.

"I'm so sorry. We're so, so sorry. Please forgive him. Please forgive us."

She continued sobbing loudly as her husband explained, "He's her brother. He lived with their parents all his life because he was so shy. It was a mistake and we can see that now. When they both died last year, he became totally isolated. We went over a couple of times and found him cleaning his guns. It just never occurred to us that something like this would happen. We're just so sorry for your family's pain."

Six months later I got a call from the judge. It was time to make a decision about charging him with a felony or a misdemeanor—and he was leaving the choice up to *me*.

"How has he been doing with his rehabilitation?" I asked.

The judge shared that he was responding exceptionally well, so I recommended a misdemeanor charge—and we never heard from him again. *Forgiveness* had freed us all.

Keeping a Clean Slate

Once you've written your *Forgiveness Letters* to wipe the slate clean, there are three ways to keep it clean.

1. Don't take things personally

Although life experiences come to us as a result of the thoughts we think, the painful actions and demeaning words from others never come to us because they are true. They come to remind us we can heal them.

2. Fast from the past

The letters I get from truly unhappy people always include long lists of the calamities that have befallen them. Recently I received one that began with: "I've tried your program, but it isn't working. I've had a terrible life. I guess I should give you more details."

Here was my response:

"You're asking for my coaching. Well, here it is: Be done with it. Don't tell these stories ever again. Fast from the past. I know of no way out of your hell as long as you continue to recite these mishaps and misfortunes."

> *A stiff appology is a second insult.... The injured party does not want to be compensated because he has been wronged; he wants to be healed because he has been hurt.*
>
> **Gilbert K. Chesterton**

I suggested she read Byron Katie's book, *Who Would You Be Without Your Story?* Then start a *Gratitude* list, adding three things to it each day. I never heard from her again.

When you're tired of your misery, you'll shed your past like an old coat and never put it on again. You're as free to do so as you believe you are.

3. Write *Forgiveness Letters* as needed

When something won't go away and you keep seeing a pattern of self-judgment, condescension, sarcasm, or judgment of others, write another *Forgiveness Letter.* It is a tool that I have used many times over the years, always with healing results.

Asking Forgiveness

Just as you can offer forgiveness to another in writing, *asking* forgiveness for yourself can be done in person or in writing. Your letter or e-mail can be as simple as: "I'm sorry. I didn't mean to hurt you. Please forgive me." Such simple words have torn down walls built over months—and even years. They are staples for healthy relationships between families and friends.

It's also possible to ask forgiveness of those who have died. Doing so with someone who is no longer in your life can help open yourself to love from those who are.

The Only Thing We Need to Forgive

While writing this chapter, I came upon a quote by Abraham-Hicks that ended with:

"The only reason you don't love them is because you're using them as your excuse to not feel good." It struck me that you could re-phrase that as: "The only reason you need to forgive them is because you gave them power over how you feel in the first place."

Let's invoke High-Way 3 and return to *Full Responsibility.* Once we realize that we were the ones who gave away our power to the other person in the first place, we can move to a new place, remember our power, and forgive ourselves for ever forgetting.

Q & A on *Forgiveness of the Past*

Finish each day and be done with it. You've done what you could.
Some blunders and absurdities no doubt crept in;
forget them as soon as you can.
Tomorrow is a new day; begin it well and serenely.
Ralph Waldo Emerson

᠁

Q: *Once I forgive myself, how do I get other people and their judgments off my back?*

A: When you truly stop judging yourself, others will stop judging you. It's how life works. In the meantime, listen to them with the same kind of listening you want them to offer you. Phrase such as "Have you got a minute to sit down and talk?" or "I know you want the best for me" may be helpful.

Q: *I find myself apologizing all the time. Is that healthy?*

A: I've always wondered why the holiest people—Gandhi, Mother Teresa, the Dalai Lama, Pope John Paul II—seemed to move slowly and talk slowly. I think I finally figured it out. That's the easiest way to stay conscious.

Years ago I started noticing how often I had been apologizing—sometimes half a dozen times a week. I wondered if I could go a whole week without doing anything I felt a need to apologize for. It slowed me down. Multiple apologies aren't bad, but they tell us we're not feeling comfortable with how we're living. Either change how you're living or learn to accept your best as good enough. Either way will help you feel better.

Q: *I just did something that was mean-spirited and dumb. How do I forgive myself?*

A: Let's call what you did "interesting." Like the child who's told not to touch the stove but touches it anyway, you didn't want to believe Mom when she said it would hurt you. Every adversity can make you *bitter* or *better*. What's going to be the verdict with this one?

As for *mean-spirited*, I'd change that word to *fear-spirited*. No one wakes up and says, "I can't wait to hurt such-and-such's feelings." We may, however, wake up and say, "I have to protect myself from that person." In the process of trying to protect ourselves from pain, we cause more. The moral of the story is that, deep down, we didn't mean to be mean. We just wanted to be safe. When we *get* that we're already safe, any meanness melts away.

> *I have never met a greater monster or miracle than myself.*
> **Montaigne**

Q: *I want to forgive, but how do I get over a death?*

A: Thank you for that courageous question. I suggest that: 1) You allow yourself to cry as much and as long as you want. 2) When you're ready, write them a goodbye letter. Then burn it and spread the ashes in a special place.

I'm of the belief system that says death isn't life-threatening. That was helpful for me to get through my father's passing. I hope that you can find solace in your belief system also.

Q: *Can you be too forgiving?*

A: No, but you can be unloving to yourself.

When I'm not sure if I'm putting up with too much from someone, I ask, "What would I want my daughter to do in this situation?"

Lord, today I am grateful that I have not been impatient, cranky, or irritable, that I haven't been jealous, rude, or judgmental, and that I haven't pouted, whined, or nagged. But soon, Lord, I'm gonna get out of bed, so I'm really gonna need your help.

Anonymous

Allow your *angergy* to rise up. It may have powerful lessons to teach you. The lesson could be to ask for a raise or to confront your landlord. If something is harming you, face it and feel it first (which often leads to healthy action) and then you'll be ready to forgive it.

Q: *I'm sad a lot because of what has happened in my past and I don't know how to change that.*

A: I was in the domestic violence shelter, one of my best friends got pregnant out of wedlock and Oprah was sexually assaulted by a family member. Each of us had an "excuse" to stay stuck in shame and guilt for the rest of our lives, but imagine this with me:

Suppose your best friend wrote you a letter yesterday that told about all the rotten things that had happened in *her* life—and they were *exactly* the same as what had happened in yours!

Now suppose that at the end of the letter she asked, "Can you still love me now that you know all of this?"

What would your answer be? You would love her, of course. Now allow yourself to love *you*.

Q: *Why don't we send the Forgiveness Letters?*

A: Your question indicates that you may still have a desire to change the other person. We do our best *Forgiveness* work when we detach with love from the other person. Sending the letter could stir up old issues they consider long gone or could get us caught up in wondering if they'll respond. Burning the letters is a powerful ritual that most people find deeply healing.

Q: *How do you celebrate another person's successes and feel compassion for their challenges if they're deceased?*

A: When you think about them, you'll feel the knot in your stomach begin to unravel and be replaced by peace.

Forgiveness is the answer to the child's dream of a miracle by which what is broken is made whole again.

Dag Hammarskjold

FGH: Gratitude for the Present

The Power of Appreciation

Defining *Gratitude for the Present*

*When a person doesn't have gratitude, something is
missing in his or her humanity.
A person can almost be defined by his or her
attitude toward gratitude.*

Elie Wiesel

⧼∞⧽

Ever notice how people with lots of love, support, health, and wealth in their lives seem to be really grateful? Which do you think came first, the success or the gratitude?

One of the most exciting discoveries of the new positive psychology research is that happiness isn't the cause of gratitude, it's the *result*. Gratitude comes *before* success in almost every case.

Growing up, most of us came to view gratitude as the "icing on the cake" of life. Back then, we thought of the "main course" as hard work, knowing the right people, or doing what others thought we "should" do every day. Now it's become clear that the main entree of a happy, healthy, and fulfilled life is choosing thoughts that feel good, and there's no easier way than being grateful.

A simple dictionary definition of gratitude is "a feeling of appreciation for something or someone." Like other emotions, it starts in our hearts and stirs up our senses. The phrase "overcome with gratitude" aptly describes our experience of welling up with tears of joy for gifts received. It is, as a high school student once described it, "a very high high."

My highest *Gratitudes* seem to be two-pronged. They acknowledge not only the gift, but also the giver, be it a person, nature, or God. In that sense, it's very similar to the feeling of love—and love is as good as it gets.

Enjoy today: this is not a dress rehearsal.

Refrigerator magnet

Why Be Grateful?

There are many good reasons to be grateful—primarily because it feels good. Like drawing back the curtains to let the sun into a dark room, it warms hearts and opens minds. Meanwhile, because it brings you happiness, others around you are blessed. I'll never forget my eight-year-old asking me what was different after I'd been doing my morning *Gratitudes* for just a few weeks. When I asked what he meant, he simply said, "You're so much happier!"

Researchers concur. According to a recent series of studies over a five-year span, gratitude positively affects practically every area of life. In *The Research Project on Gratitude and Thankfulness*, Dr. Michael McCullough and his colleagues at the University of Miami found the following attributes in adults (young and old) who kept gratitude journals or did regular gratitude interventions. They...

- ✔ had more energy and vitality.
- ✔ were more optimistic.
- ✔ were more likely to make progress toward important personal goals.
- ✔ were more alert, enthusiastic, determined, and attentive.
- ✔ were more likely to help someone by offering emotional support.
- ✔ had higher life satisfaction.
- ✔ were more generous.
- ✔ saw the interconnectedness of all life.
- ✔ were more responsible and committed.
- ✔ were less likely to judge others in terms of possessions.
- ✔ reported a heightened sense of mental well-being.

According to their research, "Even the spouses of the subjects noticed the difference in the participants who did regular gratitude writings or verbal acknowledgments." McCullough also noted that grateful people don't deny the negative aspects of life; they simply don't choose to dwell on them. Many of my clients notice that once they start making daily gratitude lists, they watch fewer newscasts. Focusing on the worst things that have happened in the past twenty-four hours is simply not a match for where they are on the **Power Pyramid**.

The Ultimate "All-Turn-ative"

Gratitude is extremely powerful because it has an immediate effect on our attitude. No matter what the situation, gratitude is the *all-turn-ative* that can turn all things around in just minutes. When we try *not* to think painful thoughts, we become a magnet for more of the same. Gratitude goes with the flow of life and gives us a new focal point. "What are you grateful for?" can yield an answer as simple as "I'm grateful I can choose to be grateful."

As a parent, my biggest disappointments haven't been in my children, but in myself. As a type A personality, I've been impatient more times than I want to remember. (Thank heavens for High-Way 6: *Forgiveness of the Past*.)

Sometimes when I ask my children for forgiveness for my sharp tone or curt word, even their saying they forgive me doesn't return me to a "95." Yet as soon as I shift our topic to what I'm grateful for about them, the air clears. One afternoon I was on my son about leaving things lying around the house and we got into a shouting match. I later asked his forgiveness and when he gave it, I was able to add, "Cool, you're reading that book I bought for you. I'm so glad you're giving it a try."

Fifteen minutes later, I met him coming from the laundry room and said, "Honey, I appreciate the fact that you're getting your laundry done so early in the weekend."

> *The question is not what you look at but what you see.*
>
> **Henry David Thoreau**

That evening at dinner, I added, "You know something I appreciate about you?" I had his attention. "When you called two friends today and neither of them wanted to go to the movie, you didn't give up. You called one more friend and now have fun plans for tonight."

A sincere "Thanks, Mom," and lively conversation was my resounding reward.

Gratitude and Work

The great little book *How Full is Your Bucket,* by Tom Rath and Donald Clifton, is full of more proof of the power of being acknowledged. One 2003 Gallup poll found that "65 percent of Americans reported receiving no recognition for good work in the past year." The poll also cited the following characteristics of co-workers who receive regular appreciation and praise:

- ✔ *increased individual productivity*
- ✔ *increased social interaction*
- ✔ *greater longevity in their jobs*
- ✔ *fewer accidents on the job*

However, perhaps their most astounding statistic was that *the #1 reason people leave their jobs is because they don't feel appreciated.* A pat on the back or recognition in a meeting can go a long way.

You'll never grow old until you've lost all your marvels.

Merry Browne

Gratitude and Health

When you incorporate gratitude into your life, almost everything improves—even your health. In recent years, McCullough and Emmons studied the effects of gratitude on psychological and physical well-being. They asked some groups of participants to list things they were grateful for once a day and others groups to make lists once a week.

As they were tracking the participants' self-reported emotional and physical states, the research partners were amazed to find that the participants who listed things they were grateful for even *once a week* not only improved in helpfulness and happiness, but spent more time exercising, slept better, and had fewer physical ailments. Those who did *daily Gratitudes* enjoyed even greater health benefits. Evidence continues to indicate that when we focus on thoughts that *feel good*, our level of wellness improves dramatically.

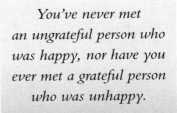

You've never met an ungrateful person who was happy, nor have you ever met a grateful person who was unhappy.

Zig Ziglar

The Top of the *Power Pyramid*

Gratitude is more than reciting thank yous. When we allow *feelings* of appreciation to flow through us, it changes us at our core. As we say in High-Way 4: *Feel All Your Feelings*, gratitude is at the very top of the **Power Pyramid**, along with joy, enthusiasm, and love.

For those who want to rise to the top of their potential for happiness, health, and success, gratitude is the ultimate "elevator." Once we're in the gratitude flow, things start changing for the better. In *Get the Picture*, we ask and believe. With *Gratitude for the Present*, we thank and receive!

Taking the Elevator to the 95th Floor

One of my favorite methods for explaining how gratitude works is to imagine being in a beautiful building with ninety-five floors. It's a building based on the **Power Pyramid** of life.

Now imagine:

Yesterday you got your spirits and hopes "up" and your feeling good put you on an elevator to the top floor of your Attitude Building. Once there, you saw life more clearly and felt "on top of the world." You soon began to ask for the "highest" good in relationships, health, work, vacations, etc. As you did, you watched helicopters take off from the helipad going to get you exactly what you'd asked for (or better).

All was well until late last evening while you were waiting for your deliveries to arrive. You became impatient and began to think about all the times you'd been disappointed. You wondered if your recent requests might not come to fruition. After all, asking and receiving seems so easy and you've always worked incredibly hard for what you wanted. You convinced yourself to be prepared for the worst and began to think of how you'd cope if you didn't receive your requests.

Before you knew it, you worked and worried your way down to the 45th floor. Once there, you got distracted by an unpleasant headline in a newspaper lying on an end table. It upset you so much that you took the wrong escalator and were soon walking around on the 25th floor. Since the folks at the 25th floor had lots of crises to tell you about from their past week, you got caught up in listening to their unfortunate mishaps and forgot all about the delivery of your requests—which were, by the way, delivered to the 95th floor around midnight.

Unfortunately, since no one was there to sign for them, they were returned to sender.

Moral of the story: once you ask for a "95" partner, job, or experience, you'll have to be in a "95" mood to receive it!

Gratitude is Natural

It can be fascinating to discover the innate gratitude of the human spirit by studying indigenous cultures. If you've ever spoken with people who have worked in the Peace Corps, for example, their stories often carry an underlying theme about the immense gratitude of the native people in their

> *At my home in Kyrgyzstan, I didn't have running water, a TV, a car, or most of the things I had when I lived in the United States, yet I was extremely happy. As a Peace Corps volunteer, you expect to go to another country where life is harder, poorer, where people need your help. Sure, most people there are poor, but those I now call my friends are so rich in character that I never noticed how poor they really were.*
> **Leslie Wakulich**

assigned countries. In describing their experiences, volunteers love to remind us that those who have nothing materially are some of the happiest people they've ever met.

Having doesn't bring happiness, but being *grateful* for what we have does. Hundreds of studies, such as those quoted in *Thank You Power,* by Deborah Norville, reveal that once our basic needs are met, the average person's level of happiness *does not increase* with our income. We don't need more fortunes to be more grateful, but once we're more grateful, more good fortune will be ours.

> *You must learn to understand the secret of gratitude. It is more than just so-called virtue. It is revealed to you as a mysterious law of existence. In obedience to it we have to fulfill our destiny.*
>
> **Albert Schweitzer**

Mutant Message Down Under

In her book, *Mutant Message Down Under,* author, physician, and former Kansas beauty queen Marlo Morgan describes her months on a walkabout through the desert with aborigines who refer to themselves as the *Real People.*

"I learned (on the walkabout) that the appearance of food was not taken for granted. It was first requested, always expected to appear, did appear, and genuine gratitude was always given.

"[One evening] the Real People explained how absurd it appeared to them when the missionaries insisted they teach their children to fold hands and give two minutes of grace before meals. They wake up being grateful! They spend the entire day never taking anything for granted. If missionaries have to teach their own children to be grateful, something that comes innately to all humans, the tribe feels they should take a very serious look at their own society. Perhaps it is they who need help."

Oceans of Gratitude

Another way to understand our intrinsically grateful nature is by watching animals. Everyone has seen the gratitude of a dog when his owner takes him out to play, but what if gratitude is natural to all mammals?

According to a *San Francisco Chronicle* article from December 14, 2005, a female humpback whale was spotted by crab fishermen just off the coast wrapped in the nylon ropes that connect crab traps to each other. The traps were heavy and the whale was struggling to stay on the surface so it could breathe. Experts assessed the situation and concluded that the only chance the whale had was if its rescuers could get into the water with her and cut her bonds, one by one. Any thrashing by the fifty-ton animal would have been deadly, but the crew decided it was a risk worth taking.

> *When we develop a right attitude of compassion and gratitude, we take a giant step towards solving our personal and international problems.*
>
> **The Dalai Lama**

One of the divers, James Moskito, described the whale as remaining peaceful during the hour or so it took them to cut the ropes. When they had finally finished and the whale realized it was free, Moskito said it began swimming in circles.

"It felt to me like it was thanking us, knowing that it was free and that we had helped it," Moskito said. But that wasn't all. After the circles, "It stopped about a foot away from me, pushed me around a little bit and had some fun."

He said after the whale nuzzled him, it swam to each of the other rescuers as well.

Teach Your Children Well

Animals and children are great teachers of the pure essence of gratitude and the power of living in the moment. So how does this natural awe and wonder ever turn into boredom? When Zach was four, his dad gave me a beautiful rose. The day I put it in a vase, it was just beginning to open up. The following morning I awoke to a blaze of colorful glory on our kitchen table. I pointed it out to Zach when he awoke.

His response was, "Yeah, Mom, I saw it yesterday."

We had somehow given him the message that a tree was "just a tree" and a flower "just a flower." I'm grateful that we caught it early enough that, as a seventeen-year-old, that same young man will often call me to the window to see a beautiful sunset.

The *Gratitude* Guarantee

Two minutes of writing *Gratitudes* each day will not only bring you new blessings, it will help you solve whatever problems you face. Imagine that your present problem is a forest fire. Standing in the middle of the blaze, you can do nothing, but with the help of gratitude to "rise above" your feelings of hopelessness or panic, you can see your options more clearly.

Gratitude doesn't make what went wrong yesterday go away, but regretting or worrying about your problems won't either. What it *will* do is make *today* better—make *right now* better. Isn't that enough? Once you understand gratitude, you'll learn that all your power and joy can only be accessed *now*.

The *Gratitude* Guarantee:
When you get grateful, you feel good.
When you feel good, good things happen!

The *Gratitude for the Present* Process:
Daily Gratitudes

Gratitude unlocks the fullness of life. It turns what we have into enough and more. It can turn a meal into a feast, a house into a home, a stranger into a friend. Gratitude makes sense of our past, brings peace for today, and creates a vision for tomorrow.

Melody Beattie

⌖

I start many of my talks with this question: "Is there anyone here who has something they could, if they wanted to, complain or worry about?"

Most hands go up.

Then I ask, "Is there anyone here who has something they could, if they wanted to, be grateful for?"

All hands go up.

I finish my point with, "Which of those categories occupy most of your thoughts? Your answer is an indicator of how your life is going these days."

The process of gratitude is simply choosing a focus of appreciation. Whether you do it at a prescribed time, such as when you first get up or before each meal, or whether you allow your thoughts to gently flow back to gratitude throughout the day, feeling appreciation is as simple as it is powerful.

> *I check myself constantly for, you know, am I appreciating this? Why not, if I'm not. I pull myself back to the now and to what's happening right now.*
>
> **Jim Carrey**

In High-Way 1 we said that a belief is "thinking it 'til you feel it." Similarly, thinking thoughts of appreciation without feeling the good feelings that go with them is like planting seeds without watering them. The fruits of gratitude are only harvested by getting to a place of humble acknowledgment of life's gifts, and that is one of the best feelings in the world.

Daily Devotion

Choose to devote yourself daily to gratitude. If you haven't started yet, begin with
writing down *three things* you're grateful for
from the past twenty-four hours. Then continue every day, with *no repeats.* If you start
to run dry, remember to include anything
you'd miss if it wasn't there, such as the co-
worker who always says good morning, the
fact that you can purchase one song off the Internet rather than buying an entire CD, that the person who cuts your hair is such a good
listener. Your smallest movement in the direction of appreciation
will reap huge rewards.

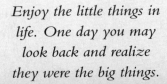

Enjoy the little things in life. One day you may look back and realize they were the big things.

Anonymous

The Worry Eraser

When someone tells me they worry all the time, the *last* thing
I suggest is that they stop worrying. That would only make them
worry about worrying. Instead, I ask them to live in the moment
rather than in the future by getting grateful.

When worry threatens to overwhelm them, I invite them to
play the *Alien Game.* Like Brad Pitt's character in the film *Meet Joe
Black*, we pretend we've just come to Earth and have been given
someone else's body for the day. As an Alien, everything is foreign to
us, not in a scary way, but in a delighting way.

Those who play this game best (by getting in touch with their
inner Alien) marvel at how toothpaste tubes work, how much teenagers laugh, how snow glistens in the moonlight, and how wonderful
butter tastes melted on homemade bread.

When we have no past and no future (and since we're going to
give this body back to its owner in a week), the moment takes over.
We know *now* in a new way, meeting life on her own terms. When
we see her in this way, we can't help but fall in love with her.

Living in the Now

Sincere gratitude helps us live in the *now*. Our life takes on a gentler pace, and time starts to feel as if it's expanding. What good is all the manifesting in the world if we never stop and appreciate our gifts once we receive them? It's like ordering a new music CD online and never listening to it! Gratitude is a "stop and smell the roses" way to savor the flowers and fruits of our dreams.

Take a few moments to do the following experiment. After you've read the instructions, put down whatever's in your hands, including this book. Now, as you breathe, start to notice a tingling beneath your skin, perhaps in your hands or feet. Kind of tickles, doesn't it? (That's the way my son used to describe it.) That's it. You're home.

So what? Being in the present means that you can't be in regret of the past or fear of the future. Without regret and bitterness, the past has no hold on you. Without anxiety and fear, the future can't concern you.

How do you come back home to the present? There are lots of ways: smell a flower, hold a baby, meditate, make love, climb a mountain. All of these are ways to live fully in the present. You can't climb a mountain while worrying about your job or regretting a past investment.

> *Worry and time have an inverse relationship. The more you have of one, the less you have of the other. Yet curiously, both are suspended when you live in the now.*
>
> **Mike Dooley**

So next time someone asks, "What's new?" you can answer, "Now. Now is always new." In this moment, we can all say, "Never been here, never done this" when we open our eyes and hit "refresh." It's in *this moment* that we can feel our feelings, taste our food, smell the coffee, and look our kids in the eye while they talk to us. In the *now* a whole new world opens up— opens *us*. There's really nothing like it. It's true freedom—and it's *free*.

Why We Don't Practice *Gratitude for the Present*

When you arise in the morning, give thanks for the morning light,
for your life and strength.
Give thanks for your food and the joy of living.
If you see no reason for giving thanks, the fault lies with yourself.

Shawnee Chief Tecumseh

⌒∞⌒

If gratitude is so glorious, why do some people read books like this one, yet never make even one daily *Gratitude* list? The excuses are many. Some people are full of resentment because they haven't practiced *Forgiveness* (High-Way 6); some are afraid of the tears of *Gratitude* that can well up (High-Way 4); some are addicted to busyness and are running *from* (High-Way 2); and others are frozen in jealousy, clueless to their own ability to manifest anything in their lives through asking and believing (High-Way 1). Fortunately, using the High-Ways can take us back home to gratitude's gifts.

We're Waiting for a Wake-Up Call

Those who remember the San Francisco earthquake of 1989 will recall a famous picture of a lone car straddling the edge of the Oakland Bay Bridge, barely hanging on. However, few people realize that the driver of that car was also in the Twin Towers on that fateful day of 9/11.

> *Life's true goodness comes not from what you have, but from how much you value and appreciate it.*
>
> **Ralph Marston**

In interviews, that gentleman noted that he hadn't gotten the first wake-up call, but he *had* gotten the second one, saying, "Now I'm changing my life and am extremely grateful for a second chance."

What's it going to take for the rest of us to finally get grateful? You may have already had a wake-up call in your own life. After speaking with thousands of individuals on this subject, I've found that the three most grateful groups on the planet tend to be:

1. Those who've come close to a loss

2. Those who've *had* a loss

3. Those who know a loss *is coming*

The third category reminds me of my father's transformation after his diagnosis with cancer. Every sunset and bird song became precious to him in those final months. Having witnessed that transformation, I swore that I wasn't going to wait to get grateful. I wanted to, as country singer Tim McGraw so beautifully puts it, "live like I was dying."

What will be *your* catalyst for developing a *Gratitude Attitude*, wisdom or woe?

"I'll Be Grateful When…"

We often believe that we can't get grateful until our present challenge passes, but our greatest teachers have shown us otherwise. One

> *In everything, give thanks.*
>
> **1 Thessalonians 5:18**

of my favorite stories of gratitude amidst adversity is that of Corrie ten Boom. In her book, *The Hiding Place*, Corrie recounts that while in Ravensbruck, a Nazi concentration camp, she and her older sister, Betsy, read to the women from a tiny bible each night.

One night, Betsy read from First Thessalonians and insisted that they thank God for *all* things—even for the lice that infested their living quarters. Corrie resisted at first, but gave it her best. As the story unfolds, the women later discover they had the freedom to pray each night because the Nazi guards hated the lice in their barracks so much that they wouldn't enter for the mandatory nightly beatings.

We Are Consumed with Work

When I ask business groups around the country what they'd like more of from their workplace, one answer tops the list. It's not more money or more time off. What they all long for is more recognition and appreciation. Our spouses and kids might say the same. Someone simply has to start that ball rolling. The result? Happier and more productive co-workers, happier and more peaceful families, and greater happiness, hope, and health for ourselves.

Still, some employers are loathe to start a Gratitude habit at meetings or during annual employee evaluations. Their excuse? "If I did it for one, I'd have to do it for everyone!"

Perhaps we can gently remind them that they have to pay everyone, too. If they didn't, everyone would eventually quit. If you don't find time to appreciate your team, your turnover rate may force you to "turn over" a new leaf.

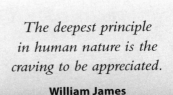

> *The deepest principle in human nature is the craving to be appreciated.*
>
> **William James**

Can We Have Too Much?

Is there such a thing as having too much? To answer that question, let's examine a topic close to many women's hearts—shoes. As the character of Carrie in *Sex and the City* once attested on our TV screens, having your heart set on a certain pair of shoes—and then one day owning them—can be delightful. However, if a scriptwriter had written an episode in which a semi dropped off a truckload of her coveted Manolo Blahnik heels in all colors and styles, what would have happened to her level of enjoyment? It would have dramatically diminished.

If you perceive that your children have become ungrateful, consider going camping, volunteering at a local shelter or food kitchen, or traveling to a third world country on a mission trip. Having some—but not all—of what we want is the human condition, and it's a condition worth giving thanks for.

We're Jealous

One of the weakest excuses for not giving thanks is that others have something we want. I recall sitting at the airport awaiting my plane when a noisy family of four—two parents and two teens—sat across from me. They were noisy in the best sense—gregarious, laughing, poking each other—and almost oblivious to those around them. I watched with fascination and eventually moved to another seat so I could "stare" a little less conspicuously.

I was most impressed with the parents. The man was physically affectionate toward his wife and there was a light in her eyes when she looked at him. As a single person open to romance, I closed my eyes and put myself in her chair, sensing what it would feel like. Rather than being green-eyed, I was grateful-eyed. She helped me *Get the Picture,* and months later I had attracted a wonderful love of my own!

We Fear We'll Lose Control

I recall working with a group of salespeople at a very successful company. Throughout the day-long seminar, many of them shared powerful insights. As the experience neared its end, I sensed a blending of minds and hearts and took a risk. I asked if there was anyone who wanted to express gratitude aloud for their team, their employer, or an individual who had helped them. The room fell silent, but I saw many people look around as they considered speaking up.

Finally, I broke the silence with, "Are you not sharing aloud because you're afraid you'll get emotional?"

"BUSTED!" yelled the largest man in the front row.

The laughter that followed was an indicator that he wasn't the only one concerned about "losing" it in front of his peers. After we regained our composure, I encouraged them to take a few minutes to write a thank-you to someone in the room or on the team. They all did, and a few even took the risk of standing and reading theirs to the group.

If tears are a concern of yours as well, writing a thank-you note to those you love and admire is a gift you'll give them—and yourself.

> *To these bounties, which are so constantly enjoyed that we are prone to forget the source from which they come, others have been added, which are of so extraordinary a nature that they cannot fail to penetrate and soften the heart...*
>
> **Abraham Lincoln**

Surrendering to *Gratitude*

One day I stopped to ask myself why I was so fascinated by the study of gratitude. Knowing that we teach best what we most need to learn, I began to understand that it's because when I surrender to gratitude, it cures what ails me.

I've referred to my propensity for wanting to control things and people. Controllers love to give, but they're uncomfortable receiving. We wear our "I don't need anyone" mindset like armor to keep ourselves from being hurt (again), yet that armor keeps us from letting love and life *in*.

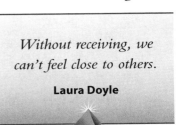

Without receiving, we can't feel close to others.

Laura Doyle

We all need each other. If we weren't receiving the gift of trees cleansing our air right now, we'd all die. Gratitude is the reaffirmation of a childlike state of acceptance that abundance is there for us, not because we've earned it, but as a *free* gift.

The idea of free gifts that we can't earn is more foreign to some people and cultures than others. In China, there's a phrase: "You honor me a foot, I will honor you ten feet in return." It's a common practice, for example, for many Chinese to refuse a gift several times before finally accepting it. Many of us can relate.

Perhaps we feel that receiving puts us in a weaker position. Yet, in receiving gratefully, we become the giver, for receiving and being grateful is one of the greatest gifts we can give another person.

In the miraculous process of conception, a man gives and a woman receives. In her willingness to receive, new life is brought forth. Receiving in gratitude puts us in touch with our receiving feminine side. It reaffirms our interconnectedness. New life is born within us and greater love and peace surround us every time we allow, receive, and give thanks.

We're Afraid We'll Forget

Like putting on a seat belt, gratitude is a habit. At first, especially if your life has been on a downward spiral, it may seem impossible or extremely awkward, but then, putting on deodorant or brushing our teeth felt foreign at first, yet they're habits we're glad we acquired.

If you're leery of starting daily *Gratitudes* for fear of forgetting to do them at some point, let me assure you, you *will* forget somewhere along the line. You may even forget for weeks or months at a time.

> *Thanksgiving pivots on our willingness to go beyond our independence and to accept the give-and-take between giver and thanksgiver. The "yes" which acknowledges our interdependence is the very "yes" to belonging, the "yes" of love.*
>
> **Brother David Steindl Rast**

But as mentioned in the first chapter, if you choose to, you can **FGH: F**orgive yourself for forgetting, be **G**rateful you remembered, and have **H**ope that you'll remember better next time. It will get easier and easier to remember. Trust me.

We Fear We'll Run Out

Another reason we stop doing *Gratitudes* is that we get bored. That's why the **8 to Great** daily ritual says "no repeats." It makes *Gratitude-ing* a lot more interesting and fun. We have to move from *who* or *what* we're grateful for to *what about* someone we're grateful for.

With a bit of brainstorming, we'll discover that we'll never run out. I have a list of "101 Ways to Open and Close a Meeting so People Will Stay Open and Close." They're all the things a meeting facilitator can use as a gratitude sharing focus to open or close meetings. Here are a few examples of Gratitude "themes:"

- ✔ *The physical environment of your workplace*
- ✔ *The person to your left*
- ✔ *Your loyal customers*
- ✔ *The gifts you bring to the workplace*

Freedom from Behind Bars

I once spoke at the largest women's prison in our state. As I was waiting to go on stage, the warden came up behind me and startled me with her demands.

"Two things we need to go over, MK."

She had my attention.

"First, no touching. I see that you touch people a lot. No reaching out with your hands and no hugging. You may not touch them in any way."

"How do they get touched?"

"They don't."

(I called half a dozen massage therapists after that event and they all volunteered their services, but none of them were allowed on the grounds.)

"The second thing is, I don't want you talking about gratitude. These women have nothing to be grateful for, so I don't want—"

I turned away and walked on stage.

"Good morning!" I shouted and was greeted by an exuberant reply.

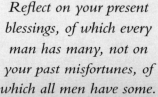

Reflect on your present blessings, of which every man has many, not on your past misfortunes, of which all men have some.

Charles Dickens

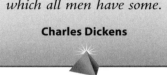

"My name is MK Mueller and they call me the Gratitude Guru. There are probably people in the world who think you have nothing to be grateful for, but of course we know better. Raise your hands right now and tell me some of the things you're grateful for."

Instantly, there were dozens of hands in the air, but a beautiful young woman in her mid-twenties had hers up fastest, so I asked her to share first. She began to tear up. We waited.

"The dew on the grass…looks like diamonds in the sunlight," she finally managed to say.

After a short silence of our appreciation, I asked how she had noticed such a glorious gift.

"I just got out of solitary."

I received one of the longest standing ovations of my career and more *thank-you notes* from that presentation than from any before or since. Those notes meant even more to me knowing the sacrifice the prisoners had made to use money they could have spent on cigarettes or candy to purchase writing paper, an envelope, and a stamp.

Gratitude for the Present Success Stories

To speak gratitude is courteous and pleasant,
to enact gratitude is generous and noble,
but to live gratitude is to touch Heaven.

Johannes A. Gaertner

⌗

As we travel the High-Ways of life, every so often we encounter individuals who live their values purely and simply. I'm privileged to call one such gentleman my brother-in-law, Colonel Bruce Hurd. The following is a reply to a letter I wrote him shortly after he finished command of a unit at Robins Air Force Base in Georgia.

The Air Force Colonel's Story

Dear MK,

Thank you for your request to share what I've found to be helpful in setting the tone for good, positive, productive meetings. While many of the things I'll mention are not original ideas, I will take credit for having the good sense to "pick and choose" those ideas and techniques that appealed to me after twenty-three years as an Air Force officer.

1) I started off each meeting by asking the unit chaplain to conduct an opening prayer. I believe this set a good tone and helped us focus on appropriate priorities.

2) My first order of business was recognizing top performers throughout the unit by presenting them with the "group commander's coin." The commander's coin was something I had specially made for the unit. The only way anyone could get one was to do something, in or out of their job, very well. For example, if someone was recognized by an outside agency as being a top performer, I gave them a coin. If a crew flew a particularly impressive mission, I gave them a coin. I believe it helped set the stage for an enjoyable, upbeat meeting and served to remind everyone present what outstanding people we have.

3) The next thing I did weekly was recognize an enlisted person (usually a junior member) as "enlisted face of the week." He/she would come to our meeting and his/her commander would introduce them and tell the assembled staff about them. This not only gave the member a chance to be front and center in a positive light, but it also served to bring them to their squadron commander's attention.

4) After asking everyone present if they had anything to add/announce at the close of a meeting, I would then announce any promotions and/or awards individuals or units had won since the previous week.

5) The last thing I would address was how much I appreciated the great work everyone was doing—particularly the leaders and supervisors who were typically present at the meeting. This would end the meeting on a positive note and send people off feeling good about themselves and seeking out award winners to congratulate them.

The things I mentioned above probably took 5–10 minutes out of our formal weekly staff meeting, but I believe it was time well spent. While typically the "kick butt" method of leading will get results in the short term, I've seen how it is very detrimental to the long term health and well-being of the unit and its members.

Appreciation Results in Appreciation

At Bruce's official going away party after his time in Georgia, he shared with me that he felt a bit overwhelmed by all the mementos and kind words. However, perhaps the greatest gift he received was seeing that the Gratitude Attitude he had lived had been picked up by his squadron. That was made clear by the final party game they played—one they named BH Bingo.

Here, again in Bruce's words, is a description of that tribute:

It revolved around a bingo sheet filled with common sayings I used every day. When I got up to talk that night, they all pulled out the bingo sheets from under their placemats. The idea was to "X out" a spot on the sheet when I would use the saying written in that block. Looking back at the sheet, I noticed that every one of the sayings was something positive, like "thank you," "thank you very much," "phenomenal," "outstanding," "great," "very great," etc. It was funny, because I really did use all of those phrases a lot.

At the end of the evening, one of my outstanding squadron commanders closed his remarks by saying, "Colonel Hurd is living proof that nice guys finish first!"

I couldn't think of a better compliment from an officer that I respect very much. My heart was and is very full.

The Assignment

One day I was picking up papers off the dinner table when I found an open notebook of my daughter's. She was a junior in high school at the time and her English teacher had asked each student to write a short note to the other students in the class.

Most of the notes began, "Hey, Jo, Whaz Up?" and ended soon after that with, "Have a great year." However, there was one note from a classmate named Pearl that stood out from the rest. It began: *Joanna, You are a beautiful ray of sunshine that lights up the lives of everyone you meet.*

I started to tear up as I read the words that were so true of my daughter. Pearl went on to say: *The world is lucky to have you around. The universe is more balanced due to your greatness. Today is sunny and beautiful just for you. You should go outside and play in the world that has been created for you. Bask in the warmth of the sun. Lay in the grass and smile. Today is yours.*

Pearl had the incredible gift of seeing the magnificence, the heroism, and the perfection within each of us. I was unfathomably grateful for her loving note to my wonderful daughter, as well as for the exceptional teacher who was aware of the power of gratitude and willing to make time for it in her classes.

Surviving the Test of Teens

The following year my daughter stopped talking to me. One day it just happened. There were no fights, as well as no more "thank you's" and no more "I love you's." I saw a lot of the back of her head and heard a lot of slammed doors. I didn't want to take it personally, so I turned to the High-Ways for answers. That led to the day I sat down and wrote her a letter.

> *If you ever want to mess your parents up, go up to them, put your arms around them, say "thank you" and walk away.*
>
> **Chris Gardner**

Dear Joanna,

I wanted to write and tell you just how much I love you and how proud I am of the young woman you're becoming. Even your questioning me is a powerful part of your finding your own way."

It went on for about a page. No mention of the arguments. I just focused on all the things I loved about her. Then I folded it, put it in an envelope, and stuck it on her pillow.

I was truly surprised the next day that I got one back. I read (through my tears) not one, but three pages of how much she loved me and how glad she was that I was her mom. I made twenty copies and stuck them in every drawer in my bedroom so I couldn't forget the grateful spirit who lived inside her body!

What Goes Around...

Salina, Kansas, pediatrician Ginger Senseman got a golden seat during a historical moment because she wrote a thank-you note. When this wife and mother found out she had breast cancer in October 2008, she and her husband canceled a family trip to Hawaii so she could begin weekly chemotherapy treatments. Their sons William (ten) and Sam (seven) were especially disappointed.

Her cancer treatment was well underway in November when her boys' favorite presidential candidate got elected. To help salve the pain of the missed vacation, Ginger decided to risk contacting her senators about getting tickets to Washington for the inauguration of Barack Obama.

Both senators responded and she received five tickets in the blue section and five in the silver section. In addition to her immediate family, she was able to offer tickets to a sister and brother and to the physician who had been commuting to Salina to help keep her practice going during her chemotherapy.

She waited in line for more than an hour to pick up her inauguration tickets at Senator Brownback's office. When it was finally her turn, she handed his staff a handwritten thank-you note. As she was leaving, the senator's chief of staff chased her down the stairs.

"Ginger, Ginger, wait!" he yelled. Once he caught up with her, he said, "Mrs. Brownback can't make it. Do you want her ticket? It's in the gold section."

"Of course, I want her ticket!" she said as she hugged him.

At five a.m. on inauguration day, her phone rang and she was told to go to Brownback's office. While her family and friends faced the challenges of an overwhelmed public transportation system and hours in the cold, Ginger drank coffee in Brownback's office for two hours and "called everybody she could think of."

While there, she asked the staff how she'd had the good fortune to be selected to receive Mrs. Brownback's ticket. A secretary told her the staff had been handing out tickets for two days to people who were often ungrateful and demanding. When she came in with her handwritten thank-you note, the staff quickly voted that she should be the one to receive the ticket that would put her fifty feet away from the swearing in of the country's first African-American president.

> *Nothing new can come into your life unless you open yourself up to being grateful for what you already have.*
>
> **Reverend Michael Beckwith**

The Best or Worst of Times?

Ginger was diagnosed with cancer, yet she lived in gratitude. No matter where I travel, I hear from individuals who believe that their problems are preventing them from being grateful. I don't argue with them, but I tell stories like Ginger's and then I offer a formula that I've fondly named *ADAM*:

A—*Adversity* is the challenge. It's the wall we run into on this bumper-car-ride of life. We always have a choice to bounce off the wall and curse or turn our car around and keep driving.

D—*Desire* is what results from such a bump-and-pivot. We can use it to briefly get very clear and passionate about what we don't want, then about what we do.

A—*Acceptance* is our next step. We forgive the bump, grateful for its resulting desire, and then come into joyful expectation of where it will all lead us.

M—*Manifestation* automatically results—a bigger and more blessed outcome than we ever could have received *had we not encountered the Adversity!*

ADAM is the reason that you rarely meet a motivational speaker who doesn't have a horrific story of overcoming a challenge. While an event that lands you flat on your back isn't required for insight, it's definitely easier to see the stars from there.

Putting *Gratitude for the Present* into Practice

When you feel grateful, you become great and
eventually attract great things.

Plato

⁓

Her name was Dana. She walked up to me after a talk at a child care conference years ago and said, "I love your idea of a *Gratitude Partner*, but I live in a small town. I'm not sure where I'd find—"

"E-mail me," I offered. "Every day—three to five *Gratitudes*. I'll write you back with mine when I can."

Her middle name must have been Faithful. For the next seven years, I was the grateful recipient of the most delightful *Gratitude* lists in my in-box, such as:

I am grateful...

for the ability to yawn.

for the sound of my husband's car in the driveway when he gets home.

for my bangs.

for being able to teach my girls how to follow a recipe.

for buttons.

Your friend,
Dana

Through the years, Dana shared that her daily *Gratitudes* improved her health, her daycare business, and her marriage. I know they also brightened *my* life immeasurably.

You can't feel blessed and stressed at the same time.

Anonymous

The *Gratitude* Rich-ual

So here is your daily homework: Three *Gratitudes* per day, no repeats, for the rest of your life (but only on the days you want to feel really good). Dana wrote five Gratitudes each morning, and you can work up to five if you'd like—but as always, no repeats.

What can you be grateful for? Anything you'd miss if you didn't have it. Why not make writing down *Gratitudes* the one thing that you do *every morning* before your first coffee? Because when you feel good, good things happen. It's that simple.

If after reading this chapter you're still not completely convinced, do the math:

Question: What have you got to lose?

Answer: Two minutes per twenty-four-hour period.

Question: What have you got to gain?

Answer: Manifesting every dream and desire for the rest of your time on the planet.

I know—it's a tough decision.

I recall a gentleman at one of my seminars remarking, "I can't wait to use *Gratitude* when I get home." We all had a good laugh as he realized what he'd just said. Gratitude can only help us be happy *now*. Living in the moment makes you more grateful. Becoming grateful helps you live in the moment. Gratitude makes every moment a very "right" now.

> *If you're feeling off balance or like your heart is broken, I guarantee you that keeping a gratitude journal will change your life. I absolutely guarantee it.*
>
> **Oprah Winfrey**

When to Say Thank You

The three most important times to say thank you are before, during, and after *everything!*

Before: As everything in *8 to Great* attests, getting to a grateful place for something *before you receive* it is the fastest way to manifest that very thing.

During: Anyone who has ever cooked a meal knows the wonderful feeling a simple thanks from someone in the midst of enjoying it can bring. One of my favorite vacation memories was when Zach turned to me and said, "Mom, if I forget later, thanks for this fun time!"

After: As a choir director, I'm grateful for the computer keyboard at my fingertips each week after our service. Most weeks I send out a quick e-mail that says something like, "Awesome work on that new song!" I've had members who've had to leave the choir remark on how much those notes meant to them.

Thirty Days to the *Gratitude Habit*

Like any other wellness activity, gratitude is a habit. Most of us are more in the habit of complaining and finding fault than we are of affirming, but that can change in a matter of weeks.

Give yourself this goal—thirty days to the *Gratitude Habit*. Here are some fun ways get your habit happening. Pick the one that feels like the best fit for your life.

1. Make a *Gratitude Calendar* with big open spaces for the days and write your *Gratitudes* each day. Hanging it where family members can see it is an extra treat for them.

2. Find a *Gratitude Partner* to phone or e-mail with your three *Gratitudes* each morning (five days a week) or ask your spouse to share *Gratitudes* with you each morning or evening.

3. Purchase my *Gratitools* CD and use one of the forty-plus ideas each week or purchase the **8 to Great** *Gratitude* handbook with lesson plans for forty activities. Visit www.8togreat.com.

4. Start a *Gratitude Group* once a week for eight weeks.

I heard from a Mom who wanted to impart the importance of gratitude to her ten-year-old daughter. They started by sharing their *Gratitudes* at dinner each evening. Two weeks into the process, she sent me this e-mail:

"MK, I wanted to let you know that when we were stuck in traffic for a long time last night, Amanda turned to me and said, 'Mom, let's do *Gratitudes*,' and we did! I'm overjoyed knowing that she now knows she can take charge of her attitude, no matter what the situation."

Gratitude **Comes Home**

As you're practicing your *Gratitudes*, make sure you put *yourself* on the list of things you're grateful for at least once a week and watch to make sure those closest to you make your list as well. Just as when you dream, it's good to dream for small, medium, and large things to manifest, so as you practice gratitude, it's good to have "Me, You, and Them" all covered.

Gratitude for Me is just what it says— finding things about yourself to be grateful for. It could be something like "I stayed calm while the baby was crying today" or "I'm really good at recruiting new folks into the Optimists."

> *You say grace before meals. But I say grace before the concert and the opera, and grace before the play and pantomime, and grace before I open a book, and grace before sketching, painting, swimming, fencing, boxing, walking, playing, dancing, and grace before I dip the pen in the ink.*
>
> **G.K. Chesterton**

The Cyrano Solution

Just as we can be a bit uncomfortable sharing gratitudes with others at first, it can bring a blush to admit what we appreciate and cherish about ourselves. I wouldn't include the following letter I wrote to myself—one of the hardest parts of this book for me to share—if I weren't absolutely convinced of its power to heal brokenness and prepare us to be loved by others.

Dear MK,

Please let me introduce myself. I've been a fan of yours for a long time. I'm not yet ready to tell you my name, but I can tell you that I'm very interested in getting to know you better.

You see, I've been watching you for years. I've seen how you came into our parish, manifested an incredible choir for more than a decade, and then gracefully turned it over when it was your time to go. I've also watched you raise two fantastic children under sometimes less than ideal circumstances, loving them no matter what they did or didn't do.

I've seen you fend off naysayers and accomplish dreams like the TV segment, the radio show, the KidSing Competition, and the Gratitude Gathering. Now look at this wonderful new book. You're amazing. Thank you for all you do for so many.

MK, I know this is a bit odd, writing you like this, but I'm not quite ready to reveal my identity. Think of me as one of your favorite literary heroes (I know this about you, too), your Cyrano, who will admire you from afar for just a bit longer. Believe me, I don't intend to stay incognito as long as he did with the fair Rosalyn.

And speaking of fair, you looked so beautiful today. I love those patchwork overalls of yours. You have such a distinctive style! I hope you'll allow me to write you again. It would give me such pleasure.

Sleep well, dearest one,

Cyrano

Take a risk and find out how wonderful it feels to have your own "inner-Cyrano." Write yourself a love letter. I promise I won't tell!

> *Appreciation of self and others are the closest match to Divine energy in the universe.*
>
> **Abraham-Hicks**

Gratitude and the Cynic

After reading the research, few people will doubt the power of gratitude for inner-transformation, but there are those who still doubt their own ability to find three blessings in their lives each day. When in doubt, write down things like, "This pen works," or "I remembered to do this," or "I woke up on time." Like putting on your shoes to go to the gym usually assures that you'll get there, so putting a small notepad and pen next to your bed or inviting your spouse or child to share daily *Gratitudes* with you will be enough to start this blissful ball rolling.

Some families put *Gratitudes* in an empty tissue box and take them out each Sunday night at their family meetings to read them. (For beautiful tissue box covers, go to www.growthegratitude.com.) Over the years, I've realized that there's effort involved in expressing appreciation. Using phrases such as "You know something I appreciate about you?" has to be our clear and strong intention.

Gratitude Games

Once you find out how good gratitude feels, you may decide to invent games to encourage it. Over the years I've created dozens of Gratitude games for the home, office, and classroom. For a complete list, see my *8 to Great Handbooks: High-Way 7—Gratitude for the Present,* which is offered on my website, www.mkmueller.com.

The Gratitude Drill is a huge favorite in *8 to Great* school classrooms and one that students repeatedly request. The facilitator first asks five or six volunteers to come forward and stand in a loose circle. Then, beginning with the person with the longest hair, each individual must come up with something they're grateful for in less than 2 ½ seconds or they'll be "gonged" (or honked) back to their seat.

The only other rule? No repeats. If the person to your right says "family," you may say "brother" or "Mom," but you may not say the word "family" or you'll be ousted from the circle. All participants can receive a prize for taking the risk of volunteering, but even if you choose to give a prize to those still standing after three minutes, be sure to have lots of prizes. Teenagers are especially hard to get down in this game.

Another favorite of mine is *Oh, Look.* Pretend something that you've taken for granted wasn't working yesterday but *is* working today. Pick something that hasn't been broken, pretend it was, then get excited about it working again. For example, you could say, "Oh, look! The windshield wipers are working!" or "Oh, look! A postal worker is leaving mail in our mailbox now!" or one of my favorites, "Oh, look! The sun is rising again!" It may be silly, but it's lots of fun!

> *Be grateful for what you have; you'll end up having more. If you concentrate on what you don't have, you will never, ever have enough.*
>
> **Oprah Winfrey**

One of the first times we played this, my son was twelve.

"Oh, look!" I shouted. "You can hear again, Zach!"

To which the smart aleck replied, "What'd you say?"

Q & A on *Gratitude for the Present*

Gratitude is not only the greatest of virtues,
but the parent of all the others.
Cicero

⌒∞⌐

Q: *I've gone back to work and am very grateful for my kids and husband making the necessary sacrifices to make it all work. How can I let them know how grateful I am and be there for them during the time we have together?*

A: In his wonderful book *The Five Languages of Love*, Gary Smalley points out that everyone speaks their own language when it comes to love and appreciation. Find out by asking your family members if they feel appreciated most by your words, your quality time, your acts of service, your touch, or your gifts. They'll appreciate being asked. Then you can "speak" your appreciation to them in a way they'll clearly hear!

Q: *How do I get my children to write thank-you notes?*

A: I have two children who are very different in this regard. Although both were raised hearing regularly about the importance of gratitude, they each have their own way of expressing it. My daughter is excellent at writing a thoughtful card or an e-mail after an event or receiving a gift, but you won't hear many thanks from her verbally.

> *We can complain that roses have thorns or be grateful that thorns have roses.*
>
> **Anonymous**

On the other hand, my son says "thanks, Mom" an average of ten times a day, yet getting him to write a thank-you note is like pulling teeth.

I've learned to encourage him to make a phone call to people he is grateful to, and that seems to work out just fine.

If your children are young, you might have them draw a picture with the words "Thank You" and send it to the person who gifted them. Meanwhile, no matter their age, write them (and your spouse) thank-you notes. Their appreciation of your taking time to do that will remind them that they can help others feel that good as well.

Q: *Where I work, our clients regularly call to complain. How are we supposed to deal with such unappreciative clients?*

A: Right now, they're ungrateful for you and you're ungrateful for them. When you're ready to see real change, get into **FGH**. First, clean the slate and show appreciation for the things your customers do right. Then start every day with your three *Gratitudes* list. For example:

I'm grateful:
1. that my phone/e-mail works.
2. that I've trained my clients to expect only the best from me.
3. that I'm learning not to let other people own my attitude.

One gentleman in a class recently added this one to his list: "I'm grateful I'm learning this now, in time to teach it to my children."

> *If you count all your assets you'll always show a profit.*
>
> **Robert Quillen**

Q: *It seems that very young children don't need to be taught gratitude. At what age do you suggest starting gratitude activities?*

A: It can be seamless. As your children hear you do your daily *Gratitudes* aloud (every time you get in a car, for example) it will be a game they love to play and will rarely tire of! I agree that we don't need to "demand" gratitude from young children; we simply need to allow and encourage it. You could even play a game of counting how many times family members say "thank you" and then raise the goal a bit each month to raise awareness. Keep it fun!

One young mother sent me this story of her four-year-old:

Noah is just getting to the point where I'll let him play outside alone. The other day—one of those beautiful blue-sky Indian summer days we've had—I peeked out the window to check on him. He was under the biggest tree in our yard. He had his arms stretched out, head thrown back, and he was singing and dancing. I could just make out the words—he was making up a song to the sky. I watched, wishing I had a camera and knowing that if I interrupted him, the moment would be gone. When he finished, I opened the door and asked what he was doing.

"I'm singing to the sky."

"How does that song go, Sweetheart?"

"It's over."

Let us be like little children and embrace this moment with gratitude, before it's gone.

> *Life is not measured by the number of breaths we take,*
> *but by the moments that take our breath away.*
> **Anonymous**

High-Way 8:
FGH: Hope for the Future
The Power of Surrender

❦

Defining *Hope for the Future*

Don't worry about the world coming to an end today...
It's already tomorrow in Australia.

Charles Schultz

◦◎◦

When I first started teaching the High-Ways, I defined *Hope for the Future* using the last two letters of the word hope: P and E—Positive Expectation. However, it soon became clear that there was more, because that definition was so close to High-Way 1, and *Get the Picture* is not the antidote to despair that *Hope* is. I continued to be open to discovering the distinction between High-Ways 1 and 8, but eventually released my search, certain that I'd know when I *knew*.

Then one day it became evident. A couple of big projects hadn't gone as I'd expected and I was frantically trying to run around and "fix" things. I started to feel myself freeze up with fear. I could still do one hundred *Gratitudes* at a sitting because I had my children, friends, family, faith, health, and the 8 High-Ways process. I was still taking risks, staying out of blaming and complaining, and feeling all my feelings, yet I could sense myself losing hope.

What amazed me during that time was that none of the High-Way 1 visualization exercises helped me feel better. I didn't *want* to dream bigger. I was spent.

Meanwhile, I had many well-meaning friends telling me what to do. Their "shoulds" only added to the din of my own. What I

> *To-do list for today:*
> *Inhale. Exhale.*
>
> **As seen on college dorm
> bulletin board**

needed wasn't advice—I needed *Hope*. One day, it came to me, sweetly, during a morning phone conversation.

"You'll be successful, sweetie. Look, you've done everything right so far. Your project will be a huge success." Even as I write this, tears come to my eyes as I remember the relief I felt from my friend's reassuring words. She knew everything about me—my past victories and my recent challenges. Her words helped lift the cloud of self-judgment I'd been living under. Every time I repeated them to myself, I could breathe deeper.

Clarity rose in me like the sun that day. I began to understand that *Get the Picture* and *Hope for the Future* both required Positive Expectation, but that *Hope for the Future* included an aspect that only BIG (Bold, Innovative, and Grand) dreamers needed. The closest word I've found to describe it is *surrender*—releasing attachment to the outcome.

BIG Dreamers

Every hero, ancient or modern, could tell you of their journey through their dark nights.

We must accept finite disappointment,
but we must never lose infinite hope.
Dr. Martin Luther King, Jr.

In the midst of winter,
I finally learned that there was in me an invincible summer.
Albert Camus

We've been warned against offering the people of this nation false hope.
But in the unlikely story that is America,
there has never been anything false about hope.
Barack Obama

I've learned from studying great men and women that goal setters don't need hope because they have a roadmap of when, where, and how. Only BIG dreamers who find themselves wandering in the desert looking for the Promised Land need it to fend off despair.

In this High-Way, we won't discuss ways to handle depression or the blues; we did that in High-Way 4: *Feel All Your Feelings*. Depression is of the mind and heart. Despair is of the spirit and soul.

Despair only happens on the way to our biggest dreams when our Positive Expectation starts to wane. When we ask, "Will it ever come?" or cry out in self-judgment, "What am I doing wrong?" we haven't done anything wrong, in fact, we're right where we need to be.

Hope for the Future and *Get the Picture*

To understand the two High-Ways better:

High-Way 1: *Get the Picture* is closer to…

Positive Expectation—feeling the excitement of the final outcome.

Confidence—the assurance that the Laws of the Universe work every time.

Visualization—imagining the end result.

Imagining—pretending that what we ask for has already arrived.

High-Way 8: *Hope for the Future i*s closer to…

Trust—the faith that there is an answer, even if it's not obvious at the moment.

Surrender—yielding to the guidance of a person, higher power or process.

Openness—relaxing into the now and allowing whatever shows up.

Time-Out—taking a break from *doing* to regroup and refresh.

> *If you want to have radical results, you must begin by displaying one the greatest human attributes—the ability to be humble enough to let go of the reins and hand them over…*
>
> **Debbie Ford**

Letting Your Dream Find You

When all my visualizing wasn't feeling good, it was because my Positive Expectations were trying to survive amid my "struggle" mentality. I needed to relax and open up to allowing new possibilities. When the process of following a dream feels painful and we're looking too hard for answers, we simply need to stop and let our answers find us.

The *Hope for the Future* Process:
Positive Expectation and Surrender of Struggle

When hope is all you have, it's all you need.
Anonymous

In order to move into *Hope for the Future* we have to open our-selves to possibilities. To illustrate this process, connect your index finger and thumb to make an "O" with one of your hands. Now imagine asking to receive a watermelon. The catch is that whatever you request, in this case, the watermelon, has to pass through that "O" to get to you. Obviously, it's not going to happen because you're not open enough for it.

Now make a new "O," this time by stretching both arms in front of you and interlacing your fingers. (This opening should be about the size of a basketball hoop.) What would happen if you asked for that watermelon now? It would slip into your life with ease. This is the gift that *Hope for the Future* offers. To become BIG dreamers, we have to expand our *allowing* and be open enough and patient enough to let our magnificent dreams come through.

High-Way 1: *Get the Picture*—Asking and Believing

To review, *Get the Picture* is about learn-ing to believe—thinking a thought until we can feel what its reality will be like. It's an *active* step that asks that we take time to vi-sualize and have fun imagining our dream's manifestation.

I recall the day I announced to my office team at our annual meeting that I'd love to host a weekly call-in radio show. We talked about it for five minutes and I was even more excited when we finished. Once we broke

*Surrender isn't passive.
It is the most active,
assertive, creative,
intelligent response
we can make to any
moment.*

Dan Millman

for lunch, I checked my voice messages. The largest radio station in the state had left me a message, asking if I wanted to host a weekly call-in show. I asked, I believed, and I quickly received. That's the power of *Get the Picture.*

High-Way 8: *Hope for the Future*—Asking and Letting Go

When our biggest dreams don't manifest when we expect them to, we can start to get frustrated. Before we get too close to despair, we must move into *Hope for the Future*, letting go of our need to control and our attachment to the outcome. *Hope for the Future* is when we free our dreams, like the release of a balloon, and find ourselves freed, as well.

The glorious "aha" of this process is that we are not surrendering *what* we want or *why* we want it. We are, however, letting go of the *how, when, where,* or *who.* The day we release and let go is the day we sleep better, laugh harder, and live more fully in the moment.

Going Along for the Ride

Once you move into *Hope for the Future*, it means you're letting something bigger than you, such as God, your counselor, or the law of attraction do the driving. Once you've set your intention (decided on a "what"), you take your focus *off* of your dream, let go of the steering wheel, and from a position in the passenger seat, get grateful for the scenery out your window.

Everyone has heard of the couple who "tried everything" to get pregnant, then finally decided to adopt, only to be surprised with a pregnancy shortly thereafter. The same universal law applies here. When you can't focus on a dream without stressing, *stop* focusing on it altogether, go along for the ride, and get into feelings of appreciation.

Surrender Samples

Surrender can take many forms. Four I've used and seen others use successfully are:

1. Stop and refocus
2. Trust a person or a process
3. Get playful
4. Get quiet

1. Stop and Refocus

I've learned the hard way that when I've done "all I can" and the end is still not in sight, I need to *stop* doing. Trying "one more thing" may result in my burning out or getting sick. Once you've come to the point of surrendering your dreams, refocus your efforts in another direction or, as the TV character Tony Soprano was known to say, "Forget about it."

There's a perfect example of this surprising road to success in a recent chapter in American history.

At the age of forty, a politician reflected, "I began feeling the way I imagine an actor or athlete must feel when, after years of commitment to a particular dream, he realizes that he's gone just about as far as talent or fortune would take him. The dream will not happen, and he now faces the choice of accepting this fact...or refusing the truth and ending up bitter.

"I refocused on my work. I spent more time at home and properly cherished my wife, exercised, and read novels. It was this acceptance, I think, that allowed me to come up with the thoroughly cockeyed idea of running for the United States Senate. One last shot to test out my ideas before I settled into a calmer, more stable existence."

After releasing attachment to the "where" "when" and "how" of his dream, it was revived. Still, he held press conferences that no one attended and drove for hours to small towns to find only two or three people waiting for him around a kitchen table. But he was not deterred. He had asked, believed, and let go. Through a series of seemingly unrelated events, he won his senate seat that year, but that wasn't the end of the story. The dream of political success came back to find Barack Obama.

> *The creative process is a process of surrender, not control.*
>
> **Julia Cameron**

2. Trust a Person or a Process

Another way to surrender the outcome is to trust a coach. Over the years I've seen half a dozen friends surrender to their AA sponsors. Sometimes their sponsors said, "Don't date him, you're not ready" or "Take that job for now." My friends' willingness to turn over the reins to another person during the first years of their recovery has been a source of inspiration to me.

My very first life coach began our initial session with, "Are you willing to be coached?" I knew my answer would commit me to her guidance. I also knew that resistance would come up at some pivotal point and I'd have to decide to surrender to her wisdom or withdraw. Knowing all that, as soon as I said *yes*, I relaxed. I felt safe and at peace. That is the gift of trust.

Just as we can let someone lead us to a new place, so faith in a process can help us lighten up and settle down. Even while we're thinking to ourselves "this will never work," following the process is in itself surrender.

> *Sometimes it's holding on that makes one strong; sometimes it's letting go.*
>
> **Sylvia Robinson**

Just as all diets work when we stick to them, surrendering to any process, whether it's for making more money, finding your soul mate, or getting back in shape opens us to allowing because we stop second-guessing ourselves. Faith in your sponsor/coach/trainer/doctor/program becomes *as important as the advice you receive* to your ultimate success. Giving up is losing *Hope* and doesn't feel good. Giving over is finding *Hope* and once we surrender to it, it feels wonderful.

My Cowboy Coach

Although depression has never visited me for long, I've had to face despair more than once. I vividly recall being so frustrated one afternoon that I threw down an issue of Oprah's magazine, thinking the last thing I needed was advice! It fell open to an article about Miraval Resort in Tucson and a man named Wyatt Webb. The article explained how he helped people by teaching them to work with horses. The idea fascinated me, and the next day I signed up to go.

That first morning at Miraval, Wyatt allowed each of us to choose a horse to work with.

"Just remember," he drawled in a throaty voice that revealed decades of hard living, "whatever challenges come up, and there's always challenges, it's not about the horse."

During my stay, I worked with Wyatt three times. I cleaned hooves next to Hollywood film producers, dancers from the New York City Ballet, butchers, secretaries, and even veterinarians. The faces changed, but each morning I saw how we all had to learn to trust our coach and be in the moment. If we didn't, we couldn't get our 1,200-pound animals to acknowledge us, let alone give up their hooves for cleaning.

The lessons that came up were unique to each individual. For one man who couldn't seem to get the horse to lift its hoof, it meant admitting he was afraid of those "bigger" than he was. As soon as he faced his fear, the horse cooperated.

For the ballerina, it meant acknowledging her fear that she'd "get the steps (of cleaning the hooves) wrong" and look like a fool. Again, the horse applauded her courage of coming clean by allowing her to clean his hooves.

For me, it was admitting that a part of me wanted the horse to like me and that I didn't want to upset him or make him uncomfortable. As soon as I figured that out, I liked *myself* better and was able to get the job done.

Our biggest challenge wasn't our animals—it was surrendering to Wyatt's coaching. Once we trusted him with our safety and psyches, insight and renewed hope were our rewards.

> *Anyone who really wants to know who they are has to travel to uncharted territories all the time. So that kind of person has to live in a world of "I don't know," which is scary, but that's the only place you learn anything.*
>
> **Wyatt Webb**

One of my favorite stories from Wyatt's first book, *It's Not About the Horse*, was of an angry young man who hated his horse—just like he hated his life. He tried for half an hour to get the horse to budge in the corral that day and finally gave up, walked away, and began to weep. At that point, the horse walked up behind him and nuzzled his neck.

3. Get Playful

Hope relaxes us into an "I've got nothing to lose by asking" mentality. Here again, even when we don't believe, as long as we don't NOT believe, we're still open to receiving.

> *The difference between an optimist and a pessimist is that an optimist laughs to forget, but a pessimist forgets to laugh.*
>
> **Tom Bodett**

Sometimes when my friends and I get playful, we put our dreams in an imaginary pink bubble, blow them out the window, and then forget about them. Sometimes we write them down in front of a roaring fire and then release them into the blaze. When the pleasure of dreaming our dreams is fun for us, it's amazing how quickly these dreams manifest.

Just as thoughts become things, *stress becomes strings*. Thinking your thoughts with no strings attached (expectations) is a glorious way to watch your *fun* become your *future*.

4. Get Quiet

Another powerful form of surrender is getting quiet—stop giving, talking, and doing—and just be still and receive. We think of "being still" as stopping movement of our physical body, but that's just the beginning. A more challenging and rewarding stillness is when we stop our mental runnings-around. We do this, not by trying *not* to think, but by focusing on something so relaxing or boring to the brain that it just rests. That focus could be on our breath, a candle flame, a mantra, or the decades of a rosary.

More and more studies are showing that when we're in a meditative state, we stop aging, our immune functions increase, our pulse slows down, and our mind gets a much-needed rest. That's on the physical plane. On the spiritual plane, we're like a cork on a beautiful ocean of love and bliss. We naturally float to the top. Check out the look in a newborn baby's eyes. We were born blissing.

> *Most people think that aging is irreversible, yet we know that there are mechanisms in the human machinery that allow for the reversal of aging through exercise, yoga, breathing techniques, and meditation.*
>
> **Deepak Chopra**

Giving Up vs. Giving Over

Remember the story of Abraham and Sarah in the Old Testament? They were so old they had given up on having kids, yet they stayed in *Hope*, and as the story goes, at the age of ninety, Sarah conceived and bore a son named Isaac.

Now let's fast forward.

Isaac is a strapping young boy. Then one day in a dream, Abraham is told that he's to sacrifice his only son to God. With the heaviest of hearts, father and son head up the mountain and once they reach the top, Abraham prepares an altar upon which to sacrifice his beloved child. Then, just at the moment when Abraham lifts the knife, an angel reaches out and stops his hand.

Father and son rejoice and they head back down the mountain with no harm done (other than the fact that Isaac most likely developed a phobia about big knives).

What does that story have to do with you? You have a dream—a big one—so big, in fact, that you don't tell most people about it because you don't want to take any teasing. Then one day you get a *piece* of your dream and start thinking, "This is *so* cool. Now I can do this and that and have these and those and—"

Then suddenly, your dream seems to be taken away from you—and it looks as if it's the end of the road. At that moment, you have

> *I know the plans I have for you. Plans of fullness, not of harm, to give you a future and a hope.*
>
> **Jeremiah 29:11**

two options—give up or give over. When you do the latter, you release your need to have something in order to be happy and find peace.

Once you release bitterness about not receiving the original dream, that is often when it's given back to you tenfold, or in Abraham's case, through generations of ancestors "as numerous as the stars."

Surrender vs. Submission

Submission is the act of giving up and often results in tears of sorrow. Surrender is the act of giving over and often results in tears of relief.

While growing up, I often struggled more than I surrendered. As a young adult, I was obsessed with "figuring out" what God's will was so I could follow it. At the age of twenty-four, that search led me to the door of a convent. It seemed the only place I hadn't tried to find the peace I was looking for. When a friend, a Presentation sister, opened the door and found out why I was there, she couldn't stop laughing, saying, I was "not nun material." (Those who know me well would add, "Can you blame her?")

I was looking hard for answers rather than *allowing* them. That day, I stopped trying. Without surrendering my desire, I surrendered my need to know my highest purpose and, sure enough, it found me.

Do not confuse surrender with submission. I thought I needed to be submissive to God and give up my dreams of theatre, music, and the big stage. Now I know that my creator's will for me is *Joy.* As I surrendered, I stopped struggling and rested by "still waters." I now do my life's work—teaching—with theatre and music interwoven on a big stage.

Hope and the Darkest Night

Hope knows there is a light, even in the darkest night. The five-year-old son of a friend of mine once asked his mom, "What is night for?"

His wise mother replied, "So we can begin new all over again the next day."

> *Develop the spirit of surrender. You will then experience bliss.*
>
> **Sri Sathya Sai Baba**

I loved her answer, and I would add this: It's also so that we can rest in "not doing," trusting that the sun will rise again and in the meantime, seeing the beauty of the stars.

Why We Don't Practice *Hope for the Future*

Hope is both the earliest and the most indispensable virtue
inherent in the state of being alive.
Erik H. Erikson

⟨∞⟩

It's rare to meet any person who hasn't lost hope at some point on their journey. The reasons are many.

We Worry

I once met a school administrator who, when I asked him what his dream was, answered, "A day with no worries." Worry felt bigger than he was and, from his intelligent and loving viewpoint, he felt that he had to fix things in order to defeat it. The good news is, the only thing we have to fix is our focus.

Worry is a form of fear, and fear is at the bottom of the **Power Pyramid**. Yet some of us have come to believe that it wards off danger "like a magical amulet," according to *Emotional Intelligence* author Daniel Goleman. We have convinced ourselves that worrying about something will stop it from happening—but nothing could be further from the truth. Worry actually makes our problems grow.

So what are you growing in your worry garden? Is it

- ✔ *bills*
- ✔ *the changing job market*
- ✔ *your children's safety*
- ✔ *your health problems*
- ✔ *the weather*
- ✔ *what others think of you*
- ✔ *making the wrong decision*
- ✔ *running out of time*

If what we think about we bring about, worry is going the wrong direction down a one-way street. We are using our imagination to *Get the Picture* of something we do not want! And not only does worry not feel good, *being worried about* feels almost as bad.

What are our options? The **FGH** formula reminds us to simply get grateful. Unplug from thoughts of what awful things could happen and plug into something you are thankful for. What else could you focus on rather than worry? The list is endless: pet your dog, buy a pet, put on your favorite song, put on your favorite outfit, call a friend, call a radio show, take a nap, take a hike, change the channel, change your hairstyle, eat an apple, drink hot tea, volunteer at a shelter, volunteer at a hospital, run a race, run for office, play eighteen holes, play the drums, write a song, write a letter to the editor, hug your kids, hug a tree...

> *The one who worries is always in worse shape than the one they worry about.*
>
> **Abraham-Hicks**

In other words, focus on anything that feels good.

Zig Ziglar often asks his audiences, "What percentage of what we worry about do we have any control over?" His answer is .06 percent! A poorer investment we *couldn't* make.

A Worry-Free Parent

Many of us have bought into the belief that the more we worry, the more it shows we care. It is a belief that does not serve us and can eventually take away from us all that we want in life. Take a moment to think of someone you know who doesn't worry much. How do you perceive them, as irresponsible and selfish or relaxed and happy?

A counselor friend of mine learned an antidote to worry from his dad when he was eight. He overheard his father talking to their neighbor at the feed store in their farming community.

"Well, aren't you worried about it?" he heard the neighbor ask.

"Heck, no. Not my problem," said his father.

"Then whose is it?"

"I got a man who does that. I hired him awhile back to do all my worrying for me. I just don't have time for such nonsense."

> *There's nothing more dreadful than the habit of doubt. It is a thorn that irritates; it is a sword that kills.*
>
> **Buddha**

My friend remembered that conversation as he got older, and he still uses his father's clever wisdom in his counseling career today.

We Doubt Ourselves

Another sign that we could use a heap of *Hope* is when we find we're doubting ourselves. Here's how it often happens:

We start to manifest wonderful things.

One day we notice that something that we've asked for hasn't arrived yet.

That leads to our starting to doubt ourselves.

That pulls us further down the **Power Pyramid**.

That slows down what we've asked for.

That gives us more reason to doubt.

That pulls us further down the **Power Pyramid**, etc.

Ask yourself: "Where has doubt ever gotten me?"

The answer is: "To the same place as worry—nowhere." If worry is fear with a shawl on, doubt is fear holding a security blanket. I once heard: "If you're going to doubt it, don't do it. If you're going to do it, don't doubt it." I say, if you must doubt, doubt your doubts.

We Don't Understand Failure/Feedback

Sometimes we use failure in a business or a relationship as our excuse for doubting ourselves. What's needed in that case is a *reframing* of failure. Successful and happy people call it "feedback." There are four options every time we experience failure/feedback:

✔ *We can choose B.C. and blame our failure/feedback on others.*

✔ *We can busy ourselves enough to run from (ignore) the failure/feedback.*

✔ *We can freeze forward movement with shame, feeling as if we're "wrong."*

✔ *We can take* Full Responsibility *for the failure/feedback, learn from it, and use it as a springboard to move forward.*

Only with the last option can the feedback feed *us*. When we start to think of failure as "free coaching," we can actually get excited and grateful for it.

Sara the CEO

Sara Blakeley wasn't exceptional by many standards. As a young woman, at first she wanted to become a lawyer, but when she failed the LSAT, she realized she wanted to try her hand at business. Five years later, though she was making an adequate living selling copiers door-to-door, Sara got an idea for a new company. Even though she'd never taken a single business course, she knew all about failure/feedback.

While growing up, her father encouraged his children to risk by asking at dinner each night, "What did you fail at today?" If they hadn't failed at anything, he was disappointed.

> *My life has been a series of endless crises...most of which never happened.*
>
> **Mark Twain**

"I'd come home sometimes and tell Dad that I had tried out for something and had failed miserably, and he'd actually high-five me," Sara said in a 2008 interview.

Sara followed her dream, producing and selling a brand new product for women. Today she's the CEO of Spanx, a multi-million dollar undergarment business.

"If I hadn't failed the LSAT, I'd have been a lawyer and there'd be no Spanx," Sara said with a smile. "I now believe that failure is nothing more than life's way of nudging you. My attitude toward failure isn't attached to outcome, but to *not trying*. It's been liberating for me. Most people attach the idea of failure to something that doesn't work out or to how people perceive them, but seeing failure in this way is about answering to myself."

When asked if she ever wanted to give up, Sara replied, "I don't think one person told me that Spanx was a workable idea until two years *after* I began pursuing it. At times I stopped for awhile out of discouragement, but I never lost confidence in the fact that it was a good idea."

Like all successful BIG dreamers, she lost her way but she never lost hope.

We Deny That We're Discouraged

Today Sara shares candidly on talk shows about the days when she was discouraged. BIG dreamers know that discouragement is just part of the menu you're going to sample along the way. Imagine trying to talk a woman giving birth out of her labor pains. Her screaming would only intensify. Discouragement is a stepping stone toward *surrender*. Rather than deny it, we can accept that we feel what we feel.

Impatience and *Hope*

Have you been reading along and wondering *when* I'm *ever* going to deal with impatience? The most impatient readers have. We all get impatient from time to time, and from that lower place on the **Power Pyramid**, we often manifest "right now" rather than "right."

I recall reading an article about how many delays the original *Star Wars* film had, how over budget it was, how many people (including members of the technical crew) thought it was a kids' movie and had no faith in it, and how it almost got *canceled* at the last minute because it was so many weeks overdue. When it was first released, only thirty-seven theatres in the entire U.S. agreed to show it, but George Lucas stuck to his guns. He could have had it *right* or he could have had it *right now*, and George released *Star Wars* five months later than promised—because he chose *right*.

When we ask, we receive, but there's also another piece of the Truth Pie that needs to be swallowed. If we had to choose between "I want it *right*" and "I want it *right now*,"

> *Most damn fools quit on the one yard line, one foot before the winning touchdown, one minute before the end of the game.*
>
> **Ross Perot**

we'd always choose the first one, *right?* So sometimes *right* comes later than we'd hoped, but it's always *right on time!*

We Get Tired

When people ask if it's truly "darkest before the dawn," I say no, but it is *coldest* before the dawn. We give up so close to the finish line because we don't know how close we really are. The final mountain we climb on the way to our dream *seems* steeper because *we're just plain tired.*

There was a college science professor who, when explaining stress management to his students, raised a glass of water and asked his students, "How heavy is this glass of water?" Answers ranged from 20g to 500g.

The professor replied, "The absolute weight doesn't matter. It depends on how long you try to hold it. If I hold it for a minute, that's not a problem. If I hold it for an hour, I'll have an ache in my right arm. If I hold it for a day, you'll have to call an ambulance. In each case, the water weighs the same, but the longer I hold it, the heavier it becomes."

He continued, "That's the way it is with stress. If we try to carry our burdens day after day, sooner or later, they will become too heavy. Sometimes it's crucial to our success to put down our burdens and rest awhile before picking them up again. When we're refreshed, we can carry on."

Surrender is putting down our work toward our dreams and resting in the knowledge that there is a reason, a purpose, a Divine Order to life.

Our Hopeless Habits

Years ago I realized that optimists believe that ill fortune is temporary, a fluke, and that it will pass, while pessimists believe that good fortune is temporary, a fluke, and that it will pass. As the marvelous work of author Martin Seligman attests, both are right some of the time, but optimists are happier, healthier, and statistically much more successful in the long run.

> *While writing **Eat Pray Love**, I fell into one of those pits of despair that we all fall into and I started thinking "I should just dump this project."*
>
> **Elizabeth Gilbert**

So what do you do if you've played the cynic over the years, debating everyone you can find to "prove" that hope is hopeless? It can feel like an overwhelming challenge to break your mold. Begin right now to forgive yourself for your pessimistic pontifications. Then you can be grateful that you now get to choose what to believe. Just as you un-learned that black cats are bad luck, you can unlearn a pessimistic attitude. One way of thinking may be how you were raised, the other will be how you will raise.

The House of Surrender

There came a day when I realized that surrender and *Hope* are good friends who live together in a serene and quiet place on a moun-tain. It's a place any of us can go when we've exhausted our reserves and resources. We simply leave the busy do-er that we usually are behind and climb to this place to listen and wait.

How long do most people stay there? It depends. The hardest part is simply admitting you're there, but then one day your resistance and denial disappear and you accept that you're right where you need to be. Time begins to pass easily and effortlessly. One day may be spent just breathing, another watching the clouds change shapes, and still another studying the beauty of your hands.

Then one day, when you least expect it and don't even have a pen handy, inspiration hits you like a lightning bolt.

"Oh, my gosh! It's so clear," you'll say to yourself. "How could I have missed it before?"

You thank your hosts and head back down the mountain—into a time of focused and intensely creative activity.

When that lightning bolt day came, I finished this *Hope for the Future* chapter. When it came, Sara Blakeley cut the feet out of her control top pantyhose. When it came, Barack Obama realized that

although his name could present a daunt-
ing barrier, he had to give politics one last
chance.

This chapter is for anyone who has been
afraid to scale the mountain of surrender,
fearing that it was a valley in disguise. Those
of us who have been there before you honor
your process.

> *So what I have to keep
> telling myself when I
> get really psyched out is,
> "Don't be afraid. Just do
> your job. Continue
> to show up."*
>
> **Elizabeth Gilbert**

Hope for the Future Success Stories

*Hope begins in the dark, the stubborn hope that if you
just show up and try to do the right thing, the dawn will come.*

Anne Lamott

൙

The Rudy Reality

If you haven't seen the movie *Rudy*, I encourage you to do so. If you have, answer this question: "Did Rudy ever quit?"

Very few of my seminar participants answer that question correctly. Rewatch the DVD and you'll see that on the biggest day of his life, Rudy didn't show up for practice.

When confronted by his custodian friend, he said, "I quit."

When asked why, he said, "I wanted to prove that I was somebody."

His friend let him have it, saying, "You're so full of crap. You're five feet nothin' and you hung in with the best college team in the land for two years. And you're also gonna walk out of here with a degree from the University of Notre Dame. In this lifetime you don't have to prove nothin' to nobody except yourself, and after what you've gone through, if you haven't done that by now, it ain't gonna never happen. Now go on back."

In that final game of the season for Notre Dame's Fighting Irish, what happened to Rudy hasn't happened before or since.

> *I overcame my
> nightmares because
> of my dreams.*
>
> **Jonas Salk**

Meanwhile, there was a behind-the-scenes story on the set of that film. The man who played that custodian—actor Charles Dutton—was an ex-con who had spent seven years in prison. While behind bars, he started to *Get the Picture* of being in movies, and to date he has acted in more than thirty feature films and has won an Emmy.

The *Rudy Reality* is that most of the greats had a time when it would have "made sense" to give up. When Rudy trusted his friend, his surrendering took him into the end zone.

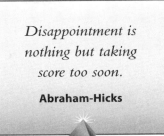

Disappointment is nothing but taking score too soon.

Abraham-Hicks

Kurtis, the Checkout Boy

I love sharing the story of a young man from my high school who had high expectations for himself as a football player. After college, he tried out for the Green Bay Packers and to his delight, he was signed as a free agent—only to be cut five weeks later.

Kurtis still had the love of his life (his girlfriend, Brenda) and the love of her two kids. One of them had been dropped by his birth father when he was four months old and had suffered severe brain damage, but Kurtis loved the child as his own.

Kurtis stayed open to life and hope, and three years after being released from the Packers, he prepared for his marriage to Brenda and another NFL tryout—this time with the Chicago Bears. The wedding was wonderful, but while on their honeymoon, Kurtis was bitten on his throwing arm by a venomous spider and wasn't able to perform at the tryout.

Fighting off despair, he went to the European league for a few months until he was picked up by the Rams as their third string quarterback. Two years later, when quarterback Trent Green was injured, Kurtis Warner stepped onto the field—and into the history books. He threw for a record 414 yards in Super Bowl XXXIV and was voted Most Valuable Player. In 2009, he played in the Super Bowl for the third time. For those who want to know where BIG dreams and *Hope* can take you, Kurt Warner's is a Most Valuable Story.

Expecting vs. Wanting

Kurt Warner didn't just want to play pro football—he expected to. *Wanting* is very different from *expectation*. When a woman wants to have a child, there's a longing which can, over time, get mixed with sadness if not realized. Once she's "expecting," even though her manifestation isn't fully realized, she has the excitement from knowing what's coming. With practice, we can get to *expectation* about anything our hearts desire.

Waiting Bells

Everyone who knew Katie knew that she'd been expecting "him" to show up all her life. She had just turned forty-eight when she found herself on her knees one Sunday after Mass, talking to God about finding a husband—again.

"Okay, God," said Katie, "I know I'm supposed to be patient, I know he's out there looking for me, too, and I know that he'll come and find me when he's ready...but dear God, isn't he about ready?"

Two weeks later Randy Lee moved to town, and two years later I sang at Katie's wedding. Randy was her perfect match. While she'd been running major department stores, he'd been managing an island for a cruise line. While she'd been living her faith in a world that often nodded condescendingly, he'd been working for an orphanage in Mexico. They both loved God, family, and the outdoors in that order, and neither had ever married. Perhaps the biggest thing they had in common was they'd both surrendered their dreams, believing that faith was enough to find true love in a small town in northern Minnesota.

These "Losers" Won Big

When teachers share **8 to Great** in schools, they give students a quiz. It's one they know the students will have trouble with because they never guess that:

- ✔ J.K. Rowling was on government assistance (the British version of welfare) when she sold her first Harry Potter book. To date, she's the second wealthiest woman in the world.
- ✔ Einstein was expelled from high school at the age of fifteen for poor academic performance.
- ✔ The Beatles were told by Decca Records that they should get a "real" job because guitar groups were on the way out.

✔ *Franklin D. Roosevelt flunked out of law school.*

✔ *Mother Teresa had dozens of articles written about her accusing her of crimes.*

✔ *Oprah had run away from home a number times when her mother tried to put her in a detention home, but all the beds were filled and she was sent home.*

Hope on the High-Ways

Sometimes our intuition can be our coach. I'll never forget the time my mom and I took a special road trip—just the two of us. I was a first-year high school teacher and wanted to scope out the Minneapolis Children's Theatre for a possible field trip with my students. She said she'd love to join me, so off we went to the Twin Cities—except that each of us thought the other one was bringing a map!

> *Most people never run far enough on their first wind to find out they've got a second. Give your dreams all you've got and you'll be amazed at the energy that comes out.*
>
> **William James**

The interstate got us to the edge of the metropolis, but we faced dozens of choices as we approached the downtown area.

For whatever reason, I turned to Mom as we were barreling down the freeway and said, "We're gonna follow that white car. She looks like she knows where she's going."

Mom wasn't convinced of my plan, but having none of her own, she just laughed and agreed. Our spirits were high as we continued on our adventure.

As the little car took one exit after another, it started to get dark, so we decided that if we passed a motel, we'd stop. Fifteen minutes later, we saw a little white motel, right in the middle of the city. We pulled in, found the rates reasonable, and called it a night.

The next morning we got up ready to continue our quest and headed to the check-in desk.

"Excuse me," I began. "We've come to Minneapolis to visit the children's theatre. Would you know where it's located?" The woman behind the counter looked at me like I was from Mars as I continued,

"I'm not sure of the name of it, but it's world-renowned. Have you ever heard of it?"

With a sly smile, the woman walked over to the front window and pulled back the curtain.

"You mean this one?"

There, across the street, was the Minneapolis Children's Theatre.

Finding My Writing Assistant

I could have given up hope in finding the perfect person to help me write this book, but because I didn't, I was blessed with one of my life's greatest gifts.

That first year, I placed ads in the newspaper three times for a part-time writing assistant. However, I go at quite a pace and the first two assistants I hired told me they couldn't keep up. I was grateful for their input, but knew I couldn't change who I was, so I simply ran the ad again, believing "the one" was out there.

> *Let your worry thoughts turn to wonder, your fears to fantasies, and your anxieties to anticipation.*
>
> **Anonymous**

The third time, the first resume I read was Tessa's. With her journalism background and the fact that she'd worked on film crews (think: handling a high maintenance individual) she was a shoo-in.

The part I remember most about her interview was when she pulled out a little slip of paper and showed me the first ad I had run for the position ten months earlier.

"I knew this was the perfect job for me," she shared, "but I was in the middle of a project and didn't want to let the person I was working with down. I've had this in my billfold ever since."

What we're looking for is looking for us *in every instance!*

I will never be able to express my gratitude for Tessa's years of dedication and her incredible gifts. When she came on board, she'd never read a self-help book or considered picking up one. Her openness to these concepts has been exciting to watch. Let me end this section with her own eloquent words:

In film and writing work, it is often feast or famine. At one point while working part-time for MK and freelancing, there was an abrupt and unexpected end to a book editing project I was working on. After devoting months to this project, I was feeling anxious and a bit daunted by another blank slate. When I came into work the next day MK and I discussed the fact that my last opportunity was plucked from thin air and the next would appear the same way. With renewed hope I sent off a couple of resumes that evening.

Two days later I got a call about editing a new book and happily accepted. The following day when I got a call about working on a film, I was over the moon. After the euphoria wore off I realized that I had a limited amount of time to properly prepare for the film and edit the book while working part-time for MK. As far as problems go, it was not a bad one to have.

Since then I have had the honor of working on many indelible films and even exploring my own passion in documentary film. As this book has evolved, so have I. The insights I've cultivated through editing these chapters have impacted my personal and professional life. I feel privileged to have been a part of this process

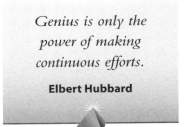

Genius is only the
power of making
continuous efforts.

Elbert Hubbard

and am forever grateful to MK for trusting me with her words. She continues to show me that everything I could ever want or need is already within. I am proud to call her a teacher and a friend.

Putting *Hope for the Future* into Practice

There is nothing with which every man is so afraid as getting to know how enormously much he is capable of doing and becoming.

Soren Kierkegaard

᠄᠁᠄

Recess-ion

In 2002, entrepreneur Maria Pinto had an employee embezzle tens of thousands of dollars from her designer clothing business. That blow, coupled with a slowing economy, led to her filing for bankruptcy in 2002. A year later she suffered major health challenges, yet she found new hope, and with new investors she restarted her business. In 2007, she became one of Michelle Obama's favorite designers.

There are thousands of stories like Maria's, where what seems to be the end of the day was just a recess break. While we entrepreneurs have to deal with uncertainty regularly, tens of thousands in the corporate world learned to face it due to the economic shift across the U.S. in 2008. While many were losing their homes and their hopes, others were using the adversity, or their furlough days, to enjoy and improve their lives. They put the "recess" back in recession.

"It Fed My Soul"

Duane was a successful motivational speaker by the time I met him years ago. His first twenty years in the work world had been spent selling vacuum sweepers door-to-door.

A day came when my family and I ran out of food. I'll never forget the day we had enough in the refrigerator for breakfast and lunch for my wife and kids, but no idea how we were going to buy food for supper. I said a prayer, putting it all in God's hands, but I was still nervous.

That day, I must have knocked on fifty doors. Not one of them even let me in for a demonstration. Finally, at 4:00, a woman was gracious enough to let me come into her home and explain what the machine

could do, but forty-five minutes later, her answer was, "No, thank you."

I thanked her, packed up my stuff, and
was halfway to my car when I heard someone
yelling.

I turned to see her on her front porch, shouting, "Young man, come back here."

Confused, I walked back toward the house.
She then asked me the most amazing thing.

> *You know what happens*
> *right before the heavens*
> *open up and all your*
> *dreams come true?*
> *Nothing.*
>
> **Mike Dooley**

"I was wondering. My husband and I just bought a side of beef
and it wouldn't all fit into the freezer. Could you use two pounds of
hamburger?"

Since I had told her nothing about my situation, this miracle not only
fed my family, it fed my soul.

Giving *Hope* a Hand

Author Mike Dooley is adamant about the power of giving *Hope*
a hand. He goes so far as to suggest that if you're looking for a job,
get up early, put on the coffee, then shower and dress for work. Then
get into your car and drive to the area where such jobs exist. Mike's
popularity and the hundreds of thousands of people who receive his
daily encouragements via e-mail are testaments to the fact that his
principles work.

Mike's enlightened "Notes from the Universe" have helped me
laugh when I wanted to cry more than once. If you'd like a love note
from "the Universe" five days a week that will make you smile, soar,
and show up, sign on for his free daily "Notes from the Universe" at
www.tut.com.

Hope is a muscle, not a magic incantation. I have found that those
who are truly committed to taking their lives to the next level not
only sign up for daily reminders like Mike's, but they also find or start
groups who help them focus more on what *can be* than what *is*.

How to Host a Magnificent Manifestations Group

Many friends of mine are in Mastermind Groups and love them. I have created my own version of this kind of weekly support group called "Magnificent Manifestations."(Feel free to call yours whatever title works.) Our weekly agenda goes as follows:

For the first ten minutes, in small groups of 4–6, share how you've marvelously manifested in the past week from any of the following areas:

1. Money
2. Time
3. Support
4. Fun and Laughter
5. Order and Organization
6. Energy, Vitality, and Health
7. Confidence and Hope
8. Romance
9. Creativity
10. Stillness, Nature Connection, Prayer, and Meditation Time

(Starting with the second meeting, you will also look back at the list of intentions you wrote out the previous meeting that have occurred during the week. It will astound you!)

For the next thirty minutes, alternate between listening to a CD on abundance/dreaming big (ten minutes) and discussing (3–5 minutes). Keep comments short and stay focused on *feel goods* and solutions rather than on pain or problems.

For the next ten minutes, write down dozens of things you want to manifest in the next week in as many areas as possible. Make some small, medium, and large intentions. Fill the page!

For the final ten minutes, read one of the future manifestations you just wrote out loud *in past tense* and invite the members to ask questions about *how it feels now that you have it!*

End with reciting a phrase such as, "When you feel good, good things happen, and we feel GREAT!" or a song such as Jana Stanfield's "Let the Change Begin" or "Whatever It Takes" or my upbeat version of "Fill Your Mind" while folks head out the door.

> *The future belongs to those who give the next generations reason for hope.*
>
> **Pierre Teilhard de Chardin**

I cannot imagine that I will ever stop participating in gatherings like the one described above, because new dreams and manifestations are what keep me young and "95-ing." It is a regular reminder that when you have a process, you have hope, and when you have hope, you have power. Added to that, the fun of gathering with friends and the thrill of watching dreams come true are a deep well of bliss that never fails to fill me up.

When new members ask for ideas of what to ask for, we encourage them to start with things they believe *could* happen. One young woman wrote down that she would receive flowers, and a bouquet was delivered the following week. As you ask and receive, your *Hope* muscle gets stronger and you begin to allow larger manifestations (like watermelons) to come into your experience. After doing this for six months, one night at the meeting I wrote that I wanted $25,000 of surprise money. I didn't expect it anytime soon, but just wrote it down for the fun of it.

The following week, my son got a letter from his university of choice that he had received a $40,000 Presidential Scholarship *that he hadn't even applied for*. While I know the scholarship was a result of *his* intending, believing, and his powerfully positive focus in high school, it was a glorious win-win for both of us. Since he had already received a financial gift, his expenses were now all covered—and I received more "surprise money" than I'd asked for!

Rediscover Your Sense of Humor

Throughout these 8 High-Ways, and especially with *Hope for the Future*, it's important to retain a spirit of playful possibility. Bill

> *Life is too important to*
> *be taken seriously.*
>
> **Oscar Wilde**

Cosby once said, "Through humor, you can soften some of the worst blows that life delivers, and once you do, you can survive them." Humorist Jean Kerr hits the nail on the head when she says, "Hope is the feeling that the feeling you have isn't permanent."

T. Marni Vos is a humorist I'm grateful to have as a personal friend. My favorite line from her presentations is: "Time heals all wounds, but I say, why wait?"

"Humor and hope are inseparable," says Michael Pritchard, parole officer and professional comedian. He goes around the country delighting young adult audiences with questions like the following ones.

Q: How many teenagers with ADD does it take to screw in a lightbulb?
A: Wanna go to a Giant's game?

Q: What is the best thing about turning 100?
A: Total lack of peer pressure!

When You Have a Process...

If you found yourself stranded one night on a country road in a car with a spare tire but with no knowledge of how to change it, you'd be stuck. If, however, someone had offered to teach you the process and you had taken time to learn it, you would be powerful. You would be free. You would be on your way.

You now know:

- ✔ *how to dream (Get the Picture: High-Way 1)*
- ✔ *how to risk (Risk: High-Way 2)*
- ✔ *how to take full responsibility (Full Responsibility: High-Way 3)*
- ✔ *how to feel all your feelings (Feel All Your Feelings: High-Way 4)*
- ✔ *how to communicate honestly (Honest Communication: High-Way 5)*
- ✔ *how to forgive the past (Forgiveness of the Past: High-Way 6)*
- ✔ *how to get and stay grateful (Gratitude for the Present: High-Way 7)*
- ✔ *how to have hope (Hope for the Future: High-Way 8)*

Now that you have these processes, my hope is that you'll use them, as I do, every day.

Thank you for being my companion on this journey. If I have shared even one insight that brings you greater joy, I am grateful, as well as hopeful that you will do the same for the next traveler you meet on the High-Ways of life.

Blissings!

MK

Do not let your fire go out, spark by irreplaceable spark,
in the hopeless swamps of the approximate, the not-quite, the not-yet.
Do not let the hero in your soul perish in lonely frustration for
the life you deserved, but have never been able to reach.
Check your road and the nature of your battle.
The world you desire can be won.
It exists, it is real, it is possible, it is yours.

Ayn Rand

Q & A on *Hope for the Future*

Q: *How can I stay motivated after I'm done with this book?*

A: At different times I've used daily gratitudes with a partner, books, magazines, true-life movies, audio CDs, and the manifestations group I described earlier in this chapter. I also offer a free monthly "Key-Mail" you can sign up for at www.mkmueller.com.

Q: *I need help. I'm not making a living for my family. I've spent lots of money on self-help materials, but still my excuses are many: not smart enough, no experience, not taking action on my goals, not worthy, and I could go on, but I think you get the message. Hope you can help.*

A: Dear One, you're experiencing "Analysis Paralysis." You're so afraid of making the wrong decision that you're not making *any* decision. Here's the great news:

There are no wrong decisions.

If you want to lose weight, *every diet works*. Just pick one and follow it. You have my *8 Steps*. Follow them. Get up every day and do *Gratitudes* and dreamings. Your life can't help but change. For your debt issues, there's a twelve-step group called Debtors Anonymous. It works—and it's *free*! If there isn't one in your area, you can join an online group. It will take you from where you are now to where you want to be financially when you follow the steps. Whatever you decide, wherever you land, allow yourself to be coached—and expect miracles!

> *This pity, insecurity, and self indulgence are unbecoming of the Great soul that you are.*
>
> **Bhagavad Gita**

Q: *How can I teach my friend or spouse* **FGH** *?*

A: Don't preach it. Live it. If you do, the joy and success that will be yours will bring that person to you begging for your secret!

Q: *If someone around you has lost hope, how do you help them hang on?*

A: If they have a plan to end their life or if they start giving away prized possessions, tell their loved ones. If it's a student, tell a school counselor. If they're an adult, call for professional help immediately or get them to a hospital. If they're not to that stage, you could invite them to go to a counselor or coaching session with you and share that you're concerned about them. In the company of that third party, brainstorm solutions. It may be as simple as learning new communication skills or giving themselves permission to feel all of their feelings.

Worrying about them twenty-four hours a day is *not* one of your options.

Finally, acknowledge that you can't change them. Surrender to that and live fully in your own here and now.

Q: *I live in a small rural community and know how depressed the town sometimes feels. I don't know what I can do to rekindle hope for our little town.*

A: One North Dakota community had a similar situation. The weeds growing around the stop signs were indicative of the mentality of apathy and discouragement.

But one day, a resident *Got the Picture* that things could be different. She took a risk and invited some friends over for coffee. She suggested that they work together to trim the weeds back. Another woman suggested putting flower pots at each stop sign. A third woman said if someone could find the pots, she'd have her art students at the high school paint them.

A fourth person added, "I don't have any pots, but my brother has a Quonset full of tubs."

As of this printing, the painted flower tubs are still there, years later, blossoming and blessing the town.

Q: *Is surrender the same as obedience?*

A: No. Obedience has more to do with submission. The word *obedience* implies an authority figure who has power over others. An evolved husband doesn't want a wife who is *obedient* to him because he's physically stronger, but men love it when a woman surrenders to their romantic advances. The person who surrenders doesn't deny their freedom and power—they *claim* it in order to willingly *give* it over for a time. The best relationships involve a dance of surrender by both parties as each one leads and follows at different times and in different situations.

Q: *Which of the High-Ways is the most important?*

A: There are many answers to your wonderful question. The High-Way I've seen have the most dramatic and immediate effect on the most lives has been *Gratitude*. It's the quickest and simplest "95" on the planet. Once it's in place, everything changes.

My other answer is that the most important High-Way for *you* could be the one you don't want to travel,

> *What President Kennedy did can be understood by analogy. It is as if he created a building named, "A man on the moon in ten years," and inside the building he put offices for all the various ideas, positions and notions that people had to do with space flight. The first office inside the front door of the building in 1961 would have been called, "It can't be done."*
>
> **Werner Erhard**

because that's the one acting as an obstacle between you and the manifestation of your dreams. It could also be the one you can't wait to travel. Follow your instincts and have fun.

Pick one. Remember, there are no wrong decisions, and every moment is the "right" now.

> *Curly: Do you know what the secret of life is?*
> *Mitch: No, what?*
> *Curly: This. (Curly holds up one finger.)*
> *Mitch: Your finger?*
> *Curly: One thing. Just one thing.*
> *You stick to that and everything else don't mean shit.*

From the film *City Slickers*

~∞~

*Our greatest happiness
comes from following our
greatest dreams.*

❧

In Conclusion...

MK, I want to apologize for doubting this program.
Now I know it is possible to be that happy
*because **I am** that happy!*

AA Member and *8 to Great* Coaching Client

I grew up hearing a lot about eternal life, thinking that I had to be patient in hopes that it would be my reward when I died. It was only as I grew into my knowing that I realized that eternity "began" a long time ago. We're all smack dab in the middle of the eternal life we've been promised. Heaven on Earth is possible for those ready to claim it.

And so many of us are. We are at the heart of a deep change in the world, watching a new generation of believers embrace the unlimited possibilities foretold ages ago. We need only open our eyes to see young and old rediscovering their passion and finding their compass in their compass-ion. It is such an exciting time to be alive.

The Final Fairy Tale

There will be those who rail against these truths with "if it were that easy…" and that is all perfect. Their rants remind me of a scene in *The Wizard of Oz*. Near the end of the film, Dorothy's friend, the Scarecrow, listens to Glinda the Good Witch's shoe-tapping instructions and challenges her with, "If it was that easy, why didn't you tell her a long time ago?"

Her simple reply reveals a great truth: "Because she wouldn't have believed me."

The Wizard Within

As you become a believer that dreams really do come true, your path from victim to victor or average to awesome will look like Mother Teresa's, Jay Leno's, Winston Churchill's, Rosa Park's, Frodo Baggin's, Thomas Edison's, and Dorothy's.

High-Way 1: *Get the Picture*—You will ask for something that feels like it exists "over the rainbow."

High-Way 2: *Risk*—You will dare to say (or sing!) your dream out loud.

High-Way 3: *Full Responsibility*—You will want to blame and complain about all the people in your life who don't understand you and your dreams, or who seem to be "monkeying around" and trying to hurt you.

High-Way 4: *Feel All Your Feelings*—You will feel elated and delighted, lost and scared, mad and sad as the new realities you've manifested with your thoughts and dreams take shape.

High-Way 5: *Honest Communication*—You will learn to be honest about what you need from the Wizards (who are all half-jerk and half-jewel) you meet along the way.

High-Way 6: *Forgiveness of the Past*—You'll start to forgive yourself for judging the Auntie Ems who make the rules and see that the Lions are just "scaredy cats" underneath all that fur.

We are all pilgrims on the same journey...but some pilgrims have better road maps.

Nelson DeMille

High-Way 7: *Gratitude for the Present*—You'll move into greater and greater appreciation for those around you as well as your own magnificent heart.

High-Way 8: *Hope for the Future*—You'll understand that the thing you have always desired in life, whether it's wisdom, courage, brains, or love, has always been within you.

Finally, you'll understand that you've never been in danger— you've never left Kansas, and all roads lead to Oz.

If you choose, this process can be your map. And although you'll be taking the same High-Ways that so many greats have taken before you, the winding roads and wonderful rewards will be uniquely your own. So don't hesitate. In-joy. Your dreams await.

Whatever you can do, or dream you can, begin it.
Boldness has genius, power and magic in it.
Goethe

8 to Great Key-Notes

The Power Pyramid

What goes around comes around.

Misery loves company, but so does joy!

We're always somewhere between "5" and "95."

"5" is only using 5 percent of your power because only 5 percent of your thoughts feel good.

"95" is using 95 percent of your power because 95 percent of your thoughts feel good.

We are more energy efficient (have more energy) when we choose thoughts that feel good!

When we are at "95," what goes around comes around faster!

When you feel good, good things happen.

High-Way 1: Get the Picture

A belief is a thought you keep thinking until you feel it.

The difference between a **dream** and a **goal** is that when you dream, you don't concern yourself with Who, When, Where, or How, only *What* you want and *Why* you want it.

High-Way 2: Risk

The four-letter word that the happiest people have been found to have in common is **Risk**.

The decision-making formula for every decision to be sure it's the right one: "If I had no fear, what would I do?"

What is a **Risk**? Running *to*, not *from*. (Running *from* is not a risk, but an escape.)

High-Way 3: Full Responsibility

What does Full Responsibility living look like? No B.C. (Blaming and Complaining) only A.D. (Acting and Dreaming)

You spot it, you got it, so exchange "You should" with "I could."

High-Way 4: Feel All Your Feelings

Mad (Angergy) and Sad (Release) are two sides of the same coin. You always feel them together to the same extent.

To stay out of depression, feel your anger (fire).

To stay out of rage, feel your sadness (water).

Mad and Sad Bowls Theory

When someone says, "You never," "You always," or "You are such a..." it is never about the match. They simply need AVA. (See High-Way 5 below.)

High-Way 5: Honest Communication

4 Steps for asking for what you want:

Pre-step: (Have you got a minute?)

1. When you... (1 time and 1 place)
2. I felt a little...
3. Because...
4. Therefore...

How to prevent defensiveness with Deep Listening (AVA):

1. Acknowledge
2. Validate
3. Ask the million dollar question

How to stop 3rd party communication

If you're X, go to Z.
If you're Y, tell X to go to Z.
If you're Z, ask X if they agree with Y.

High-Ways 6, 7, 8

Positive Attitude is **FGH:**

> **F**orgiveness of the Past
> **G**ratitude for the Present
> **H**ope for the Future

High-Way 6: Forgiveness of the Past

The Forgiveness Formula: We were all doing the best we could at the time with the information we had.

How to balance pride and humility: We're all half-jerk, half-jewel, no better, no worse than anyone else.

The Three Steps of Forgiveness:

> Face it
> Feel it
> Forgive it

How to tell if you've forgiven someone: If when something bad happens to them, you commiserate rather than celebrate.

High-Way 7: Gratitude for the Present

The Gratitude "Richual:" Write down 3 gratitudes from the past 24 hours, with no repeats ever!

The Three Most Grateful Groups:

> Those who just had a loss
> Those who have come close to a loss
> Those who know a loss is coming

High-Way 8: Hope for the Future

> Hope is Positive Expectation and Surrender
> *The Road to Success is **never** a straight line.*

Index of Quotes